HE LIVED AMONG US:

A Look at Christ's Life on Earth

BOB CRAIG

LUCIDBOOKS

He Lived Among Us: A Look at Christ's Life on Earth

Published by Lucid Books in Houston, TX.
www.LucidBooks.net

First Printing 2016

ISBN 10: 1-63296-088-5
ISBN 13: 978-1-63296-088-7
eISBN 10: 1-63296-089-3
eISBN 13: 978-1-63296-089-4

Special Sales: Most Lucid Books titles are available in special quantity discounts. Custom imprinting or excerpting can also be done to fit special needs. Contact Lucid Books at info@lucidbooks.net.

Table of Contents

Introduction

Jesus Christ came to Earth in fulfillment of prophecies God had delivered through various men in times of old. His birth was unique and miraculous. The four Gospels tell the story of His life and ministry. It has been called "the greatest story ever told," and we can't know it too well.

In 1922, Dr. A. T. Robertson wrote a helpful book called *A Harmony of The Gospels*. It's a chronological outline of the life of Christ based on all four Gospel accounts. The book you have in your hands is a commentary roughly based on Dr. Robertson's outline of the Gospels. The biblical references (with minor variations) come from Dr. Robertson's book; the additional comments are mine. It is my hope and prayer that studying the life of Christ in this way will be a transformative experience as you get to know the Savior better through a careful examination of the things He said and did during His earthly sojourn.

Chapter 1

THE BEGINNING OF CHRIST'S PUBLIC MINISTRY

Rather than starting with the miraculous birth of Jesus and His growing-up years, we're going to jump ahead a little in the story to the beginning of His ministry, which followed on the heels of the ministry of his cousin, John. The birth of John was extraordinary also in that both of John's parents were beyond the age of normal childbearing. Gabriel, an angel, who, according to Luke 1:19, "stands in the very presence of God," assured Zacharias (John's father-to-be) that he and his wife Elizabeth would have this special child.

John, or "John the Baptist," as he came to be known, was a special messenger sent to announce the coming of the Messiah. As the "voice of one crying in the wilderness," John preached a powerful message of repentance and the coming kingdom. Many of the people who heard John's message confessed their sins and were baptized by John in the Jordan River (Matthew 3:1–13). Despite not having any sin of His own to confess, Jesus came to John to be baptized. And that's where we'll pick up the story, highlighting the major events in the life of Christ.

The Baptism of Jesus

Matthew 3:13–17

*13 Then Jesus arrived from Galilee at the Jordan coming
to John, to be baptized by him. 14 But John tried to
prevent Him, saying, "I have need to be baptized by You,*

> *and do You come to me?"* [15] *But Jesus answering said to him, "Permit it at this time; for in this way it is fitting for us to fulfill all righteousness." Then he permitted Him.* [16] *After being baptized, Jesus came up immediately from the water; and behold, the heavens were opened, and he saw the Spirit of God descending as a dove and lighting on Him,* [17] *and behold, a voice out of the heavens said, "This is My beloved Son, in whom I am well-pleased."*

We don't know that much about the life of Jesus between the time of His birth and the time when He came to John asking for baptism. There's the occasion recorded in Luke 2:41–51 in which Jesus stayed behind (unbeknownst to his parents) after visiting the temple with His parents during a religious holiday. Even at the young age of 12, He was focused on His mission. When His parents asked where He had been, Jesus replied, "Why is it that you were looking for Me? Did you not know that I had to be in My Father's house?" (v. 49).

As an adult, Jesus must have heard about John's message and mission because Matthew tells us that Jesus journeyed down from Galilee to request baptism. John had evidently heard about Jesus—he knew that his mission was to prepare the way for the Messiah—and when Jesus showed up to be baptized, John protested, saying Jesus should baptize him instead. Jesus insisted that it was necessary for Him to be baptized by John. In saying, "Permit this . . . to fulfill all righteousness" (v. 15), Jesus was identifying Himself with John and John's mission. In making this public commitment of baptism, Jesus modeled for us how important it is for us to do the same.

John agreed to baptize Jesus and was part of the amazed crowd who heard God's voice from heaven say, "This is My beloved Son, in whom I am well-pleased" (v. 17). As far as they knew, this was just another man whom John happened to know, not the Son of Man who had come to be baptized. God's voice affirmed Jesus' decision to be baptized. We may not hear a voice from heaven, but God affirms our choice to be baptized too.

Mark 1:9–11

> [9] *In those days Jesus came from Nazareth in Galilee and was baptized by John in the Jordan.* [10] *Immediately coming up out of the water, He saw the heavens opening, and the Spirit like a dove descending upon Him;* [11] *and a voice came out of the heavens: "You are My beloved Son, in You I am well-pleased."*

We diminish the impact of Jesus' life and choices if we don't see His humanity as clearly as we see His divinity. As the Son of Man, Jesus decided to have John baptize Him. God, His Father, affirmed that decision with a miraculous sign. A dove descended upon Jesus, while a voice stated, "You are My beloved Son. In You I am well-pleased" (v. 11). Witnesses must have wondered at this divine endorsement.

Luke 3:21–22

> [21] *Now when all the people were baptized, Jesus was also baptized, and while He was praying, heaven was opened,* [22] *and the Holy Spirit descended upon Him in bodily form like a dove, and a voice came out of heaven, "You are My beloved Son, in You I am well-pleased."*

According to Luke, other people were being baptized, and Jesus is identified with them. Luke suggests this baptism was a deep and meaningful experience for Jesus, noting that He was praying.

As mentioned above, when Jesus was only 12, He said He had to be in His Father's house (Luke 2:49), demonstrating He had some understanding of His identity and purpose here on earth even at an early age. This step of baptism further revealed His relationship to His Father and His commitment to the mission. It was a key public step for Jesus to take at the onset of His ministry.

Certainly the people who witnessed Jesus' baptism were amazed by what they saw and heard. John had correctly identified Jesus as the promised Messiah, and John's baptism of Jesus marked the beginning of the end of his own ministry, while serving as a launching point for Jesus' ministry.

John 1:29–34

[29] *The next day he saw Jesus coming to him and said,*
"Behold, the Lamb of God who takes away the sin of the
world! [30] *This is He on behalf of whom I said, 'After me*
comes a Man who has a higher rank than I, for He existed
before me.' [31] *I did not recognize Him, but so that He*
might be manifested to Israel, I came baptizing in water."
[32] *John testified saying, "I have seen the Spirit descending*
as a dove out of heaven, and He remained upon Him. [33] *I*
did not recognize Him, but He who sent me to baptize
in water said to me, 'He upon whom you see the Spirit
descending and remaining upon Him, this is the One who
baptizes in the Holy Spirit.' [34] *I myself have seen, and have*
testified that this is the Son of God."

A couple of quick observations. First, it appears that John's account begins after John the Baptist had baptized Jesus in the Jordan River, unlike the accounts in Matthew and Mark. Notice also that John refers to the dove as a "He" rather than an "it." The dove was a tangible manifestation of the person of the Holy Spirit.

John knew the mission he had received from God, and he faithfully fulfilled it. As the forerunner to Jesus' ministry, John gave powerful testimony that Jesus was indeed the long-awaited Messiah, the Son of God sent from heaven.

The Temptations of Christ

Matthew 4:1–11

1 Then Jesus was led up by the Spirit into the wilderness
to be tempted by the devil. 2 And after He had fasted forty
days and forty nights, He then became hungry. 3 And
the tempter came and said to Him, "If You are the Son
of God, command that these stones become bread." 4 But
He answered and said, "It is written, 'MAN SHALL NOT
LIVE ON BREAD ALONE, BUT ON EVERY WORD
THAT PROCEEDS OUT OF THE MOUTH OF GOD.'"

5 Then the devil took Him into the holy city and had
Him stand on the pinnacle of the temple, 6 and said to
Him, "If You are the Son of God, throw Yourself down;
for it is written, 'HE WILL COMMAND HIS ANGELS
CONCERNING YOU'; and 'ON their HANDS THEY
WILL BEAR YOU UP, SO THAT YOU WILL NOT
STRIKE YOUR FOOT AGAINST A STONE.'" 7 Jesus said
to him, "On the other hand, it is written, 'YOU SHALL
NOT PUT THE LORD YOUR GOD TO THE TEST.'"

8 Again, the devil took Him to a very high mountain and
showed Him all the kingdoms of the world and their glory;
9 and he said to Him, "All these things I will give You, if
You fall down and worship me." 10 Then Jesus said to him,
"Go, Satan! For it is written, 'YOU SHALL WORSHIP
THE LORD YOUR GOD, AND SERVE HIM ONLY.'"
11 Then the devil left Him; and behold, angels came and
began to minister to Him.

The temptations of Jesus in the wilderness were desperate attempts by the devil to distract and derail Jesus from His mission. Studying how Jesus overcame these temptations can give us insight into Satan's methods, as well as hope for overcoming the temptations we face.

Satan attempted to introduce doubt into Jesus' mind about His purpose and whether God could be trusted. The devil has been using that same method since the Garden of Eden (Genesis 3:1–4).

The devil came to Jesus after Jesus had been fasting for 40 days. Obviously, Jesus would have been hungry, so the devil's first temptation was for Jesus to satisfy His hunger in a way that was outside the will of God. Jesus didn't fall for it, relying on God's Word instead.

From there, Satan challenged Jesus to prove His divine Sonship by throwing Himself off the temple and relying on God to rescue Him. Again, Jesus answered back with truth from the Word of God, saying we're not to put God to the test.

Finally, Satan tempted Jesus to take a shortcut to glory and power, which Jesus rejected once more through reliance on the Word of God. Satan tempts us to take shortcuts to success and glory too, but he never delivers on what he promises.

From the example of Jesus, we can derive some principles for fighting temptation. First, recognize temptation for what it is. Second, don't give it serious consideration. And, third, answer temptation with biblical truth.

Mark 1:12–13

[12] *Immediately the Spirit impelled Him to go out into the wilderness.* [13] *And He was in the wilderness forty days being tempted by Satan; and He was with the wild beasts, and the angels were ministering to Him.*

Mark uses the word *immediately* frequently throughout his Gospel. It is a fast-moving account of the life of Jesus. Here, Jesus was impelled by the Spirit to go to the wilderness. His testing was part of God's plan.

Mark says that Jesus was *repeatedly* tempted during His time in the wilderness. The three temptations mentioned in Matthew's Gospel may have been typical of what Jesus endured during this 40-day trial. It's possible that Jesus was tempted toward pride after receiving heavenly assurance at His baptism that He was the Son of God. That's certainly one of Satan's favorite tempting strategies. As we've seen, though, Jesus humbly submitted to the Word of God.

Mark includes another interesting detail—Jesus was "with the wild beasts." God kept Jesus from danger and comforted Him through the ministering presence of His angels. Later, Jesus says that His followers are as "sheep in the midst of wolves" (Matthew 10:16). The protective presence of God keeps us from harm and enables us to persevere through testing.

Luke 4:1–13

1 *Jesus, full of the Holy Spirit, returned from the Jordan*
and was led around by the Spirit in the wilderness 2 *for*
forty days, being tempted by the devil. And He ate nothing
during those days, and when they had ended, He became
hungry. 3 *And the devil said to Him, "If You are the Son of*
God, tell this stone to become bread." 4 *And Jesus answered*
him, "It is written, 'MAN SHALL NOT LIVE ON BREAD
ALONE.'"

5 *And he led Him up and showed Him all the kingdoms*
of the world in a moment of time. 6 *And the devil said to*
Him, "I will give You all this domain and its glory; for it
has been handed over to me, and I give it to whomever I
wish. 7 *Therefore if You worship before me, it shall all be*
Yours." 8 *Jesus answered him, "It is written, 'YOU SHALL*
WORSHIP THE LORD YOUR GOD AND SERVE HIM
ONLY.'"

9 *And he led Him to Jerusalem and had Him stand on the*
pinnacle of the temple, and said to Him, "If You are the Son

of God, throw Yourself down from here; [10] for it is written, 'HE WILL COMMAND HIS ANGELS CONCERNING YOU TO GUARD YOU,'

[11] and, 'ON their HANDS THEY WILL BEAR YOU UP, SO THAT YOU WILL NOT STRIKE YOUR FOOT AGAINST A STONE.'" [12] And Jesus answered and said to him, "It is said, 'YOU SHALL NOT PUT THE LORD YOUR GOD TO THE TEST.'"

[13] When the devil had finished every temptation, he left Him until an opportune time.

Like Mark, Luke suggests that Jesus was tempted during the entire 40 days, culminating with the three temptations that are recorded. Mark and Luke would have us recognize how necessary it is for our character and commitment to be tested over an extended period of time.

Notice the phrase, "until an opportune time." The devil would be back. He is not so easily defeated. He merely backed off until a time he considered more promising. Peter, who was certainly familiar with temptation, wrote in 1 Peter 5:8, "Be of sober spirit, be on the alert. Your adversary, the devil, prowls around like a roaring lion, seeking someone to devour." The tempter is looking for that "opportune time." We learn from this passage that while Satan may turn back for a while, he won't give up. He looks for an opportune time to attack us again.

The temptations of Jesus in the wilderness help us understand the meaning of Hebrews 4:15: "For we do not have a high priest who cannot sympathize with our weaknesses, but One who has been tempted in all things as we are, yet without sin." Jesus endured—and conquered—the same kinds of temptations we face. He understands the battle we're in and will help us in our time of need.

The Miracle at Cana

John 2:1–11

1 *On the third day there was a wedding in Cana of Galilee, and the mother of Jesus was there;* 2 *and both Jesus and His disciples were invited to the wedding.* 3 *When the wine ran out, the mother of Jesus said to Him, "They have no wine."* 4 *And Jesus said to her, "Woman, what does that have to do with us? My hour has not yet come."* 5 *His mother said to the servants, "Whatever He says to you, do it."* 6 *Now there were six stone waterpots set there for the Jewish custom of purification, containing twenty or thirty gallons each.* 7 *Jesus said to them, "Fill the waterpots with water." So they filled them up to the brim.* 8 *And He said to them, "Draw some out now and take it to the headwaiter." So they took it to him.* 9 *When the headwaiter tasted the water which had become wine, and did not know where it came from (but the servants who had drawn the water knew), the headwaiter called the bridegroom,* 10 *and said to him, "Every man serves the good wine first, and when the people have drunk freely, then he serves the poorer wine; but you have kept the good wine until now."* 11 *This beginning of His signs Jesus did in Cana of Galilee, and manifested His glory, and His disciples believed in Him.*

When John notes that "both Jesus and His disciples were invited to the wedding" we get a glimpse into how "making disciples" (Matthew 28:18–20) works. It flows out of personal relationships. Disciples share their experiences with friends, who become disciples, and they share their experiences with their friends, and so the process widens and deepens.

Initially, Jesus was reluctant to address His mother's request, though she appeared confident that He would do something since she said to the servants, "Whatever He says to you, do it" (v. 5). This miracle at Cana was, as John notes, "the beginning of His signs." Jesus was very conscious of timing, as He initially said, "My hour has not yet come" (v. 4). After calm consideration, He stepped up to do what no one else could do and provided more wine for the celebration.

The miracle at Cana marked the beginning of Jesus' ministry; it was His first in the public light. It certainly illustrates the power of God in what might be considered ordinary, non-religious situations. Following the miracle at Cana, some people began to realize that Jesus was more than just another man.

The servants must have been reluctant to follow Jesus' instructions about the waterpots. However, Mary had instructed them to "do whatever He says," so they did. They might have been a little nervous when told to "draw some out and take it to the headwaiter" (v. 8). A miracle followed, and it seems that the only ones who really appreciated it—and expressed their appreciation—were the disciples, Mary, the servants who filled the waterpots, and the headwaiter. Despite the limited audience, Jesus performed the miracle, benefitting everyone at the reception.

Note that the headwaiter commented on the quality of the wine (formerly water). The guests must have noticed also. It seems that many times God's provision is enjoyed, but is not attributed to Him. The people at the reception knew they were drinking the best wine, but they didn't know from where it came. They must have asked questions. We can see in this miracle and the reaction to it, a picture of the human tendency to accept God's gracious provision without any real concern for expressing appreciation.

This miracle helped to affirm the disciples' belief and trust in Jesus. "The disciples believed in Him" (v.11), we're told. It was a step in the process of their maturation and trust.

Jesus Purges the Temple

John 2:13–22

[13] The Passover of the Jews was near, and Jesus went up to
Jerusalem. [14] And He found in the temple those who were
selling oxen and sheep and doves, and the money changers
seated at their tables. [15] And He made a scourge of cords,
and drove them all out of the temple, with the sheep
and the oxen; and He poured out the coins of the money
changers and overturned their tables; [16] and to those who
were selling the doves He said, "Take these things away;
stop making My Father's house a place of business." [17] His
disciples remembered that it was written, "ZEAL FOR
YOUR HOUSE WILL CONSUME ME." [18] The Jews then
said to Him, "What sign do You show us as your authority
for doing these things?" [19] Jesus answered them, "Destroy
this temple, and in three days I will raise it up." [20] The Jews
then said, "It took forty-six years to build this temple, and
will You raise it up in three days?" [21] But He was speaking
of the temple of His body. [22] So when He was raised from
the dead, His disciples remembered that He said this; and
they believed the Scripture and the word which Jesus had
spoken.

Jesus saw the commercialization of an important religious holiday and was furious. The Passover had great significance in Jewish society, and participants were required to have certain elements with them to observe the function. Merchants took advantage of the opportunity to make a profit, setting up shop inside the temple. A place of worship had been turned into a marketplace. Worship that was meant to help people release their burdens actually resulted in them taking on more.

Jesus had made the journey (about 80 miles or so) from Capernaum to Jerusalem to participate in the Passover with His disciples, stopping along the way to visit His family for a few days. His first miracle had been at the wedding in Cana. Now His ministry was about to become much more public. His purging of the temple was anything but a low-key affair. He referred to the temple as "My Father's house" (v. 16). We can understand His anger at seeing it being so badly misused.

His zeal grabbed the attention of everyone there. Some saw the presence of God in what took place. Others saw someone interfering with business as usual and were indignant.

Regarding the process of the temple degenerating into a marketplace instead of a place of worship, what may have begun as a convenience for visiting worshipers to get what they needed had turned into a greedy means of profiteering for some. Worship and celebration were receding into the background. The lesson for our day is that worship should always be at the center of our church gatherings.

Keep in mind that this event followed Jesus' identity-strengthening baptism, His severe testing in the wilderness, and the miracle He performed at Cana. He was stepping more and more into His mission, whatever the cost.

And it seems He knew what was coming, for He said, "Destroy this temple, and in three days I will raise it up" (v. 19). That proved to be prophetic. We're told in verse 22 that after Jesus had been raised from the dead, the disciples recalled what He had said and their faith was strengthened.

Jesus' Meeting with Nicodemus

John 3:1–21

[3:1] *Now there was a man of the Pharisees, named Nicodemus, a ruler of the Jews;* [2] *this man came to Jesus by night and said to Him, "Rabbi, we know that You have come from God as a teacher; for no one can do these signs that You do unless God is with him."* [3] *Jesus answered and*

said to him, "Truly, truly, I say to you, unless one is born
again he cannot see the kingdom of God."

4 *Nicodemus said to Him, "How can a man be born when*
he is old? He cannot enter a second time into his mother's
womb and be born, can he?" 5 *Jesus answered, "Truly,*
truly, I say to you, unless one is born of water and the
Spirit he cannot enter into the kingdom of God. 6 *That*
which is born of the flesh is flesh, and that which is born
of the Spirit is spirit. 7 *Do not be amazed that I said to you,*
'You must be born again.' 8 *The wind blows where it wishes*
and you hear the sound of it, but do not know where it
comes from and where it is going; so is everyone who is
born of the Spirit."

9 *Nicodemus said to Him, "How can these things be?"*
10 *Jesus answered and said to him, "Are you the teacher of*
Israel and do not understand these things? 11 *Truly, truly,*
I say to you, we speak of what we know and testify of
what we have seen, and you do not accept our testimony.
12 *If I told you earthly things and you do not believe, how*
will you believe if I tell you heavenly things? 13 *No one*
has ascended into heaven, but He who descended from
heaven: the Son of Man. 14 *As Moses lifted up the serpent*
in the wilderness, even so must the Son of Man be lifted
up; 15 *so that whoever believes will in Him have eternal*
life.

16 *"For God so loved the world, that He gave His only*
begotten Son, that whoever believes in Him shall not
perish, but have eternal life. 17 *For God did not send the*
Son into the world to judge the world, but that the world
might be saved through Him. 18 *He who believes in Him*
is not judged; he who does not believe has been judged
already, because he has not believed in the name of the
only begotten Son of God. 19 *This is the judgment, that*

the Light has come into the world, and men loved the darkness rather than the Light, for their deeds were evil.
[20] *For everyone who does evil hates the Light, and does not come to the Light for fear that his deeds will be exposed.*
[21] *But he who practices the truth comes to the Light, so that his deeds may be manifested as having been wrought in God."*

We aren't told how Nicodemus knew of Jesus. Perhaps he was in the audience of John the Baptist. Maybe he was one of the guests at the wedding. In his position of leadership, he certainly would have heard about the incident at the temple. And as a "ruler of the Jews," Nicodemus probably had people keeping him informed about what was going on in the area. In any case, his curiosity was high.

Commentators offer different possible reasons as to why Nicodemus came to see Jesus at night. It may have been that he was very concerned about what the meeting could do to his political career. It might have been a politically incorrect move for him to meet with someone as controversial as Jesus. Whatever the reasons, that he desired an undisturbed conversation seems clear.

It's interesting that such a profound discussion was held in private. (Or at least we don't know if anyone else was there to hear it.) Jesus took the time to talk with a curious and seeking politician. Jesus could have asked Nicodemus to come back another time, but He didn't. As it turned out, Nicodemus became a follower of Jesus at some point.

Jesus' Ministry in Samaria

John 4:5–42

[5] *So He came to a city of Samaria called Sychar, near the parcel of ground that Jacob gave to his son Joseph;* [6] *and Jacob's well was there. So Jesus, being wearied from His*

journey, was sitting thus by the well. It was about the sixth
hour. [7] *There came a woman of Samaria to draw water.*
Jesus said to her, "Give Me a drink." [8] *For His disciples*
had gone away into the city to buy food. [9] *Therefore the*
Samaritan woman said to Him, "How is it that You,
being a Jew, ask me for a drink since I am a Samaritan
woman?" (For Jews have no dealings with Samaritans.)
[10] *Jesus answered and said to her, "If you knew the gift*
of God, and who it is who says to you, 'Give Me a drink,'
you would have asked Him, and He would have given you
living water." [11] *She said to Him, "Sir, You have nothing to*
draw with and the well is deep; where then do You get that
living water? [12] *You are not greater than our father Jacob,*
are You, who gave us the well, and drank of it himself
and his sons and his cattle?" [13] *Jesus answered and said to*
her, "Everyone who drinks of this water will thirst again;
[14] *but whoever drinks of the water that I will give him shall*
never thirst; but the water that I will give him will become
in him a well of water springing up to eternal life."

[15] *The woman said to Him, "Sir, give me this water, so I*
will not be thirsty nor come all the way here to draw." [16] *He*
said to her, "Go, call your husband and come here." [17] *The*
woman answered and said, "I have no husband." Jesus
said to her, "You have correctly said, 'I have no husband';
[18] *for you have had five husbands, and the one whom you*
now have is not your husband; this you have said truly."
[19] *The woman said to Him, "Sir, I perceive that You are a*
prophet. [20] *Our fathers worshiped in this mountain, and*
you people say that in Jerusalem is the place where men
ought to worship." [21] *Jesus said to her, "Woman, believe*
Me, an hour is coming when neither in this mountain nor
in Jerusalem will you worship the Father. [22] *You worship*
what you do not know; we worship what we know, for
salvation is from the Jews. [23] *But an hour is coming, and*

now is, when the true worshipers will worship the Father in spirit and truth; for such people the Father seeks to be His worshipers. [24] God is spirit, and those who worship Him must worship in spirit and truth." [25] The woman said to Him, "I know that Messiah is coming (He who is called Christ); when that One comes, He will declare all things to us." [26] Jesus said to her, "I who speak to you am He."

[27] At this point His disciples came, and they were amazed that He had been speaking with a woman, yet no one said, "What do You seek?" or, "Why do You speak with her?" [28] So the woman left her waterpot, and went into the city and said to the men, [29] "Come, see a man who told me all the things that I have done; this is not the Christ, is it?" [30] They went out of the city, and were coming to Him.

[31] Meanwhile the disciples were urging Him, saying, "Rabbi, eat." [32] But He said to them, "I have food to eat that you do not know about." [33] So the disciples were saying to one another, "No one brought Him anything to eat, did he?" [34] Jesus said to them, "My food is to do the will of Him who sent Me and to accomplish His work. [35] Do you not say, 'There are yet four months, and then comes the harvest'? Behold, I say to you, lift up your eyes and look on the fields, that they are white for harvest. [36] Already he who reaps is receiving wages and is gathering fruit for life eternal; so that he who sows and he who reaps may rejoice together. [37] For in this case the saying is true, 'One sows and another reaps.' [38] I sent you to reap that for which you have not labored; others have labored and you have entered into their labor."

[39] From that city many of the Samaritans believed in Him because of the word of the woman who testified, "He told me all the things that I have done." [40] So when the Samaritans came to Jesus, they were asking Him to stay

> *with them; and He stayed there two days.* [41] *Many more believed because of His word;* [42] *and they were saying to the woman, "It is no longer because of what you said that we believe, for we have heard for ourselves and know that this One is indeed the Savior of the world."*

This important work for which God had sent John the Baptist, then Jesus, and now us, is not competitive but cooperative. Note that Jesus moved on when the public began competitive talk about whether Jesus was baptizing more disciples than John (4:1–3). There was more than enough work for John and Jesus to do without fostering a competition between the two. It's the same for faithful churches today—the body of Christ is meant to work together.

At this point, the scope of Jesus' mission was expanding. He went from Judea to Samaria, from a comfortable culture to a foreign one. He went from a private conversation with a Jewish politician to a more public location to talk with a promiscuous lady. The gospel is for all people, not just the Jews.

The work of redemption is pressing and urgent. The fields are "white for harvest" (v. 35). The disciples, and the church today, reap what others have sown (v. 38).

This scene with the woman from Samaria shows us how our work is to be done. We have to meet people where they are, seek to have spiritual conversations, and explain our faith in easy-to-understand ways.

Chapter 2

THE GREAT GALILEAN MINISTRY: THE DISCIPLES CALLED

Jesus' Interaction with Nobility

John 4:46–54

> *46 Therefore He came again to Cana of Galilee where He had made the water wine. And there was a royal official whose son was sick at Capernaum. 47 When he heard that Jesus had come out of Judea into Galilee, he went to Him and was imploring Him to come down and heal his son; for he was at the point of death. 48 So Jesus said to him, "Unless you people see signs and wonders, you simply will not believe." 49 The royal official said to Him, "Sir, come down before my child dies." 50 Jesus said to him, "Go; your son lives." The man believed the word that Jesus spoke to him and started off. 51 As he was now going down, his slaves met him, saying that his son was living. 52 So he inquired of them the hour when he began to get better. Then they said to him, "Yesterday at the seventh hour the fever left him." 53 So the father knew that it was at that hour in which Jesus said to him, "Your son lives"; and he himself believed and his whole household. 54 This is again a second sign that Jesus performed when He had come out of Judea into Galilee.*

We aren't sure how this nobleman knew about Jesus. Apparently, he knew enough about Him to believe that Jesus could do something about his son's illness. Since the man lived in Cana, he might have been a guest at the wedding where Jesus performed His first miracle. It's probably safe to assume he had at least heard about it. In any case, he believed Jesus, heard his son had been healed, and put his faith in Jesus.

Unlike Jesus' first miracle at the wedding in Cana, which was a private event, this was a very public sign. The man was a public official, and it appears that his request was made in a very public venue. The miracle itself is another example of Jesus using His divine power in service to His mission. While we must never lose sight of Jesus' humanity, we must also keep in mind that Jesus is God in the flesh.

Jesus Threatened in His Home Synagogue

Luke 4:16–31

> 16 *And He came to Nazareth, where He had been brought up; and as was His custom, He entered the synagogue on the Sabbath, and stood up to read.* 17 *And the book of the prophet Isaiah was handed to Him. And He opened the book and found the place where it was written,*
>
> 18 *"THE SPIRIT OF THE LORD IS UPON ME, BECAUSE HE ANOINTED ME TO PREACH THE GOSPEL TO THE POOR. HE HAS SENT ME TO PROCLAIM RELEASE TO THE CAPTIVES, AND RECOVERY OF SIGHT TO THE BLIND, TO SET FREE THOSE WHO ARE OPPRESSED,* 19 *TO PROCLAIM THE FAVORABLE YEAR OF THE LORD."*
>
> 20 *And He closed the book, gave it back to the attendant and sat down; and the eyes of all in the synagogue were fixed on Him.* 21 *And He began to say to them, "Today this Scripture has been fulfilled in your hearing."* 22 *And all were speaking well of Him, and wondering at the gracious words which were falling from His lips; and they were saying, "Is this not Joseph's son?"* 23 *And He said*

> *to them, "No doubt you will quote this proverb to Me, 'Physician, heal yourself! Whatever we heard was done at Capernaum, do here in your hometown as well.'"* 24 *And He said, "Truly I say to you, no prophet is welcome in his hometown.* 25 *But I say to you in truth, there were many widows in Israel in the days of Elijah, when the sky was shut up for three years and six months, when a great famine came over all the land;* 26 *and yet Elijah was sent to none of them, but only to Zarephath, in the land of Sidon, to a woman who was a widow.* 27 *And there were many lepers in Israel in the time of Elisha the prophet; and none of them was cleansed, but only Naaman the Syrian."* 28 *And all the people in the synagogue were filled with rage as they heard these things;* 29 *and they got up and drove Him out of the city, and led Him to the brow of the hill on which their city had been built, in order to throw Him down the cliff.* 30 *But passing through their midst, He went His way.*
>
> 31 *And He came down to Capernaum, a city of Galilee, and He was teaching them on the Sabbath.*

Jesus was accustomed to attending the synagogue on the Sabbath. People there knew Him. After all, he had grown up in Nazareth.

Jesus read from Isaiah, announcing Himself as the person fulfilling that prophecy. This probably wasn't the first time they heard that passage, but it was definitely the most impactful. At first, "all were speaking well of Him, and wondering at the gracious words which were falling from His lips" (v. 22), but that didn't last long.

Jesus went on to tell a couple stories from the Old Testament that the people in the congregation understood to be an unflattering comparison between rebellious Israel and themselves. They became enraged and attempted to do away with Jesus. Somehow He escaped through the crowd. (God can rescue us, too, from what seem like impossible situations.)

The reaction of this congregation shouldn't surprise us. A "kill the messenger" attitude is alive and well both inside and outside the church. Sometimes we prefer blissful ignorance to hearing the truth and having to change.

Jesus Recruits His Disciples

Matthew 4:18–22

> 18 *Now as Jesus was walking by the Sea of Galilee, He saw two brothers, Simon who was called Peter, and Andrew his brother, casting a net into the sea; for they were fishermen.* 19 *And He said to them, "Follow Me, and I will make you fishers of men."* 20 *Immediately they left their nets and followed Him.* 21 *Going on from there He saw two other brothers, James the son of Zebedee, and John his brother, in the boat with Zebedee their father, mending their nets; and He called them.* 22 *Immediately they left the boat and their father, and followed Him.*

Matthew's account does not include some of the events we've discussed so far (e.g., the wedding at Cana, the purging of the temple). No one person could keep up with all that was happening in Jesus' life. Second Timothy 3:16 says that "all Scripture is given by inspiration of God." We must believe that God was leading Matthew to record what he did, just as He was leading the other Gospel writers to record what they did.

Matthew saw the unfolding events in light of prophecy. The relocation of Jesus to Galilee was a fulfillment of Isaiah 9:1–2: "But there will be no more gloom for her who was in anguish; in earlier times He treated the land of Zebulun and the land of Naphtali with contempt, but later on He shall make it glorious, by the way of the sea, on the other side of Jordan, Galilee of the Gentiles. The people who walk in darkness will see a great light; those who live in a dark land, the light will shine on them."

Jesus began calling His disciples shortly after He started His ministry. Andrew had heard John the Baptist announce who Jesus was, and along with another disciple, he followed after Jesus. Jesus invited them to spend the day where He was staying. Andrew shared what he had learned with his brother, Peter (John 1:35–40).

Andrew and Peter were fishermen, as were James and John. It's not unreasonable to think that they must have talked with each other about their meeting with Jesus. They all had some prior knowledge of Jesus before He called them.

Mark 1:16–20

16 *As He was going along by the Sea of Galilee, He saw Simon and Andrew, the brother of Simon, casting a net in the sea; for they were fishermen.* 17 *And Jesus said to them, "Follow Me, and I will make you become fishers of men."* 18 *Immediately they left their nets and followed Him.* 19 *Going on a little farther, He saw James the son of Zebedee, and John his brother, who were also in the boat mending the nets.* 20 *Immediately He called them; and they left their father Zebedee in the boat with the hired servants, and went away to follow Him.*

Like Matthew's Gospel, Mark's Gospel goes from the temptations in the wilderness to Jesus' public ministry, picking up after the arrest of John the Baptist.

Luke 5:1–11

1 *Now it happened that while the crowd was pressing around Him and listening to the word of God, He was standing by the lake of Gennesaret;* 2 *and He saw two boats*

> *lying at the edge of the lake; but the fishermen had gotten out of them and were washing their nets. [3] And He got into one of the boats, which was Simon's, and asked him to put out a little way from the land. And He sat down and began teaching the people from the boat. [4] When He had finished speaking, He said to Simon, "Put out into the deep water and let down your nets for a catch." [5] Simon answered and said, "Master, we worked hard all night and caught nothing, but I will do as You say and let down the nets." [6] When they had done this, they enclosed a great quantity of fish, and their nets began to break; [7] so they signaled to their partners in the other boat for them to come and help them. And they came and filled both of the boats, so that they began to sink. [8] But when Simon Peter saw that, he fell down at Jesus' feet, saying, "Go away from me Lord, for I am a sinful man!" [9] For amazement had seized him and all his companions because of the catch of fish which they had taken; [10] and so also were James and John, sons of Zebedee, who were partners with Simon. And Jesus said to Simon, "Do not fear, from now on you will be catching men." [11] When they had brought their boats to land, they left everything and followed Him.*

Luke's Gospel includes some detail that neither Matthew nor Mark mention. We know from John's Gospel that Jesus knew Peter—Andrew had introduced them. He may have assumed that James and John were friends of Peter's, since they were fishing together.

Jesus tested their readiness to follow Him. First, He requested permission to use one of their boats as a pulpit—a platform from which to address the crowd. Then He asked Peter and Andrew to try fishing in a particular spot. Luke notes their reluctance. After all, they were fishermen and they knew that spot wasn't a good place to catch fish. Jesus was just a carpenter. How should He know? But they obeyed and were amazed with the results.

When Peter, Andrew, James, and John expressed their amazement at the catch, Jesus said to them (paraphrase): "If you follow My instructions, you'll see results, even in the lives of people."

These disciples were common men, not exceptional or especially learned. They seem to be the sort of disciples described in 1 Corinthians 1:26–27: "For consider your calling, brethren, that there were not many wise according to the flesh, not many mighty, not many noble; but God has chosen the foolish things of the world to shame the wise, and God has chosen the weak things of the world to shame the things which are strong." Their example assures us that God is capable of using any person who will answer the call to follow Jesus.

Jesus Heals Peter's Mother-in-law and Many Others

Matthew 8:14–17

14 When Jesus came into Peter's home, He saw his mother-in-law lying sick in bed with a fever. 15 He touched her hand, and the fever left her; and she got up and waited on Him. 16 When evening came, they brought to Him many who were demon-possessed; and He cast out the spirits with a word, and healed all who were ill. 17 This was to fulfill what was spoken through Isaiah the prophet: "HE HIMSELF TOOK OUR INFIRMITIES AND CARRIED AWAY OUR DISEASES."

Matthew tells us that Jesus visited Peter's home. The visit took place shortly after Peter had accepted Jesus' invitation to become a disciple. Perhaps Peter invited Jesus over because his mother-in-law was sick. After witnessing the fishing miracle, he might have thought Jesus could do something to help her.

Notice Jesus' absolute authority over disease. He touched the hand of Peter's mother-in-law and she was healed. He merely spoke a word of healing to the multitudes, and they were healed. The method of healing didn't seem to matter. These diseases were subject to His authority.

Matthew quotes Isaiah 53:4: "He Himself took our infirmities and carried away our diseases." Christ deals with the problems that we can't deal with ourselves—our sin and our weaknesses. God is a merciful, rescuing God.

Mark 1:29–34

29 *And immediately after they came out of the synagogue,*
they came into the house of Simon and Andrew, with
James and John. 30 *Now Simon's mother-in-law was lying*
sick with a fever; and immediately they spoke to Jesus
about her. 31 *And He came to her and raised her up, taking*
her by the hand, and the fever left her, and she waited on
them.

32 *When evening came, after the sun had set, they began*
bringing to Him all who were ill and those who were
demon-possessed. 33 *And the whole city had gathered at*
the door. 34 *And He healed many who were ill with various*
diseases, and cast out many demons; and He was not
permitting the demons to speak, because they knew who
He was.

According to Mark, all four of them (Peter, Andrew, James, and John) went to Peter's house. Mark says they spoke to Jesus about Peter's sick mother-in-law. They had all seen His ability to do the miraculous with the amazing catch they hauled in thanks to Jesus' fishing tips.

Mark's account adds the detail that Jesus helped Peter's mother-in-law out of bed, showing His compassion. Additionally, the four men, and perhaps others, brought many others to Jesus for healing and to be freed from demon possession. Jesus' mercy and power are both on display in this episode.

Luke 4:38–41

[38] *Then He got up and left the synagogue, and entered Simon's home. Now Simon's mother-in-law was suffering from a high fever, and they asked Him to help her.* [39] *And standing over her, He rebuked the fever, and it left her; and she immediately got up and waited on them.*

[40] *While the sun was setting, all those who had any who were sick with various diseases brought them to Him; and laying His hands on each one of them, He was healing them.* [41] *Demons also were coming out of many, shouting, "You are the Son of God!" But rebuking them, He would not allow them to speak, because they knew Him to be the Christ.*

Luke says in verse 38 that Jesus "rebuked the fever" (with a word), while He laid hands on others. Both methods illustrate His absolute authority, and both wonderfully illustrate His attention to individuals. The kingdom spreads relationally, one person at a time.

There are small differences in what each Gospel writer recorded about this incident. These differences can be accounted for by realizing that each writer wrote down what was most important to him as he either observed the healing or heard about it.

The Disciples' First Preaching Tour

Matthew 4:23–25

[23] *Jesus was going throughout all Galilee, teaching in their synagogues and proclaiming the gospel of the kingdom, and healing every kind of disease and every kind of sickness among the people.*

[24] The news about Him spread throughout all Syria; and they brought to Him all who were ill, those suffering with various diseases and pains, demoniacs, epileptics, paralytics; and He healed them. [25] Large crowds followed Him from Galilee and the Decapolis and Jerusalem and Judea and from beyond the Jordan.

Jesus taught in Galilee's synagogues, proclaiming the kingdom of God to people who would have some understanding of the Scriptures. Matthew doesn't record it, but Jesus likely announced that He was the fulfillment of Isaiah's prophecies (see Luke 4:18–21). Jesus understood His audience and could speak the right word of challenge.

Jesus' ministry was certainly not restricted to buildings, though. He went to where the people were. His ministry seemed to be more "go and tell" than "come and hear."

We can imagine that many who were healed began following Jesus, helping to spread the good news among family, friends, and whoever else would listen.

Mark 1:35–39

[35] In the early morning, while it was still dark, Jesus got up, left the house, and went away to a secluded place, and was praying there. [36] Simon and his companions searched for Him; [37] they found Him, and said to Him, "Everyone is looking for You." [38] He said to them, "Let us go somewhere else to the towns nearby, so that I may preach there also; for that is what I came for." [39] And He went into their synagogues throughout all Galilee, preaching and casting out the demons.

Jesus slipped out of Peter's house early in the morning to pray in a secluded place. We aren't told how much time passed before Peter and the others found Him. He was in high demand, so they came looking for Him.

After this period in private prayer, Jesus was intent on continuing His ministry in nearby towns. Perhaps the urgency of His mission became even more clear after spending time in prayer with His Father. Jesus was focused on doing His Father's will and fulfilling His ministry. That is a constant theme throughout the Gospels.

Luke 4:42–44

[42] *When day came, Jesus left and went to a secluded place;*
and the crowds were searching for Him, and came to Him
and tried to keep Him from going away from them. [43] *But*
He said to them, "I must preach the kingdom of God to
the other cities also, for I was sent for this purpose."

[44] *So He kept on preaching in the synagogues of Judea.*

The group looking for Jesus included more than Peter's household; it also included the crowds He had ministered to.

Again we see how Jesus' time alone with His Father assured Him of His mission and compelled Him to pursue it. While Jesus never seemed rushed, there was an urgency to His mission. He was sent to preach the kingdom, and that remained His focus.

Matthew Becomes a Follower

Matthew 9:9–13

[9] *As Jesus went on from there, He saw a man called*
Matthew, sitting in the tax collector's booth; and He said
to him, "Follow Me!" And he got up and followed Him.

[10] *Then it happened that as Jesus was reclining at the table*
in the house, behold, many tax collectors and sinners
came and were dining with Jesus and His disciples.
[11] *When the Pharisees saw this, they said to His disciples,*

"Why is your Teacher eating with the tax collectors and sinners?" [12] *But when Jesus heard this, He said, "It is not those who are healthy who need a physician, but those who are sick.* [13] *But go and learn what this means: 'I DESIRE COMPASSION, AND NOT SACRIFICE,' for I did not come to call the righteous, but sinners."*

Matthew's account of how he became a follower of Jesus is a first-person testimony told in third person. As a disrespected tax collector, Matthew must have been surprised that Jesus took an interest in him. After all, Jesus was the talk of the town, and Matthew would have heard of Him. Upon receiving Jesus' invitation, Matthew "got up and followed Him" (v. 9).

Following his interaction with Jesus, Matthew invited some of his friends and fellow workers to spend time with Jesus. The Pharisees were upset that Jesus would eat with some of the most despised people in society.

We can assume the events Matthew recorded prior to his entering the story at this point came from the inspired testimony of others.

Mark 2:13–17

[13] *And He went out again by the seashore; and all the people were coming to Him, and He was teaching them.*

[14] *As He passed by, He saw Levi the son of Alphaeus sitting in the tax booth, and He said to him, "Follow Me!" And he got up and followed Him.*

[15] *And it happened that He was reclining at the table in his house, and many tax collectors and sinners were dining with Jesus and His disciples; for there were many of them,*
and they were following Him. [16] *When the scribes of the*
Pharisees saw that He was eating with the sinners and tax collectors, they said to His disciples, "Why is He eating

and drinking with tax collectors and sinners?" [17] *And hearing this, Jesus said to them, "It is not those who are healthy who need a physician, but those who are sick; I did not come to call the righteous, but sinners."*

Matthew may have told his story to Mark. If so, he probably said something about Jesus coming to his place of work and offering the invitation to follow Him. Mark seems to be impressed that Jesus came over to Matthew's house for a meal.

Mark says many tax collectors and sinners showed up for the meal. Jesus didn't screen out the riffraff of society. Instead, He said he came for "sinners," not the "righteous"; the "sick," not the "healthy" (v. 17).

A form of sickness is revealed when religious people disassociate themselves from the very people who most need the healing Jesus offers.

Luke 5:27–32

[27] *After that He went out and noticed a tax collector named Levi sitting in the tax booth, and He said to him, "Follow Me."* [28] *And he left everything behind, and got up and began to follow Him.*

[29] *And Levi gave a big reception for Him in his house; and there was a great crowd of tax collectors and other people who were reclining at the table with them.* [30] *The Pharisees and their scribes began grumbling at His disciples, saying, "Why do you eat and drink with the tax collectors and sinners?"* [31] *And Jesus answered and said to them, "It is not those who are well who need a physician, but those who are sick.* [32] *I have not come to call the righteous but sinners to repentance."*

Luke says Matthew threw a big reception for Jesus. Matthew was celebrating his new allegiance to Jesus, and he wanted to share his discovery with all his friends. That's a great description of evangelism.

We should point out the obvious here: the scribes and Pharisees were sinners too, just as we all are. They needed repentance just as much as the people they were criticizing. They had excluded themselves from needing what Jesus came to offer—forgiveness and life. Religious blindness can be the most difficult blindness to overcome.

Jesus Designates the Twelve for a Special Assignment

Mark 3:13–19

> 13 *And He went up on the mountain and summoned those*
> *whom He Himself wanted, and they came to Him.* 14 *And*
> *He appointed twelve, so that they would be with Him and*
> *that He could send them out to preach,* 15 *and to have*
> *authority to cast out the demons.* 16 *And He appointed the*
> *twelve: Simon (to whom He gave the name Peter),* 17 *and*
> *James, the son of Zebedee, and John the brother of James*
> *(to them He gave the name Boanerges, which means,*
> *"Sons of Thunder");* 18 *and Andrew, and Philip, and*
> *Bartholomew, and Matthew, and Thomas, and James the*
> *son of Alphaeus, and Thaddaeus, and Simon the Zealot;*
> 19 *and Judas Iscariot, who betrayed Him.*

Jesus found a private place to share His vision and plans with the twelve men He had called to help Him accomplish God's mission. From among the men Jesus summoned, He selected twelve for intensive training. These men would follow Him everywhere (as compared with the other disciples who had local constraints that required their attention). One can be a follower of Jesus and not forsake home and job. In fact, He needs disciples to follow Him in their homes and jobs, too. Each of us needs to discern what the Lord is calling us to.

These twelve disciples would be given specific assignments, so they would need intensive training. You may have heard the saying, "God doesn't call the qualified; He qualifies the called." That was the case with these guys. They would later be known as the twelve apostles, or "sent ones."

Mark's account helps us see the intimate familiarity Jesus has with His followers. Not only did He know them by name, He gave personal nicknames to some of them. When we are following Jesus, we are not "lost in the crowd." We are known individually and personally.

Luke 6:12–16

12 *It was at this time that He went off to the mountain*
to pray, and He spent the whole night in prayer to God.
13 *And when day came, He called His disciples to Him*
and chose twelve of them, whom He also named as
apostles: 14 *Simon, whom He also named Peter, and*
Andrew his brother; and James and John; and Philip and
Bartholomew; 15 *and Matthew and Thomas; James the*
son of Alphaeus, and Simon who was called the Zealot;
16 *Judas the son of James, and Judas Iscariot, who became*
a traitor.

Jesus' decision to expand His ministry into Galilee followed an all-night session of prayer with His Father. He was always seeking to do the Father's will, and He needed wisdom for what was next. If prayer was that important to Jesus, it certainly should be a priority for us, too.

Have you ever noticed that there is no mention of anyone feeling hurt, neglected, or overlooked after Jesus chose the twelve? That is how the church should work—each person concerned with fulfilling his or her own ministry for the good of everyone.

Chapter 3

THE GREAT GALILEAN MINISTRY: THE SERMON ON THE MOUNT

The Beatitudes

Matthew 5:1–11

1 When Jesus saw the crowds, He went up on the mountain;
and after He sat down, His disciples came to Him. 2 He
opened His mouth and began to teach them, saying,
3 "Blessed are the poor in spirit, for theirs is the kingdom of
heaven. 4 "Blessed are those who mourn, for they shall be
comforted. 5 "Blessed are the gentle, for they shall inherit
the earth. 6 "Blessed are those who hunger and thirst for
righteousness, for they shall be satisfied. 7 "Blessed are
the merciful, for they shall receive mercy. 8 "Blessed are
the pure in heart, for they shall see God. 9 "Blessed are
the peacemakers, for they shall be called sons of God.
10 "Blessed are those who have been persecuted for the
sake of righteousness, for theirs is the kingdom of heaven.
11 "Blessed are you when people insult you and persecute
you, and falsely say all kinds of evil against you because
of Me. 12 Rejoice and be glad, for your reward in heaven
is great; for in the same way they persecuted the prophets
who were before you.

The Beatitudes describe life in the kingdom for followers of Jesus. The attitudes and behaviors listed are countercultural—that is, the world doesn't consider being "poor in spirit" a "blessed" condition (v. 3), but in God's kingdom, it is. Note, these descriptions aren't entrance requirements for the kingdom, but ways of living for those who have trusted Christ.

Disciples and the World

Matthew 5:13–20

[13] "You are the salt of the earth; but if the salt has become tasteless, how can it be made salty again? It is no longer good for anything, except to be thrown out and trampled under foot by men.

[14] "You are the light of the world. A city set on a hill cannot
be hidden; [15] nor does anyone light a lamp and put it
under a basket, but on the lampstand, and it gives light to
all who are in the house. [16] Let your light shine before men
in such a way that they may see your good works, and glorify your Father who is in heaven.

[17] "Do not think that I came to abolish the Law or the
Prophets; I did not come to abolish but to fulfill. [18] For
truly I say to you, until heaven and earth pass away, not the smallest letter or stroke shall pass from the Law until
all is accomplished. [19] Whoever then annuls one of the
least of these commandments, and teaches others to do the same, shall be called least in the kingdom of heaven; but whoever keeps and teaches them, he shall be called great in the kingdom of heaven.

[20] "For I say to you that unless your righteousness surpasses that of the scribes and Pharisees, you will not enter the kingdom of heaven.

Followers of Jesus are meant to challenge the values and goals of the world, showing that life apart from a vital relationship with God through Jesus is not really life at all. The "light" believers shine into a dark world is not always welcomed. Jesus challenges His followers to understand that they cannot shirk the assignment given them to provide a bright contrast to this dismal world.

Personal Relationships

Matthew 5:21–48

[21] *"You have heard that the ancients were told, 'YOU*
SHALL NOT COMMIT MURDER' and 'Whoever
commits murder shall be liable to the court.' [22] *But I say to*
you that everyone who is angry with his brother shall be
guilty before the court; and whoever says to his brother,
'You good-for-nothing,' shall be guilty before the supreme
court; and whoever says, 'You fool,' shall be guilty enough
to go into the fiery hell. [23] *Therefore if you are presenting*
your offering at the altar, and there remember that your
brother has something against you, [24] *leave your offering*
there before the altar and go; first be reconciled to your
brother, and then come and present your offering.
[25] *Make friends quickly with your opponent at law*
while you are with him on the way, so that your opponent
may not hand you over to the judge, and the judge to the
officer, and you be thrown into prison. [26] *Truly I say to*
you, you will not come out of there until you have paid
up the last cent.

[27] *"You have heard that it was said, 'YOU SHALL NOT*
COMMIT ADULTERY'; [28] *but I say to you that everyone*
who looks at a woman with lust for her has already
committed adultery with her in his heart. [29] *If your right*
eye makes you stumble, tear it out and throw it from you;
for it is better for you to lose one of the parts of your body,
than for your whole body to be thrown into hell. [30] *If your*
right hand makes you stumble, cut it off and throw it from
you; for it is better for you to lose one of the parts of your
body, than for your whole body to go into hell.

[31] *"It was said, 'WHOEVER SENDS HIS WIFE AWAY,*
LET HIM GIVE HER A CERTIFICATE OF DIVORCE';
[32] *but I say to you that everyone who divorces his wife,*

except for the reason of unchastity, makes her commit
adultery; and whoever marries a divorced woman
commits adultery.

33 *"Again, you have heard that the ancients were told,*
'YOU SHALL NOT MAKE FALSE VOWS, BUT SHALL
FULFILL YOUR VOWS TO THE LORD.' 34 *But I say to*
you, make no oath at all, either by heaven, for it is the
throne of God, 35 *or by the earth, for it is the footstool of His*
feet, or by Jerusalem, for it is THE CITY OF THE GREAT
KING. 36 *Nor shall you make an oath by your head, for*
you cannot make one hair white or black. 37 *But let your*
statement be, 'Yes, yes' or 'No, no'; anything beyond these
is of evil.

38 *"You have heard that it was said, 'AN EYE FOR AN*
EYE, AND A TOOTH FOR A TOOTH.' 39 *But I say to*
you, do not resist an evil person; but whoever slaps you on
your right cheek, turn the other to him also. 40 *If anyone*
wants to sue you and take your shirt, let him have your
coat also. 41 *Whoever forces you to go one mile, go with*
him two. 42 *Give to him who asks of you, and do not turn*
away from him who wants to borrow from you.

Redemption, rather than retaliation is the expectation for followers of Christ. Grace has a powerful voice.

43 *"You have heard that it was said, 'YOU SHALL LOVE*
YOUR NEIGHBOR and hate your enemy.' 44 *But I say to*
you, love your enemies and pray for those who persecute
you, 45 *so that you may be sons of your Father who is in*
heaven; for He causes His sun to rise on the evil and the
good, and sends rain on the righteous and the unrighteous.
46 *For if you love those who love you, what reward do you*
have? Do not even the tax collectors do the same? 47 *If you*
greet only your brothers, what more are you doing than

others? Do not even the Gentiles do the same? [48] *Therefore you are to be perfect, as your heavenly Father is perfect.*

Sin goes beyond the letter of the law to the actual motivations of our hearts. In that sense, Jesus raises the bar on the Mosaic Law, calling for a transformed heart. For example, regarding vows (or oaths), followers of Christ should live with such integrity that making a vow is completely unnecessary. A simple yes or no reply ought to be enough.

Jesus challenges His followers to practice unconditional love (v. 44), even toward enemies. This kind of love distinguishes Christians from the rest of the world and is representative of the kind of love God offers the world.

Giving to the Poor and Prayer

Matthew 6:1–15

[1] *"Beware of practicing your righteousness before men to be noticed by them; otherwise you have no reward with your Father who is in heaven.*

[2] *"So when you give to the poor, do not sound a trumpet before you, as the hypocrites do in the synagogues and in the streets, so that they may be honored by men. Truly I say to you, they have their reward in full.* [3] *But when you give to the poor, do not let your left hand know what your right hand is doing,* [4] *so that your giving will be in secret; and your Father who sees what is done in secret will reward you.*

[5] *"When you pray, you are not to be like the hypocrites; for they love to stand and pray in the synagogues and on the street corners so that they may be seen by men. Truly I say to you, they have their reward in full.* [6] *But you, when you pray, go into your inner room, close your door and pray*

to your Father who is in secret, and your Father who sees what is done in secret will reward you.

7 *"And when you are praying, do not use meaningless repetition as the Gentiles do, for they suppose that they will be heard for their many words.* 8 *So do not be like them; for your Father knows what you need before you ask Him.*

9 *"Pray, then, in this way: 'Our Father who is in heaven, Hallowed be Your name.* 10 *'Your kingdom come. Your will be done, On earth as it is in heaven.* 11 *'Give us this day our daily bread.* 12 *'And forgive us our debts, as we also have forgiven our debtors.* 13 *'And do not lead us into temptation, but deliver us from evil. [For Yours is the kingdom and the power and the glory forever. Amen.']*
14 *For if you forgive others for their transgressions, your heavenly Father will also forgive you.* 15 *But if you do not forgive others, then your Father will not forgive your transgressions.*

When light shines into the darkness, not much attention is given to the bulb producing the light. Jesus expects that those who follow Him will be so persistent in authentic practice and devotion that what they do will be more apparent than who is doing it. God rewards what is done in secret (v. 4).

Jesus taught that prayer is conversation with God. It is an intimate encounter with our Heavenly Father that is not to be entered into for the purpose of impressing others.

Because real prayer is a conversation between a child of God and the Father, meaningless repetition is out of place. Prayer is not a matter of unlocking God's blessing through the recitation of some special words; it is a matter of cultivating the relationship through honest communication.

The Lord's Prayer is a basic outline for praying. We start with the recognition that we are God's children and that He is great. We submit ourselves to His will and ask for His daily provision. We acknowledge our need for forgiveness and our need to forgive others. We plead for His protection from the enemy and praise Him for ruling and reigning both now and forever. It's a great prayer to reorient us to reality.

Fasting; The True Treasure; Wealth (Mammon)

Matthew 6:16–24

16 *"Whenever you fast, do not put on a gloomy face as the hypocrites do, for they neglect their appearance so that they will be noticed by men when they are fasting. Truly I say to you, they have their reward in full.* 17 *But you, when you fast, anoint your head and wash your face* 18 *so that your fasting will not be noticed by men, but by your Father who is in secret; and your Father who sees what is done in secret will reward you.*

19 *"Do not store up for yourselves treasures on earth, where moth and rust destroy, and where thieves break in and steal.* 20 *But store up for yourselves treasures in heaven, where neither moth nor rust destroys, and where thieves do not break in or steal;* 21 *for where your treasure is, there your heart will be also.*

22 *"The eye is the lamp of the body; so then if your eye is clear, your whole body will be full of light.* 23 *But if your eye is bad, your whole body will be full of darkness. If then the light that is in you is darkness, how great is the darkness!*

24 *"No one can serve two masters; for either he will hate the one and love the other, or he will be devoted to one and despise the other. You cannot serve God and wealth.*

Apparently, Jesus expected that His followers would fast because He said "whenever you fast" (v. 16), not "if" you fast.

Fasting is a spiritual exercise between a person and God. It's not meant to show others how spiritually dedicated we are. The impact of fasting will be experienced by the person who fasts for the right reasons.

Jesus expects that His followers will work and live productively for the benefit of others. However, Christians understand that this present world is temporary (v. 20), and we shouldn't be focused on worldly gain at the expense of doing God's will.

Christians are cautioned to monitor what we allow into our minds. Our perspective and desires are shaped by what we focus on, so it's important to keep our focus on the things of God.

Christ insists that His followers not split their devotion between Him and any other competing loyalty, especially the pursuit of wealth. The allure of material things in this world is strong and must be guarded against.

The Cure for Anxiety

Matthew 6:25–34

[25] *"For this reason I say to you, do not be worried about
your life, as to what you will eat or what you will drink;
nor for your body, as to what you will put on. Is not life
more than food, and the body more than clothing?* [26] *Look
at the birds of the air, that they do not sow, nor reap nor
gather into barns, and yet your heavenly Father feeds
them. Are you not worth much more than they?* [27] *And
who of you by being worried can add a single hour to his
life?* [28] *And why are you worried about clothing? Observe
how the lilies of the field grow; they do not toil nor do
they spin,* [29] *yet I say to you that not even Solomon in all
his glory clothed himself like one of these.* [30] *But if God
so clothes the grass of the field, which is alive today and
tomorrow is thrown into the furnace, will He not much*

more clothe you? You of little faith! [31] Do not worry then,
saying, 'What will we eat?' or 'What will we drink?'
or 'What will we wear for clothing?' [32] For the Gentiles
eagerly seek all these things; for your heavenly Father
knows that you need all these things. [33] But seek first His
kingdom and His righteousness, and all these things will
be added to you.

[34] "So do not worry about tomorrow; for tomorrow will
care for itself. Each day has enough trouble of its own.

The concern for having enough is natural, but it can cause a lot of unnecessary anxiety. That's why Jesus includes praying for daily provision in the Lord's Prayer. In this beautiful section of Scripture, He reminds His followers that God sees our needs and is able to meet those needs, so we don't need to be too concerned about having enough. Our focus should be on seeking His kingdom and His righteousness (v. 33).

Judging Others

Matthew 7:1–16

[1] "Do not judge so that you will not be judged. [2] For in the
way you judge, you will be judged; and by your standard
of measure, it will be measured to you. [3] Why do you look
at the speck that is in your brother's eye, but do not notice
the log that is in your own eye? [4] Or how can you say to
your brother, 'Let me take the speck out of your eye,' and
behold, the log is in your own eye? [5] You hypocrite, first
take the log out of your own eye, and then you will see
clearly to take the speck out of your brother's eye.

[6] "Do not give what is holy to dogs, and do not throw your
pearls before swine, or they will trample them under their
feet, and turn and tear you to pieces.

Judging people and their behavior is God's job, not ours. The truth is, we're often blind to our own faults, and the blindness makes it difficult for us to make fair judgments of others.

We are called to share the gospel with others, recognizing that not everyone will receive our message. There is a time to move on.

Prayer and the Golden Rule

Matthew 7:7–12

7 *"Ask, and it will be given to you; seek, and you will find;*
knock, and it will be opened to you. 8 *For everyone who*
asks receives, and he who seeks finds, and to him who
knocks it will be opened. 9 *Or what man is there among*
you who, when his son asks for a loaf, will give him a
stone? 10 *Or if he asks for a fish, he will not give him a*
snake, will he? 11 *If you then, being evil, know how to give*
good gifts to your children, how much more will your
Father who is in heaven give what is good to those who
ask Him!

12 *"In everything, therefore, treat people the same way*
you want them to treat you, for this is the Law and the
Prophets.

Our Heavenly Father instructs us to pray with faith and expectation. We are to "ask," "seek," and "knock," knowing that He desires to answer our prayers and bless us with what we need. Another way to say this is we are to make our requests known, pursue the will of God through faithful action, and persist in praying until we discern God's answer.

Verse 12, often referred to as "the Golden Rule," is a summary of the Law and the Prophets.

The Narrow and Wide Gates

Matthew 7:13–14

13 *"Enter through the narrow gate; for the gate is wide and*
the way is broad that leads to destruction, and there are
many who enter through it. 14 *For the gate is small and the*
way is narrow that leads to life, and there are few who
find it.

The way of salvation is narrow—only through Jesus. And the path of discipleship is difficult. But it is the only way to true life, beginning now and lasting forever.

A Tree and Its Fruit

Matthew 7:15–23

15 *"Beware of the false prophets, who come to you in*
sheep's clothing, but inwardly are ravenous wolves. 16 *You*
will know them by their fruits. Grapes are not gathered
from thorn bushes nor figs from thistles, are they? 17 *So*
every good tree bears good fruit, but the bad tree bears
bad fruit. 18 *A good tree cannot produce bad fruit, nor can*
a bad tree produce good fruit. 19 *Every tree that does not*
bear good fruit is cut down and thrown into the fire. 20 *So*
then, you will know them by their fruits.

21 *"Not everyone who says to Me, 'Lord, Lord,' will enter*
the kingdom of heaven, but he who does the will of My
Father who is in heaven will enter. 22 *Many will say to*
Me on that day, 'Lord, Lord, did we not prophesy in Your
name, and in Your name cast out demons, and in Your
name perform many miracles?' 23 *And then I will declare*
to them, 'I never knew you; DEPART FROM ME, YOU
WHO PRACTICE LAWLESSNESS.'

Jesus warned His followers that the world is full of deceivers with bad motives. The way to identify the truthfulness of a person or ministry is through the fruit produced. Is the person living a life of integrity and faithfulness to the Scriptures? That's the test.

Many who appeared to be following Jesus were really pursuing their own agendas. The day of judgment will reveal the truth.

The Two Foundations

Matthew 7:24–29

[24] *"Therefore everyone who hears these words of Mine and acts on them, may be compared to a wise man who built his house on the rock.* [25] *And the rain fell, and the floods came, and the winds blew and slammed against that house; and yet it did not fall, for it had been founded on the rock.* [26] *Everyone who hears these words of Mine and does not act on them, will be like a foolish man who built his house on the sand.* [27] *The rain fell, and the floods came, and the winds blew and slammed against that house; and it fell—and great was its fall."*

[28] *When Jesus had finished these words, the crowds were amazed at His teaching;* [29] *for He was teaching them as one having authority, and not as their scribes.*

What a person builds his or her life upon is a matter is of eternal importance. The world offers what appears to be an attractive alternative to faith in Christ, but Jesus warns that what is offered is not adequate. He likens the world's offer to a house built on sand; it may look good on the outside, but when storms come it will be collapse. By contrast, lives founded upon a personal relationship with Christ will survive even the fiercest of storms.

The Beatitudes

Luke 6:20–45

[20] *And turning His gaze toward His disciples, He began to say, "Blessed are you who are poor, for yours is the kingdom of God.* [21] *Blessed are you who hunger now, for you shall be satisfied. Blessed are you who weep now, for you shall laugh.* [22] *Blessed are you when men hate you, and ostracize you, and insult you, and scorn your name as evil, for the sake of the Son of Man.* [23] *Be glad in that day and leap for joy, for behold, your reward is great in heaven. For in the same way their fathers used to treat the prophets.* [24] *But woe to you who are rich, for you are receiving your comfort in full.* [25] *Woe to you who are well-fed now, for you shall be hungry. Woe to you who laugh now, for you shall mourn and weep.* [26] *Woe to you when all men speak well of you, for their fathers used to treat the false prophets in the same way*

"But I say to you who hear, love your enemies, do good to those who hate you, [28] *bless those who curse you, pray for those who mistreat you.* [29] *Whoever hits you on the cheek, offer him the other also; and whoever takes away your coat, do not withhold your shirt from him either.* [30] *Give to everyone who asks of you, and whoever takes away what is yours, do not demand it back.* [31] *Treat others the same way you want them to treat you.* [32] *If you love those who love you, what credit is that to you? For even sinners love those who love them.* [33] *If you do good to those who do good to you, what credit is that to you? For even sinners do the same.* [34] *If you lend to those from whom you expect to receive, what credit is that to you? Even sinners lend to sinners in order to receive back the same amount.* [35] *But love your enemies, and do good, and lend, expecting nothing in return; and your reward will be great, and*

> *you will be sons of the Most High; for He Himself is kind to ungrateful and evil men. 36 Be merciful, just as your Father is merciful.*
>
> *37 "Do not judge, and you will not be judged; and do not condemn, and you will not be condemned; pardon, and you will be pardoned. 38 Give, and it will be given to you. They will pour into your lap a good measure—pressed down, shaken together, and running over. For by your standard of measure it will be measured to you in return."*
>
> *39 And He also spoke a parable to them: "A blind man cannot guide a blind man, can he? Will they not both fall into a pit? 40 A pupil is not above his teacher; but everyone, after he has been fully trained, will be like his teacher.*
> *41 Why do you look at the speck that is in your brother's eye, but do not notice the log that is in your own eye? 42 Or how can you say to your brother, 'Brother, let me take out the speck that is in your eye,' when you yourself do not see the log that is in your own eye? You hypocrite, first take the log out of your own eye, and then you will see clearly to take out the speck that is in your brother's eye.*
> *43 For there is no good tree which produces bad fruit, nor, on the other hand, a bad tree which produces good fruit.*
> *44 For each tree is known by its own fruit. For men do not gather figs from thorns, nor do they pick grapes from a briar bush. 45 The good man out of the good treasure of his heart brings forth what is good; and the evil man out of the evil treasure brings forth what is evil; for his mouth speaks from that which fills his heart.*

Luke says that Jesus focused His attention upon His disciples (v. 20). While aware of the crowd, His message was primarily directed at His disciples.

Luke also includes Jesus' key teaching to "treat others the same way you want them to treat you" (v. 31).

Luke was inspired to make a special note about generosity. Followers of Christ should not be motivated by meeting minimal standards for giving. As recipients of lavish grace, we have the opportunity to give lavishly. In God's economy, the generous person is richly blessed.

It's essential for followers of Christ to be persistent learners. Over time, we will become more like our great Teacher.

We are not qualified to judge other people or try to change them. That's God's job.

Authentic faith is evidenced by how we live. What's in a person's heart will be revealed through their actions.

Builders and Foundations

Luke 6:46–49

46 *"Why do you call Me, 'Lord, Lord,' and do not do what*
I say? 47 *Everyone who comes to Me and hears My words*
and acts on them, I will show you whom he is like: 48 *he*
is like a man building a house, who dug deep and laid a foundation on the rock; and when a flood occurred, the torrent burst against that house and could not shake
it, because it had been well built. 49 *But the one who has*
heard and has not acted accordingly, is like a man who built a house on the ground without any foundation; and the torrent burst against it and immediately it collapsed, and the ruin of that house was great."

We must realize what Jesus expects of us while also realizing how completely incapable we are of meeting those expectations in our own strength. We are entirely dependent on the grace of God to obey and live out our calling as kingdom citizens. We will never reach a point of perfection or perfect obedience in this life, but we're called to keep following Jesus and keep looking to Him for the grace and forgiveness we need.

The Anointing of Jesus' Feet and the Parable of the Two Debtors

Luke 7:36–50

[36] Now one of the Pharisees was requesting Him to dine with him, and He entered the Pharisee's house and reclined at the table. [37] And there was a woman in the city who was a sinner; and when she learned that He was reclining at the table in the Pharisee's house, she brought an alabaster vial of perfume, [38] and standing behind Him at His feet, weeping, she began to wet His feet with her tears, and kept wiping them with the hair of her head, and kissing His feet and anointing them with the perfume. [39] Now when the Pharisee who had invited Him saw this, he said to himself, "If this man were a prophet He would know who and what sort of person this woman is who is touching Him, that she is a sinner."

[40] And Jesus answered him, "Simon, I have something to say to you." And he replied, "Say it, Teacher." [41] "A moneylender had two debtors: one owed five hundred denarii, and the other fifty. [42] When they were unable to repay, he graciously forgave them both. So which of them will love him more?" [43] Simon answered and said, "I suppose the one whom he forgave more." And He said to him, "You have judged correctly." [44] Turning toward the woman, He said to Simon, "Do you see this woman? I entered your house; you gave Me no water for My feet, but she has wet My feet with her tears and wiped them with her hair. [45] You gave Me no kiss; but she, since the time I came in, has not ceased to kiss My feet. [46] You did not anoint My head with oil, but she anointed My feet with perfume. [47] For this reason I say to you, her sins, which are many, have been forgiven, for she loved much; but he who is forgiven little, loves little." [48] Then He said to her,

"Your sins have been forgiven." [49] *Those who were reclining at the table with Him began to say to themselves, "Who is this man who even forgives sins?"* [50] *And He said to the woman, "Your faith has saved you; go in peace."*

In this incident we see a contrast between a formal relationship and an intimate one. Simon's relationship with Jesus was formal—Simon had no personal closeness with Jesus. It seems like Simon was primarily interested in having a celebrity over to his place. His motive was not kind hospitality, but personal self-interest.

The woman (identified as "a sinner") wanted a close, personal relationship with Jesus. She had messed up her life, and she knew it. So, Jesus' forgiveness was very sweet to her, and her gratitude to Him overflowed in an act of great humility and great cost to herself, for the perfume she used was expensive.

When Jesus said to her, "Your faith has saved you, go in peace" (v. 50), He reassured her that she was fully forgiven and fully accepted. She could get on with her life, leaving behind all regrets. He says the same thing to everyone who comes to Him for forgiveness today.

Jesus' Second Trip Through Galilee

Luke 8:1–3

[1] *Soon afterwards, He began going around from one city and village to another, proclaiming and preaching the kingdom of God. The twelve were with Him,* [2] *and also some women who had been healed of evil spirits and sicknesses: Mary who was called Magdalene, from whom seven demons had gone out,* [3] *and Joanna the wife of Chuza, Herod's steward, and Susanna, and many others who were contributing to their support out of their private means.*

The twelve disciples chosen for intensive training and to be with Jesus accompanied Him on this trip. Along with the twelve, Luke mentions that several women whom Jesus had healed were with them. These women were helping to support the ministry financially, and they might have shared their testimony along the way.

Luke's gospel highlights the importance of women to Jesus' ministry. They were key partners and participants in the work Christ was doing. While not part of the twelve, their lives had been changed by Jesus too, and they were following Him just as the disciples were, though with different responsibilities.

Chapter 4

THE GREAT GALILEAN MINISTRY: PARABLES OF THE KINGDOM

Jesus Teaches in Parables

Matthew 13:1–9

1 That day Jesus went out of the house and was sitting by
the sea. 2 And large crowds gathered to Him, so He got into
a boat and sat down, and the whole crowd was standing
on the beach.

3 And He spoke many things to them in parables, saying,
"Behold, the sower went out to sow; 4 and as he sowed,
some seeds fell beside the road, and the birds came and
ate them up. 5 Others fell on the rocky places, where they
did not have much soil; and immediately they sprang up,
because they had no depth of soil. 6 But when the sun had
risen, they were scorched; and because they had no root,
they withered away. 7 Others fell among the thorns, and
the thorns came up and choked them out. 8 And others fell
on the good soil and yielded a crop, some a hundredfold,
some sixty, and some thirty. 9 He who has ears, let him hear."

Notice Jesus isn't teaching in a synagogue, but is sitting seaside. His ministry isn't confined to a building—it extends "outside the walls." Notice also that Jesus is teaching the crowds, not just His disciples. His parables are less about the expectations and aspirations of kingdom citizens and more about grasping the nature of His kingdom. They are for people who haven't yet decided to follow Jesus, as well as for those who have.

Jesus taught profound realities through simple stories. Hearers must listen with open ears and open hearts.

An Explanation

Matthew 13:10–17

[10] *And the disciples came and said to Him, "Why do You*
speak to them in parables?" [11] *Jesus answered them, "To*
you it has been granted to know the mysteries of the
kingdom of heaven, but to them it has not been granted.
[12] *For whoever has, to him more shall be given, and he*
will have an abundance; but whoever does not have, even
what he has shall be taken away from him. [13] *Therefore I*
speak to them in parables; because while seeing they do
not see, and while hearing they do not hear, nor do they
understand. [14] *In their case the prophecy of Isaiah is being*
fulfilled, which says, 'YOU WILL KEEP ON HEARING,
BUT WILL NOT UNDERSTAND; YOU WILL KEEP
ON SEEING, BUT WILL NOT PERCEIVE; [15] *FOR*
THE HEART OF THIS PEOPLE HAS BECOME DULL,
WITH THEIR EARS THEY SCARCELY HEAR, AND
THEY HAVE CLOSED THEIR EYES, OTHERWISE
THEY WOULD SEE WITH THEIR EYES, HEAR WITH
THEIR EARS, AND UNDERSTAND WITH THEIR
HEART AND RETURN, AND I WOULD HEAL THEM.'

[16] *But blessed are your eyes, because they see; and your*
ears, because they hear. [17] *For truly I say to you that many*
prophets and righteous men desired to see what you see,
and did not see it, and to hear what you hear, and did not
hear it.

The disciples asked Jesus why He often spoke in parables, and He seemed to say that they reveal what's really in someone's heart, yet they can't be understood without God's help. Even the disciples didn't have a complete understanding of Jesus' parables, for they needed Him to explain their meaning. The difference was they had open, teachable hearts, unlike many in the crowd.

Keep in mind that Matthew was not a rabbi; he was a tax collector. Yet, like many Jewish men, he probably had a pretty thorough knowledge of the Old Testament. So when Jesus quoted from Isaiah (vv. 14–15), Matthew, and many in the crowd, would have had some context for what Jesus was saying. When we share the gospel with others, we've got to make sure we're using language and concepts they can understand.

The Sower Explained

Matthew 13:18–23

18 *"Hear then the parable of the sower.* 19 *When anyone*
hears the word of the kingdom and does not understand
it, the evil one comes and snatches away what has been
sown in his heart. This is the one on whom seed was sown
beside the road. 20 *The one on whom seed was sown on*
the rocky places, this is the man who hears the word and
immediately receives it with joy; 21 *yet he has no firm root*
in himself, but is only temporary, and when affliction or
persecution arises because of the word, immediately he
falls away. 22 *And the one on whom seed was sown among*
the thorns, this is the man who hears the word, and the
worry of the world and the deceitfulness of wealth choke
the word, and it becomes unfruitful. 23 *And the one on*
whom seed was sown on the good soil, this is the man
who hears the word and understands it; who indeed bears
fruit and brings forth, some a hundredfold, some sixty,
and some thirty."

The "seed," or "word of the kingdom" (v. 18), is powerful to produce the fruit of a changed life. It just needs to be planted in good soil—that is, in a person with a willing, receptive heart who understands the message of the gospel. Seed sown in shallow soil or rocky soil or among the thorns, will not produce fruit. A lack of understanding, worry, and the pursuit of other things, prevents the gospel from taking root in someone's life.

Tares Among Wheat

Matthew 13:24–30

24 Jesus presented another parable to them, saying, "The kingdom of heaven may be compared to a man who sowed good seed in his field. 25 But while his men were sleeping, his enemy came and sowed tares among the wheat, and went away. 26 But when the wheat sprouted and bore grain, then the tares became evident also. 27 The slaves of the landowner came and said to him, 'Sir, did you not sow good seed in your field? How then does it have tares?' 28 And he said to them, 'An enemy has done this!' The slaves said to him, 'Do you want us, then, to go and gather them up?' 29 But he said, 'No; for while you are gathering up the tares, you may uproot the wheat with them. 30 Allow both to grow together until the harvest; and in the time of the harvest I will say to the reapers, "First gather up the tares and bind them in bundles to burn them up; but gather the wheat into my barn."'

God is the landowner in this parable. He will, in His time, separate the good from the bad.

The Mustard Seed

Matthew 13:31–32

31 He presented another parable to them, saying, "The kingdom of heaven is like a mustard seed, which a man took and sowed in his field; [32] *and this is smaller than all other seeds, but when it is full grown, it is larger than the garden plants and becomes a tree, so that THE BIRDS OF THE AIR come and NEST IN ITS BRANCHES."*

While the mission of Jesus might appear somewhat insignificant, it transforms lives and will outgrow and outlast everything else.

The Leaven

Matthew 13:33–35

[33] *He spoke another parable to them, "The kingdom of heaven is like leaven, which a woman took and hid in three pecks of flour until it was all leavened."*

[34] *All these things Jesus spoke to the crowds in parables, and He did not speak to them without a parable.* [35] *This was to fulfill what was spoken through the prophet: "I WILL OPEN MY MOUTH IN PARABLES; I WILL UTTER THINGS HIDDEN SINCE THE FOUNDATION OF THE WORLD."*

Unless you were there when she mixed up the batter, you wouldn't know about the yeast she included. That the yeast is there is seen in the baking of the bread. In the same way, the kingdom grows almost imperceptibly. It starts small but keeps growing.

The Tares Explained

Matthew 13:36–43

[36] *Then He left the crowds and went into the house. And His disciples came to Him and said, "Explain to us the*

> *parable of the tares of the field."* [37] *And He said, "The one who sows the good seed is the Son of Man,* [38] *and the field is the world; and as for the good seed, these are the sons of the kingdom; and the tares are the sons of the evil one;*
> [39] *and the enemy who sowed them is the devil, and the harvest is the end of the age; and the reapers are angels.*
> [40] *So just as the tares are gathered up and burned with fire, so shall it be at the end of the age.* [41] *The Son of Man will send forth His angels, and they will gather out of His kingdom all stumbling blocks, and those who commit lawlessness,* [42] *and will throw them into the furnace of fire; in that place there will be weeping and gnashing of teeth.* [43] *Then THE RIGHTEOUS WILL SHINE FORTH AS THE SUN in the kingdom of their Father. He who has ears, let him hear.*

God will allow the wheat and the tares to grow together until the judgment at the end of the age. At that time the world will be divided into children of the kingdom and children of the evil one (v. 38). Again, we are told to listen closely with a receptive heart. The parables both reveal and conceal the truth.

Hidden Treasure

Matthew 13:44

> [44] *"The kingdom of heaven is like a treasure hidden in the field, which a man found and hid again; and from joy over it he goes and sells all that he has and buys that field.*

The kingdom is worth more than all we have. The man in the parable gladly sells everything he has so that he can buy the "field" of the kingdom.

A Costly Pearl

Matthew 13:45–46

[45] "Again, the kingdom of heaven is like a merchant seeking fine pearls, [46] and upon finding one pearl of great value, he went and sold all that he had and bought it.

This merchant was seeking after fine pearls and discovered one of "great value" (v. 46). Like the man in the hidden treasure parable, he gladly sold all he had in order to purchase it. What Jesus offers cannot be purchased at any price, but it can be received—relationship with God—and it is immeasurably valuable for all eternity.

The Parable of the Net

Matthew 13:47–52

[47] "Again, the kingdom of heaven is like a dragnet cast into the sea, and gathering fish of every kind; [48] and when it was filled, they drew it up on the beach; and they sat down and gathered the good fish into containers, but the bad they threw away. [49] So it will be at the end of the age; the angels will come forth and take out the wicked from among the righteous, [50] and will throw them into the furnace of fire; in that place there will be weeping and gnashing of teeth.

[51] "Have you understood all these things?" They said to Him, "Yes." [52] And Jesus said to them, "Therefore every scribe who has become a disciple of the kingdom of heaven is like a head of a household, who brings out of his treasure things new and old."

The parable of the net is similar to the parable of the tares. God will sort out the good from the bad at the end of the age. Only He can do that.

Jesus said, "A disciple of the kingdom of heaven is like a head of a household, who brings out of his treasure things new and old" (v. 52). Followers of Jesus can see and understand the "new" revelation Jesus came to bring while also seeing that He is the fulfillment of the "old" promises in the Jewish Scriptures (Old Testament).

Parable of the Sower and Soils

Mark 4:1–12

1 He began to teach again by the sea. And such a very large
crowd gathered to Him that He got into a boat in the sea
and sat down; and the whole crowd was by the sea on
the land. 2 And He was teaching them many thing s in
parables, and was saying to them in His teaching, 3 "Listen
to this! Behold, the sower went out to sow; 4 as he was
sowing, some seed fell beside the road, and the birds came
and ate it up. 5 Other seed fell on the rocky ground where
it did not have much soil; and immediately it sprang
up because it had no depth of soil. 6 And after the sun
had risen, it was scorched; and because it had no root, it
withered away. 7 Other seed fell among the thorns, and
the thorns came up and choked it, and it yielded no crop.
8 Other seeds fell into the good soil, and as they grew up
and increased, they yielded a crop and produced thirty,
sixty, and a hundredfold." 9 And He was saying, "He who
has ears to hear, let him hear."

10 As soon as He was alone, His followers, along with the
twelve, began asking Him about the parables. 11 And He was
saying to them, "To you has been given the mystery of the
kingdom of God, but those who are outside get everything
in parables, 12 so that WHILE SEEING, THEY MAY SEE
AND NOT PERCEIVE, AND WHILE HEARING, THEY

> *MAY HEAR AND NOT UNDERSTAND, OTHERWISE THEY MIGHT RETURN AND BE FORGIVEN."*

Mark notes that the crowd was so large Jesus had to move into a boat in order to address them.

We don't know how many "followers" (v. 10) were there in addition to the twelve disciples, but Jesus explained the meaning of the parables to all of them once the crowd had dissipated. These followers may not have been part of the twelve disciples called to be with Jesus for intensive training, but they were still disciples of Jesus. Like all of us, they needed to learn the meaning of His teaching and how to follow Him. The parables were understood by those who wanted to understand and were given the ability to do so (v. 11), but those with hard hearts remained ignorant.

Explanation

Mark 4:13–25

> 13 *And He said to them, "Do you not understand this*
> *parable? How will you understand all the parables?* 14 *The*
> *sower sows the word.* 15 *These are the ones who are beside*
> *the road where the word is sown; and when they hear,*
> *immediately Satan comes and takes away the word which*
> *has been sown in them.* 16 *In a similar way these are the*
> *ones on whom seed was sown on the rocky places, who,*
> *when they hear the word, immediately receive it with joy;*
> 17 *and they have no firm root in themselves, but are only*
> *temporary; then, when affliction or persecution arises*
> *because of the word, immediately they fall away.* 18 *And*
> *others are the ones on whom seed was sown among the*
> *thorns; these are the ones who have heard the word,* 19 *but*
> *the worries of the world, and the deceitfulness of riches,*
> *and the desires for other things enter in and choke the*

> *word, and it becomes unfruitful.* [20] *And those are the ones on whom seed was sown on the good soil; and they hear the word and accept it and bear fruit, thirty, sixty, and a hundredfold."*
>
> [21] *And He was saying to them, "A lamp is not brought to be put under a basket, is it, or under a bed? Is it not brought to be put on the lampstand?* [22] *For nothing is hidden, except to be revealed; nor has anything been secret, but that it would come to light.* [23] *If anyone has ears to hear, let him hear."* [24] *And He was saying to them, "Take care what you listen to. By your standard of measure it will be measured to you; and more will be given you besides.*
> [25] *For whoever has, to him more shall be given; and whoever does not have, even what he has shall be taken away from him."*

When Jesus asked His disciples and the other followers, "Do you not understand this parable?" (v. 13), it was likely less out of annoyance at their slowness and more as a challenge to pay attention, for He had just told them that they had been given the ability to understand the mystery of the kingdom (vv. 10–12). Even so, the fact that He had to explain the parables to them indicates that they didn't have complete understanding yet (vv. 33–34).

There can be ready acceptance of God's Word (good soil, v. 20) and much fruit as a result, or something less than that depending on the condition of the listener's heart. We are assured that the planted Word is capable of producing ample results.

As followers of Christ, we cannot avoid our obligation to society. God has placed us here to compassionately challenge a confused and lost world. As Jesus said, one doesn't light a lamp and then hide it under a basket (v. 21). Christians must let their light shine.

Parable of the Seed

Mark 4:26–29

26 And He was saying, "The kingdom of God is like a man
who casts seed upon the soil; 27 and he goes to bed at night
and gets up by day, and the seed sprouts and grows—how,
he himself does not know. 28 The soil produces crops by
itself; first the blade, then the head, then the mature grain
in the head. 29 But when the crop permits, he immediately
puts in the sickle, because the harvest has come."

Followers of Christ don't know how effective their witness will be in any given situation. We are called to plant the seed of God's Word in the lives of others and trust that it will bear fruit in God's timing and by His power. It is not the job of the witness to understand precisely how the process works. If the seed is planted, it will eventually produce fruit.

Parable of the Mustard Seed

Mark 4:30–34

30 And He said, "How shall we picture the kingdom of
God, or by what parable shall we present it? 31 It is like a
mustard seed, which, when sown upon the soil, though it
is smaller than all the seeds that are upon the soil, 32 yet
when it is sown, it grows up and becomes larger than all
the garden plants and forms large branches; so that THE
BIRDS OF THE AIR can NEST UNDER ITS SHADE."

33 With many such parables He was speaking the word to
them, so far as they were able to hear it; 34 and He did not
speak to them without a parable; but He was explaining
everything privately to His own disciples.

From an almost unnoticed initiation into the kingdom, a life that accepts the Word of God grows into a very visible witness. Seekers find refuge through the gospel message God's people share with the world.

As we get opportunities to preach, teach, or share the gospel with others, we must be aware of how much our listeners are able to comprehend what we're saying. The goal is to challenge without overwhelming or confusing.

Parable of the Sower

Luke 8:4–15

4 *When a large crowd was coming together, and those*
from the various cities were journeying to Him, He spoke
by way of a parable: 5 *"The sower went out to sow his seed;*
and as he sowed, some fell beside the road, and it was
trampled under foot and the birds of the air ate it up.
6 *Other seed fell on rocky soil, and as soon as it grew up, it*
withered away, because it had no moisture. 7 *Other seed*
fell among the thorns; and the thorns grew up with it and
choked it out. 8 *Other seed fell into the good soil, and grew*
up, and produced a crop a hundred times as great." As He
said these things, He would call out, "He who has ears to
hear, let him hear."

9 *His disciples began questioning Him as to what this*
parable meant. 10 *And He said, "To you it has been granted*
to know the mysteries of the kingdom of God, but to the rest
it is in parables, so that SEEING THEY MAY NOT SEE,
AND HEARING THEY MAY NOT UNDERSTAND.

11 *"Now the parable is this: the seed is the word of God.*
12 *Those beside the road are those who have heard; then*
the devil comes and takes away the word from their heart,
so that they will not believe and be saved. 13 *Those on*

> *the rocky soil are those who, when they hear, receive the word with joy; and these have no firm root; they believe for a while, and in time of temptation fall away.*
> 14 *The seed which fell among the thorns, these are the ones who have heard, and as they go on their way they are choked with worries and riches and pleasures of this life, and bring no fruit to maturity.*
> 15 *But the seed in the good soil, these are the ones who have heard the word in an honest and good heart, and hold it fast, and bear fruit with perseverance.*

Luke mentions that people were journeying from "various cities" (v. 4) to hear what Jesus was teaching. He had accumulated quite a following at this point of His ministry.

When Jesus says, "He who has ears to hear," (v. 8), He is searching for people who will exercise their ability to respond to a spiritual conversation.

In answer to the disciples' question as to what this parable meant, Jesus said they had been given the ability to understand. Ready and willing listeners grasped His message. Their relationship to Jesus and their faith gave them ears to hear His teaching. Our finite wisdom severely limits what we can understand apart from God's help. God gives understanding to those who desire it and ask for it.

Parable of the Lamp

Luke 8:16–18

> 16 *"Now no one after lighting a lamp covers it over with a container, or puts it under a bed; but he puts it on a lampstand, so that those who come in may see the light.*
> 17 *For nothing is hidden that will not become evident, nor anything secret that will not be known and come to light.*
> 18 *So take care how you listen; for whoever has, to him*

more shall be given; and whoever does not have, even what he thinks he has shall be taken away from him."

Jesus Himself is the light of the world, and His followers are called to let their light—their understanding of the gospel and the kingdom—shine brightly for others to see the glory of Christ. Indeed, it is our calling and responsibility.

Jesus Calms the Storm

Matthew 8:23–27

[23] *When He got into the boat, His disciples followed Him.*
[24] *And behold, there arose a great storm on the sea, so that the boat was being covered with the waves; but Jesus Himself was asleep.* [25] *And they came to Him and woke Him, saying, "Save us, Lord; we are perishing!"* [26] *He said to them, "Why are you afraid, you men of little faith?" Then He got up and rebuked the winds and the sea, and it became perfectly calm.* [27] *The men were amazed, and said, "What kind of a man is this, that even the winds and the sea obey Him?"*

According to Matthew, Jesus was tired after an evening of healing and being pressed in by the crowds. When He got into the boat, the disciples followed. A fierce storm came up and threatened the boat. After Jesus calmed the storm, the disciples asked, "What kind of man is this?" (v. 27). Though they had been with Him for some time now, they were still having trouble understanding His divine power. We shouldn't be too critical of their slowness to understand, for we have difficulty comprehending His power also.

Mark 4:35–41

[35] *On that day, when evening came, He said to them, "Let us go over to the other side."* [36] *Leaving the crowd,*

they took Him along with them in the boat, just as He was; and other boats were with Him. [37] *And there arose a fierce gale of wind, and the waves were breaking over the boat so much that the boat was already filling up.* [38] *Jesus Himself was in the stern, asleep on the cushion; and they woke Him and said to Him, "Teacher, do You not care that we are perishing?"* [39] *And He got up and rebuked the wind and said to the sea, "Hush, be still." And the wind died down and it became perfectly calm.* [40] *And He said to them, "Why are you afraid? Do you still have no faith?"* [41] *They became very much afraid and said to one another, "Who then is this, that even the wind and the sea obey Him?"*

At the conclusion of another very busy day, Jesus suggested to His disciples that they boat over to the other side of the lake. While Matthew had Jesus going into the boat and the disciples following, Mark has the disciples going into the boat and bringing Jesus with them. Also, Mark mentions that there were more boats than just the one Jesus was in. Apparently, some in the crowd followed in their own boats.

Mark doesn't say, but it's probably safe to assume that the storm that threatened the boat Jesus was in was a threat to other boats too. Jesus spoke to the raging storm, and it calmed down. The "hush" He spoke is like a parent quieting a rowdy child. Jesus has that kind of control over the "rowdy" elements of wind and sea!

After they had seen what He could do, Jesus challenged His followers to not be afraid and to have faith.

Luke 8:22–25

[22] *Now on one of those days Jesus and His disciples got into a boat, and He said to them, "Let us go over to the other side of the lake." So they launched out.* [23] *But as they were sailing along He fell asleep; and a fierce gale of wind descended*

on the lake, and they began to be swamped and to be in danger. [24] They came to Jesus and woke Him up, saying, "Master, Master, we are perishing!" And He got up and rebuked the wind and the surging waves, and they stopped, and it became calm. [25] And He said to them, "Where is your faith?" They were fearful and amazed, saying to one another, "Who then is this, that He commands even the winds and the water, and they obey Him?"

This story reveals both the humanity and divinity of Jesus. He fell asleep in the boat, exhausted from ministry. But He also spoke to the wind and waves, and they obeyed! There is wonder in knowing the God-man. There is much more to Him than we can possibly understand, and that causes us to worship.

Jesus Raises Jairus's Daughter from the Dead

Matthew 9:18–26

[18] While He was saying these things to them, a synagogue official came and bowed down before Him, and said, "My daughter has just died; but come and lay Your hand on her, and she will live." [19] Jesus got up and began to follow him, and so did His disciples.

[20] And a woman who had been suffering from a hemorrhage for twelve years, came up behind Him and touched the fringe of His cloak; [21] for she was saying to herself, "If I only touch His garment, I will get well." [22] But Jesus turning and seeing her said, "Daughter, take courage; your faith has made you well." At once the woman was made well.

[23] When Jesus came into the official's house, and saw the flute-players and the crowd in noisy disorder, [24] He said, "Leave; for the girl has not died, but is asleep." And they

> *began laughing at Him.* [25] *But when the crowd had been sent out, He entered and took her by the hand, and the girl got up.* [26] *This news spread throughout all that land.*

Jairus was a synagogue official. Perhaps that's how he knew Jesus. Regardless, he believed that Jesus could heal his daughter (v. 18).

The trip to Jairus's house was interrupted by another need. "And a woman who had been suffering from a hemorrhage for twelve years, came up behind Him and touched the fringe of His cloak" (v. 20). This woman had faith that just touching Jesus' cloak would suffice for her healing.

There is no indication that Jesus was stressed by attending to both needs. God isn't limited by what we'd consider normal limitations. That's not to say Jesus didn't grow tired—He did—but He was ministering in the power of the Spirit and wasn't rushed or overwhelmed by the needs He saw.

We see a demonstration of Jesus' power over death when He entered Jairus's house. The gathering crowd of grievers laughed in scorn when Jesus said the girl was merely sleeping. The mourners were sure she was dead. Jesus quietly took her hand and lifted her from death back to life. Like His own resurrection, the miracle was private, but the evidence became very public (v. 26).

Mark 5:21–43

> [21] *When Jesus had crossed over again in the boat to the other side, a large crowd gathered around Him; and so He stayed by the seashore.* [22] *One of the synagogue officials named Jairus came up, and on seeing Him, fell at His feet*
> [23] *and implored Him earnestly, saying, "My little daughter is at the point of death; please come and lay Your hands on her, so that she will get well and live."* [24] *And He went off with him; and a large crowd was following Him and pressing in on Him.*

25 A woman who had had a hemorrhage for twelve years, 26 and had endured much at the hands of many physicians, and had spent all that she had and was not helped at all, but rather had grown worse— 27 after hearing about Jesus, she came up in the crowd behind Him and touched His cloak. 28 For she thought, "If I just touch His garments, I will get well." 29 Immediately the flow of her blood was dried up; and she felt in her body that she was healed of her affliction. 30 Immediately Jesus, perceiving in Himself that the power proceeding from Him had gone forth, turned around in the crowd and said, "Who touched My garments?" 31 And His disciples said to Him, "You see the crowd pressing in on You, and You say, 'Who touched Me?'" 32 And He looked around to see the woman who had done this. 33 But the woman fearing and trembling, aware of what had happened to her, came and fell down before Him and told Him the whole truth. 34 And He said to her, "Daughter, your faith has made you well; go in peace and be healed of your affliction."

35 While He was still speaking, they came from the house of the synagogue official, saying, "Your daughter has died; why trouble the Teacher anymore?" 36 But Jesus, overhearing what was being spoken, said to the synagogue official, "Do not be afraid any longer, only believe." 37 And He allowed no one to accompany Him, except Peter and James and John the brother of James. 38 They came to the house of the synagogue official; and He saw a commotion, and people loudly weeping and wailing. 39 And entering in, He said to them, "Why make a commotion and weep? The child has not died, but is asleep." 40 They began laughing at Him. But putting them all out, He took along the child's father and mother and His own companions, and entered the room where the child was. 41 Taking the child by the hand, He said to her, "Talitha kum!" (which translated

means, "Little girl, I say to you, get up!"). [42] *Immediately the girl got up and began to walk, for she was twelve years old. And immediately they were completely astounded.* [43] *And He gave them strict orders that no one should know about this, and He said that something should be given her to eat.*

In Mark's account, Jairus's daughter was at the point of death. Matthew takes up the story when she is already dead. In Mark's telling, it appears Jairus asked Jesus to heal his daughter, and in Matthew's Gospel he asked for Jesus to restore life to her. Differences aside, a miracle was about to take place.

When the house staff came to give the news to Jairus that his daughter had died, Jesus overheard and told him not to be afraid, but to believe (v. 36). He then brought her back to life, demonstrating His power over death.

Mark mentions that only Peter, James, and John accompanied Jesus to Jairus's home. Jesus asked everyone to leave except immediate family and the three disciples. Mark notes that Jesus spoke to the girl in Aramaic—a detail showing the eyewitness nature of this testimony.

After her revival, Jesus saw to it that her physical needs were met. He told the onlookers to get her something to eat (v. 43). This is another example of the Gospels showing both the miraculous and the mundane.

Luke 8:40–56

[40] *And as Jesus returned, the people welcomed Him, for they had all been waiting for Him.* [41] *And there came a man named Jairus, and he was an official of the synagogue; and he fell at Jesus' feet, and began to implore Him to come to his house;* [42] *for he had an only daughter, about twelve years old, and she was dying. But as He went, the crowds were pressing against Him.*

43 *And a woman who had a hemorrhage for twelve years,*
and could not be healed by anyone, 44 *came up behind*
Him and touched the fringe of His cloak, and immediately
her hemorrhage stopped. 45 *And Jesus said, "Who is the*
one who touched Me?" And while they were all denying it,
Peter said, "Master, the people are crowding and pressing
in on You." 46 *But Jesus said, "Someone did touch Me, for*
I was aware that power had gone out of Me." 47 *When the*
woman saw that she had not escaped notice, she came
trembling and fell down before Him, and declared in the
presence of all the people the reason why she had touched
Him, and how she had been immediately healed. 48 *And*
He said to her, "Daughter, your faith has made you well;
go in peace."

49 *While He was still speaking, someone came from the*
house of the synagogue official, saying, "Your daughter
has died; do not trouble the Teacher anymore." 50 *But*
when Jesus heard this, He answered him, "Do not be
afraid any longer; only believe, and she will be made well."
51 *When He came to the house, He did not allow anyone*
to enter with Him, except Peter and John and James, and
the girl's father and mother. 52 *Now they were all weeping*
and lamenting for her; but He said, "Stop weeping, for she
has not died, but is asleep." 53 *And they began laughing at*
Him, knowing that she had died. 54 *He, however, took her*
by the hand and called, saying, "Child, arise!" 55 *And her*
spirit returned, and she got up immediately; and He gave
orders for something to be given her to eat. 56 *Her parents*
were amazed; but He instructed them to tell no one what
had happened.

Luke (a doctor) affirms that no one could heal this woman with the issue of blood (v. 43). She had exhausted all available resources and possibilities. Jesus was her last hope. Similarly, at Jairus's house, the girl needed a miracle. In both cases, Jesus is shown to be powerful and effective. He could, as testified by these witnesses, do what no one else could do—He healed a desperate woman from an illness and brought a young girl back to life.

Chapter 5

THE GREAT GALILEAN MINISTRY: THE DISCIPLES ON MISSION

Miracles of Healing

Matthew 9:35–38

> [35] *Jesus was going through all the cities and villages,
> teaching in their synagogues and proclaiming the gospel of
> the kingdom, and healing every kind of disease and every
> kind of sickness.*
>
> [36] *Seeing the people, He felt compassion for them, because
> they were distressed and dispirited like sheep without a
> shepherd.* [37] *Then He said to His disciples, "The harvest is
> plentiful, but the workers are few.* [38] *Therefore beseech the
> Lord of the harvest to send out workers into His harvest."*

Jesus illustrated what He wanted His followers to do—teach, proclaim the gospel of the kingdom, and heal (9:35). He was compelled by an awesome vision of the kingdom and moved by mercy (9:36). He communicated His vision to His followers, expecting them to carry on the good work. "The harvest is plentiful, but the workers are few. Therefore beseech the Lord of the harvest to send out workers into His harvest" (9:37–38).

By Jesus sharing the work with His disciples, He ensured that the kingdom would spread more quickly. The apostle Paul would later write: "We are laborers together with God" (1 Corinthians 3:9). Today, the church is called to continue the good work of spreading the gospel.

The Twelve Disciples; Instructions for Service

Matthew 10:1–15

*1 Jesus summoned His twelve disciples and gave them
authority over unclean spirits, to cast them out, and to
heal every kind of disease and every kind of sickness.*

*2 Now the names of the twelve apostles are these: The
first, Simon, who is called Peter, and Andrew his brother;
and James the son of Zebedee, and John his brother;
3 Philip and Bartholomew; Thomas and Matthew the
tax collector; James the son of Alphaeus, and Thaddaeus;
4 Simon the Zealot, and Judas Iscariot, the one who
betrayed Him.*

*5 These twelve Jesus sent out after instructing them: "Do
not go in the way of the Gentiles, and do not enter any
city of the Samaritans; 6 but rather go to the lost sheep
of the house of Israel. 7 And as you go, preach, saying,
'The kingdom of heaven is at hand.' 8 Heal the sick, raise
the dead, cleanse the lepers, cast out demons. Freely you
received, freely give. 9 Do not acquire gold, or silver, or
copper for your money belts, 10 or a bag for your journey,
or even two coats, or sandals, or a staff; for the worker is
worthy of his support. 11 And whatever city or village you
enter, inquire who is worthy in it, and stay at his house
until you leave that city. 12 As you enter the house, give it
your greeting. 13 If the house is worthy, give it your blessing
of peace. But if it is not worthy, take back your blessing
of peace. 14 Whoever does not receive you, nor heed your
words, as you go out of that house or that city, shake the
dust off your feet. 15 Truly I say to you, it will be more
tolerable for the land of Sodom and Gomorrah in the day
of judgment than for that city.*

When Matthew listed the twelve disciples, he referred to himself as "the tax collector" (10:3), perhaps because he was amazed that Jesus would select a person in his position to be a disciple.

The team was instructed to start where they were—at home. Later, when the remaining disciples were visiting with the resurrected Jesus, He told them that they were to be His "witnesses both in Jerusalem, and in all Judea and Samaria, and even to the remotest part of the earth" (Acts 1:8). Similarly, our mission starts at home but expands into all the world.

The message they were to share is given to them (and us): "And as you go, preach, saying, 'The kingdom of heaven is at hand'" (10:7). They were expected to *do* something as well as *say* something. "Heal the sick, raise the dead, cleanse the lepers, cast out demons. Freely you received, freely give" (10:8).

They were to be sustained by the fruits of the harvest: "Do not acquire gold, or silver, or copper for your money belts, or a bag for your journey, or even two coats, or sandals, or a staff; for the worker is worthy of his support" (10:9–10).

A Hard Road Before Them

Matthew 10:16–23

16 *"Behold, I send you out as sheep in the midst of wolves;
so be shrewd as serpents and innocent as doves.* 17 *But
beware of men, for they will hand you over to the courts
and scourge you in their synagogues;* 18 *and you will even
be brought before governors and kings for My sake, as a
testimony to them and to the Gentiles.* 19 *But when they
hand you over, do not worry about how or what you are
to say; for it will be given you in that hour what you are
to say.* 20 *For it is not you who speak, but it is the Spirit of
your Father who speaks in you.*

[21] "Brother will betray brother to death, and a father his child; and children will rise up against parents and cause them to be put to death. [22] You will be hated by all because of My name, but it is the one who has endured to the end who will be saved.

[23] "But whenever they persecute you in one city, flee to the next; for truly I say to you, you will not finish going through the cities of Israel until the Son of Man comes.

These missionaries had to be alert and aware—they were like "sheep amidst wolves" (10:16). Their work had to carry on despite opposition and even persecution. "But whenever they persecute you in one city, flee to the next; for truly I say to you, you will not finish going through the cities of Israel until the Son of Man comes" (10:23). The work of spreading the gospel will not be completed until Jesus returns to earth.

The Meaning of Discipleship

Matthew 10:24–39

[24] "A disciple is not above his teacher, nor a slave above his master. [25] It is enough for the disciple that he become like his teacher, and the slave like his master. If they have called the head of the house Beelzebul, how much more will they malign the members of his household!

[26] "Therefore do not fear them, for there is nothing concealed that will not be revealed, or hidden that will not be known. [27] What I tell you in the darkness, speak in the light; and what you hear whispered in your ear, proclaim upon the housetops. [28] Do not fear those who kill the body but are unable to kill the soul; but rather fear Him who is able to destroy both soul and body in hell. [29] Are not two

sparrows sold for a cent? And yet not one of them will fall to the ground apart from your Father. [30] But the very hairs of your head are all numbered. [31] So do not fear; you are more valuable than many sparrows.

[32] "Therefore everyone who confesses Me before men, I will also confess him before My Father who is in heaven. [33] But whoever denies Me before men, I will also deny him before My Father who is in heaven.

[34] "Do not think that I came to bring peace on the earth; I did not come to bring peace, but a sword. [35] For I came to SET A MAN AGAINST HIS FATHER, AND A DAUGHTER AGAINST HER MOTHER, AND A DAUGHTER-IN-LAW AGAINST HER MOTHER-IN-LAW; [36] and A MAN'S ENEMIES WILL BE THE MEMBERS OF HIS HOUSEHOLD.

[37] "He who loves father or mother more than Me is not worthy of Me; and he who loves son or daughter more than Me is not worthy of Me. [38] And he who does not take his cross and follow after Me is not worthy of Me. [39] He who has found his life will lose it, and he who has lost his life for My sake will find it.

Disciples working with God (1 Corinthians 3:9) need not be intimidated. We must remember who our Master is! "It is enough for the disciple that he become like his teacher, and the slave like his master. If they have called the head of the house Beelzebub, how much more will they malign the members of his household!" (10:24–25).

The message must not be hidden. "What I tell you in the darkness, speak in the light; and what you hear whispered in your ear, proclaim upon the housetops" (10:27).

Disciples are coworkers with God and are of great value to Him. Jesus spoke a strong word of encouragement and hope when He said, "So, do not fear; you are more valuable than many sparrows" (10:31). If the death of a sparrow doesn't go unnoticed by Jesus, His followers certainly won't go unnoticed either.

An assuring hymn published in 1892 by an anonymous author has a chorus that goes: "No, never alone; No, never alone. He promised never to leave me, Never to leave me alone." Jesus will never abandon His people.

These missionaries confronted people with the claims of Christ, and their message was often met with resistance. Conditions are about the same now as when Jesus addressed these disciples. Jesus warned His followers about the nature of gospel work: "Do not think that I came to bring peace on the earth; I did not come to bring peace, but a sword" (10:34).

Followers of Jesus should not underestimate the challenges they may face. Opposition could come from close relations, including family members. A disciple's highest allegiance must be to Christ.

The Reward of Service

Matthew 10:40–11:1

40 *"He who receives you receives Me, and he who receives*
Me receives Him who sent Me. 41 *He who receives a*
prophet in the name of a prophet shall receive a prophet's
reward; and he who receives a righteous man in the name
of a righteous man shall receive a righteous man's reward.
42 *And whoever in the name of a disciple gives to one of*
these little ones even a cup of cold water to drink, truly I
say to you, he shall not lose his reward."

11:1 *When Jesus had finished giving instructions to His*
twelve disciples, He departed from there to teach and
preach in their cities.

Despite resistance and even persecution, there will be people who will accept our message. Even the smallest effort will be noted and appreciated by our Lord. It's not up to us to determine the results. God just calls us to be faithful.

Discipleship includes both instruction and example. Jesus did what He asked His followers to do. "When Jesus had finished giving instructions to His twelve disciples, He departed from there to teach and preach in their cities" (11:1).

The Twelve Sent Out

Mark 6:7–13

[7] And He summoned the twelve and began to send them out in pairs, and gave them authority over the unclean spirits; [8] and He instructed them that they should take nothing for their journey, except a mere staff—no bread, no bag, no money in their belt— [9] but to wear sandals; and He added, "Do not put on two tunics." [10] And He said to them, "Wherever you enter a house, stay there until you leave town. [11] Any place that does not receive you or listen to you, as you go out from there, shake the dust off the soles of your feet for a testimony against them." [12] They went out and preached that men should repent. [13] And they were casting out many demons and were anointing with oil many sick people and healing them.

What Jesus was capable of doing He was unable to do because of the rampant unbelief among the people of His hometown. "He could do no miracle there except that He laid His hands on a few sick people and healed them" (6:5). Jesus was astounded at the epidemic of unbelief among them.

Jesus summoned the twelve, gave them instructions, and sent them out in pairs. He understood that there is strength in numbers, and they would need the encouragement and support of one another. "Two are better than one because they have a good return for their labor. For if either of them falls, the one will lift up his companion. But woe to the one who falls when there is not another to lift him up" (Ecclesiastes 4:9–10).

These missionaries were to depend on God and the people they were ministering to for food, shelter, and everything else they needed.

Ministry of the Twelve

Luke 9:1–6

[1] *And He called the twelve together, and gave them power and authority over all the demons and to heal diseases.*
[2] *And He sent them out to proclaim the kingdom of God and to perform healing.* [3] *And He said to them, "Take*
nothing for your journey, neither a staff, nor a bag, nor bread, nor money; and do not even have two tunics
apiece. [4] *Whatever house you enter, stay there until you*
leave that city. [5] *And as for those who do not receive you,*
as you go out from that city, shake the dust off your feet as a testimony against them." [6] *Departing, they began going*
throughout the villages, preaching the gospel and healing everywhere.

Again, we see that what Jesus called these disciples to do, He also empowered them to do. "He . . . gave them power and authority over all the demons and to heal diseases" (v. 1). God empowers His people for ministry as they trust Him and rely on His promises.

John the Baptist Executed

Matthew 14:1–12

1 At that time Herod the tetrarch heard the news about
Jesus, 2 and said to his servants, "This is John the Baptist;
he has risen from the dead, and that is why miraculous
powers are at work in him."

3 For when Herod had John arrested, he bound him and
put him in prison because of Herodias, the wife of his
brother Philip. 4 For John had been saying to him, "It is
not lawful for you to have her." 5 Although Herod wanted
to put him to death, he feared the crowd, because they
regarded John as a prophet.

6 But when Herod's birthday came, the daughter of
Herodias danced before them and pleased Herod, 7 so
much that he promised with an oath to give her whatever
she asked. 8 Having been prompted by her mother, she said,
"Give me here on a platter the head of John the Baptist."
9 Although he was grieved, the king commanded it to
be given because of his oaths, and because of his dinner
guests. 10 He sent and had John beheaded in the prison.
11 And his head was brought on a platter and given to the
girl, and she brought it to her mother. 12 His disciples came
and took away the body and buried it; and they went and
reported to Jesus.

What Jesus was doing had reached the ears of the palace. When Herod heard about it he said, "This is John the Baptist; he has risen from the dead, and that is why miraculous powers are at work in him" (v. 2). Herod had been concerned about John since John challenged him about taking his brother Philip's wife, Herodias. Herod wanted to do something to John, but he knew it could be politically dangerous. But

Herodias and her daughter had a different plan—they asked for John's head on a platter, and Herod agreed.

The danger of letting your emotions rule your actions is seen in Herod's rash decision to have John executed. He had his "reputation" to consider. What he said, he had said in the hearing of dinner guests, and he felt honor-bound to abide by his oath. He had to do what he didn't want to do because he spoke foolishly and publicly. His pride was at stake, so he sent executioners to the prison to behead John the Baptist.

Jesus was deeply impacted when He heard of John's death. "Now when Jesus heard about John, He withdrew from there in a boat to a secluded place by Himself; and when the people heard of this, they followed Him on foot from the cities" (14:13–14). Jesus' popularity sometimes made it difficult for Him to get alone.

Mark 6:14–29

14 *And King Herod heard of it, for His name had become*
well known; and people were saying, "John the Baptist has
risen from the dead, and that is why these miraculous
powers are at work in Him." 15 *But others were saying, "He*
is Elijah." And others were saying, "He is a prophet, like
one of the prophets of old." 16 *But when Herod heard of it,*
he kept saying, "John, whom I beheaded, has risen!"

17 *For Herod himself had sent and had John arrested and*
bound in prison on account of Herodias, the wife of his
brother Philip, because he had married her. 18 *For John*
had been saying to Herod, "It is not lawful for you to have
your brother's wife." 19 *Herodias had a grudge against*
him and wanted to put him to death and could not do
so; 20 *for Herod was afraid of John, knowing that he was*
a righteous and holy man, and he kept him safe. And
when he heard him, he was very perplexed; but he used
to enjoy listening to him. 21 *A strategic day came when*

Herod on his birthday gave a banquet for his lords and military commanders and the leading men of Galilee;
[22] and when the daughter of Herodias herself came in and danced, she pleased Herod and his dinner guests; and the king said to the girl, "Ask me for whatever you want and I will give it to you."
[23] And he swore to her, "Whatever you ask of me, I will give it to you; up to half of my kingdom."
[24] And she went out and said to her mother, "What shall I ask for?" And she said, "The head of John the Baptist."
[25] Immediately she came in a hurry to the king and asked, saying, "I want you to give me at once the head of John the Baptist on a platter."
[26] And although the king was very sorry, yet because of his oaths and because of his dinner guests, he was unwilling to refuse her.
[27] Immediately the king sent an executioner and commanded him to bring back his head. And he went and had him beheaded in the prison,
[28] and brought his head on a platter, and gave it to the girl; and the girl gave it to her mother.
[29] When his disciples heard about this, they came and took away his body and laid it in a tomb.

Mark said that "Herod was afraid of John, knowing that he was a righteous and holy man, and he kept him safe. And when he heard him, he was very perplexed; but he used to enjoy listening to him" (v. 20). Herod respected, even feared, John. John was a source of intellectual entertainment for him.

John was innocent of any crime other than being honest with the ruler of his area. Like some of the prophets of old and disciples throughout the history of the church, John paid with his life in order to be faithful to his message and calling.

Luke 9:7–9

[7] Now Herod the tetrarch heard of all that was happening; and he was greatly perplexed, because it was said by some that John had risen from the dead,
[8] and by some

> *that Elijah had appeared, and by others that one of the prophets of old had risen again.* [9] *Herod said, "I myself had John beheaded; but who is this man about whom I hear such things?" And he kept trying to see Him.*

Luke doesn't give us any of the story leading up to John's execution. He picks it up with a statement from Herod about having John beheaded.

Luke notes that Herod kept trying to meet with Jesus but was unable to do so. Jesus was focused on His mission, not on meeting with Herod, however important a figure he might have been. Jesus didn't pay much attention to worldly power structures.

Chapter 6

THE SPECIAL TRAINING OF THE TWELVE IN DISTRICTS AROUND GALILEE

The Feeding of the 5,000

Matthew 14:13–21

13 Now when Jesus heard about John, He withdrew from
there in a boat to a secluded place by Himself; and when
the people heard of this, they followed Him on foot from
the cities. 14 When He went ashore, He saw a large crowd,
and felt compassion for them and healed their sick.
15 When it was evening, the disciples came to Him and
said, "This place is desolate and the hour is already late;
so send the crowds away, that they may go into the villages
and buy food for themselves." 16 But Jesus said to them,
"They do not need to go away; you give them something
to eat!" 17 They said to Him, "We have here only five loaves
and two fish." 18 And He said, "Bring them here to Me."
19 Ordering the people to sit down on the grass, He took
the five loaves and the two fish, and looking up toward
heaven, He blessed the food, and breaking the loaves He
gave them to the disciples, and the disciples gave them to
the crowds, 20 and they all ate and were satisfied. They
picked up what was left over of the broken pieces, twelve
full baskets. 21 There were about five thousand men who
ate, besides women and children.

Jesus withdrew to deal with the execution of John (v. 13). His solitude was quickly interrupted as word got out about where He was. It wasn't just a few people who found him; Matthew says there were about five thousand men, and there would have been many women and children, too.

Matthew notes that Jesus felt compassion for the crowds. This compassion compelled Him to set aside His grief and minister to hurting people.

The disciples wanted to send the crowds home so they could get something to eat. The shortage of food became the occasion for one of Jesus' most well-known miracles. The disciples had a measly five loaves and two fish among them. That's a rather scant supply for a crowd numbered in the thousands.

Jesus asked them to give Him what they had and He blessed the meager offering. Then He instructed the disciples to share what He had blessed with this hungry crowd. Everyone was fed, and they even had some left over. God is able to multiply our small offerings beyond what we can imagine.

Mark 6:30–44

[30] *The apostles gathered together with Jesus; and they*
reported to Him all that they had done and taught. [31] *And*
He said to them, "Come away by yourselves to a secluded
place and rest a while." (For there were many people
coming and going, and they did not even have time to
eat.) [32] *They went away in the boat to a secluded place by*
themselves.

[33] *The people saw them going, and many recognized them*
and ran there together on foot from all the cities, and got
there ahead of them. [34] *When Jesus went ashore, He saw*
a large crowd, and He felt compassion for them because
they were like sheep without a shepherd; and He began
to teach them many things. [35] *When it was already quite*
late, His disciples came to Him and said, "This place is
desolate and it is already quite late; [36] *send them away so*
that they may go into the surrounding countryside and

> *villages and buy themselves something to eat." 37 But He answered them, "You give them something to eat!" And they said to Him, "Shall we go and spend two hundred denarii on bread and give them something to eat?" 38 And He said to them, "How many loaves do you have? Go look!" And when they found out, they said, "Five, and two fish." 39 And He commanded them all to sit down by groups on the green grass. 40 They sat down in groups of hundreds and of fifties. 41 And He took the five loaves and the two fish, and looking up toward heaven, He blessed the food and broke the loaves and He kept giving them to the disciples to set before them; and He divided up the two fish among them all. 42 They all ate and were satisfied, 43 and they picked up twelve full baskets of the broken pieces, and also of the fish. 44 There were five thousand men who ate the loaves.*

Matthew's account seems to focus on Jesus' need for some space following the death of John. Mark says Jesus arranged a retreat for His disciples to have some time to recover from a very busy schedule.

When Jesus challenged the disciples to feed the crowds, they immediately came up with natural solutions. "Shall we go and spend two hundred denarii on bread and give them something to eat?" they asked (v. 37). Jesus insisted that they inventory their own resources. It wasn't much, but it didn't matter. A supernatural solution was coming.

Jesus had the crowd grouped into sizes His disciples could handle. It's an example of the practical mixed with the supernatural. Jesus used both.

The disciples had been concerned about the crowd having something to eat. It turned out that they all ate and were satisfied. It seems that there was more left over than what they had started with (v. 43). Our heavenly Father is a God of abundance.

Luke 9:10–17

10 When the apostles returned, they gave an account to
Him of all that they had done. Taking them with Him,
He withdrew by Himself to a city called Bethsaida.
11 But the crowds were aware of this and followed Him;
and welcoming them, He began speaking to them about
the kingdom of God and curing those who had need of
healing.

12 Now the day was ending, and the twelve came and said
to Him, "Send the crowd away, that they may go into the
surrounding villages and countryside and find lodging
and get something to eat; for here we are in a desolate
place." 13 But He said to them, "You give them something
to eat!" And they said, "We have no more than five loaves
and two fish, unless perhaps we go and buy food for all
these people." 14 (For there were about five thousand men.)
And He said to His disciples, "Have them sit down to eat
in groups of about fifty each." 15 They did so, and had them
all sit down. 16 Then He took the five loaves and the two
fish, and looking up to heaven, He blessed them, and broke
them, and kept giving them to the disciples to set before
the people. 17 And they all ate and were satisfied; and the
broken pieces which they had left over were picked up,
twelve baskets full.

Luke assures us that Jesus welcomed the crowds. We might be inclined to think that the constant crowds would become a bother, but that's not how Jesus saw them.

When Jesus instructed the disciples to feed the crowds, they felt that what they were being asked to do was beyond their ability to do. And they were right. From a human perspective, they didn't have enough to feed the crowds. It would take a miracle. Many times we look at our own insufficient resources and either despair or attempt to come up with our own solutions apart from God. When we're coming up short, the best thing we can do is turn to God in prayer.

John 6:1–14

1 *After these things Jesus went away to the other side of the*
Sea of Galilee (or Tiberias). 2 *A large crowd followed Him,*
because they saw the signs which He was performing
on those who were sick. 3 *Then Jesus went up on the*
mountain, and there He sat down with His disciples. 4 *Now*
the Passover, the feast of the Jews, was near. 5 *Therefore*
Jesus, lifting up His eyes and seeing that a large crowd
was coming to Him, said to Philip, "Where are we to buy
bread, so that these may eat?" 6 *This He was saying to test*
him, for He Himself knew what He was intending to do.
7 *Philip answered Him, "Two hundred denarii worth of*
bread is not sufficient for them, for everyone to receive
a little." 8 *One of His disciples, Andrew, Simon Peter's*
brother, said to Him, 9 *"There is a lad here who has five*
barley loaves and two fish, but what are these for so many
people?" 10 *Jesus said, "Have the people sit down." Now*
there was much grass in the place. So the men sat down,
in number about five thousand. 11 *Jesus then took the*
loaves, and having given thanks, He distributed to those
who were seated; likewise also of the fish as much as they
wanted. 12 *When they were filled, He said to His disciples,*
"Gather up the leftover fragments so that nothing will be
lost." 13 *So they gathered them up, and filled twelve baskets*
with fragments from the five barley loaves which were left
over by those who had eaten. 14 *Therefore when the people*
saw the sign which He had performed, they said, "This is
truly the Prophet who is to come into the world."

John's Gospel doesn't deal with either the execution of John the Baptist or the retreat Mark mentions. When John begins his story, he refers to conflicts and confrontations with the religious leaders of the day. The note that "Jesus went away" (v. 1) suggests that He was looking for a place where He and His disciples could rest for a while.

Jesus told Philip that He expected the disciples to feed the crowds. Philip estimated how much money it would take, but Jesus had a better idea in mind (vv. 6–7). John's account indicates that the disciples didn't have anything of their own to offer. The "five barley loaves and two fish" (v. 9) were offered to Andrew by one of the young boys in the crowd. We don't bring much to God either, but He can use whatever we bring.

The crowd was amazed by Jesus' miracle and recognized that he was a food-providing prophet in the way of Moses and the manna (v. 14).

When the crowd was done eating, Jesus told His disciples, "Gather up the leftover fragments so that nothing will be lost" (v. 13). We might wish to speculate on what they did with these leftovers. Was it for the disciples or for future crowds? We don't know. All we know is that Jesus instructed the disciples to save what was left. Perhaps the lesson is that while God offers great abundance, He doesn't waste anything either.

Jesus Walks on Water

Matthew 14:22–33

22 *Immediately He made the disciples get into the boat and*
go ahead of Him to the other side, while He sent the crowds
away. 23 *After He had sent the crowds away, He went up*
on the mountain by Himself to pray; and when it was
evening, He was there alone. 24 *But the boat was already*
a long distance from the land, battered by the waves; for
the wind was contrary. 25 *And in the fourth watch of the*
night He came to them, walking on the sea. 26 *When the*
disciples saw Him walking on the sea, they were terrified,
and said, "It is a ghost!" And they cried out in fear. 27 *But*

> *immediately Jesus spoke to them, saying, "Take courage, it is I; do not be afraid."*
>
> [28] *Peter said to Him, "Lord, if it is You, command me to come to You on the water."* [29] *And He said, "Come!" And Peter got out of the boat, and walked on the water and came toward Jesus.* [30] *But seeing the wind, he became frightened, and beginning to sink, he cried out, "Lord, save me!"* [31] *Immediately Jesus stretched out His hand and took hold of him, and said to him, "You of little faith, why did you doubt?"* [32] *When they got into the boat, the wind stopped.* [33] *And those who were in the boat worshiped Him, saying, "You are certainly God's Son!"*

Matthew was the only Gospel writer actually in the boat to witness this miracle. You can imagine this incident would have stuck with Him whenever he was tempted to fear.

Apparently, the disciples wanted to stay with Jesus after feeding the 5,000, but Jesus had them get into the boat and go ahead of Him to the other side of the lake. He then went up on the mountain to pray by Himself. Again and again we see that prayer was a priority for Jesus. He was strengthened by time spent alone with His Father.

When the disciples saw Jesus walking on the surface of the water they were terrified. They thought they were seeing a ghost. They didn't have a category in their minds for men walking on water. Even though they had seen Jesus do plenty of miraculous things, they didn't have perfect faith. None of us do.

To calm their fears, Jesus identified Himself to them. We may experience fear, too, whenever God deals with us in an unexpected way. That's how our faith is stretched.

Peter asked Jesus if he could walk on the water out to where Jesus was. We don't know how far Peter got before the blustering wind got his attention and he began to sink. Peter appeared to have enough faith to get out of the boat, but not enough faith to continue walking on the water. When he took his eyes off Jesus, he began to sink. The same principle applies to all of us: focus on external circumstances and down we go; focus on Jesus and anything is possible.

Jesus asked Peter why he doubted, but we don't get an answer. It was probably meant to challenge Peter to trust Him more. In our human weakness, we continue to struggle to trust the Lord despite His faithfulness to us. We have a tendency to lean on our own understanding (Proverbs 3:5) rather than the Word of God.

Mark 6:45–52

45 *Immediately Jesus made His disciples get into the boat*
and go ahead of Him to the other side to Bethsaida, while
He Himself was sending the crowd away. 46 *After bidding*
them farewell, He left for the mountain to pray.

47 *When it was evening, the boat was in the middle of the*
sea, and He was alone on the land. 48 *Seeing them straining*
at the oars, for the wind was against them, at about the
fourth watch of the night He came to them, walking on the
sea; and He intended to pass by them. 49 *But when they*
saw Him walking on the sea, they supposed that it was
a ghost, and cried out; 50 *for they all saw Him and were*
terrified. But immediately He spoke with them and said to
them, "Take courage; it is I, do not be afraid." 51 *Then He*
got into the boat with them, and the wind stopped; and
they were utterly astonished, 52 *for they had not gained*
any insight from the incident of the loaves, but their heart
was hardened.

We know Jesus had compassion on the crowds, but there were times when He needed to get away to pray. His prayers were essential to His mission.

From His position on the land, Jesus could see His disciples "straining at the oars" (vv. 47–48). He could see they were in trouble. We can take comfort in knowing that God sees our struggles and is able to rescue us from whatever it is we're straining against.

Mark says Jesus "intended to pass by them" (v. 48). If He was coming to help them, why did He want to pass by them? It was probably so He could reveal more of His glory to them. He intended to rescue them, but also to amaze them. His miracles weren't just neat tricks, but were meant to grow the faith of the disciples. They would need strong faith in the challenging days that were ahead.

Mark writes that the disciples were "utterly astonished" (v. 51) by this incident. Apparently, they hadn't fully processed the miraculous nature of the feeding of 5,000 yet.

John 6:16–21

> [16] *Now when evening came, His disciples went down to*
> *the sea,* [17] *and after getting into a boat, they started to*
> *cross the sea to Capernaum. It had already become dark,*
> *and Jesus had not yet come to them.* [18] *The sea began to*
> *be stirred up because a strong wind was blowing.* [19] *Then,*
> *when they had rowed about three or four miles, they saw*
> *Jesus walking on the sea and drawing near to the boat;*
> *and they were frightened.* [20] *But He said to them, "It is I;*
> *do not be afraid."* [21] *So they were willing to receive Him*
> *into the boat, and immediately the boat was at the land to*
> *which they were going.*

According to John, they had rowed three or four miles when they saw Jesus walking on the sea and drawing near to the boat. It was about five miles across, so they were more than half way there.

We can understand their being frightened, but they were—after assurance from Jesus—"willing to receive Him into the boat" (v. 21). The text says the boat immediately made it to the other side. Either they had made it most of the way to the other side and Jesus walked almost all the way across the Sea of Galilee, or their arrival was sped up by the arrival of Jesus in their boat.

Jesus Retreats to Tyre and Sidon

Matthew 15:21–28

21 *Jesus went away from there, and withdrew into the district*
of Tyre and Sidon. 22 *And a Canaanite woman from that*
region came out and began to cry out, saying, "Have mercy
on me, Lord, Son of David; my daughter is cruelly demon-
possessed." 23 *But He did not answer her a word. And His*
disciples came and implored Him, saying, "Send her away,
because she keeps shouting at us." 24 *But He answered and*
said, "I was sent only to the lost sheep of the house of Israel."
25 *But she came and began to bow down before Him, saying,*
"Lord, help me!" 26 *And He answered and said, "It is not*
good to take the children's bread and throw it to the dogs."
27 *But she said, "Yes, Lord; but even the dogs feed on the*
crumbs which fall from their masters' table." 28 *Then Jesus*
said to her, "O woman, your faith is great; it shall be done
for you as you wish." And her daughter was healed at once.

Tyre and Sidon may have been as far north as Jesus traveled. These cities were notorious for their pagan religions. Apparently, the distance hadn't kept the population from hearing of this new rabbi named Jesus.

In this encounter, a woman of a different culture acknowledged Jesus as "Lord, Son of David" (v. 22) and pleaded with Him to heal her daughter. The disciples thought she was a nuisance and wanted Jesus to send her away. Jesus responded that He was sent "only to the lost sheep of the house of Israel" (v. 24).

More desperate than ever, the woman came to the feet of Jesus with her request. She may not have been from Israel, but she had great faith, and Jesus answered her request. Her hope was not based upon her worthiness, but upon His mercy. Jesus was impressed with the strength of this foreign woman's faith. Because of that faith, her request was granted and the disciples learned a vital lesson—God's kingdom is open to all people.

Mark 7:24–30

[24] Jesus got up and went away from there to the region of
Tyre. And when He had entered a house, He wanted no
one to know of it; yet He could not escape notice. [25] But
after hearing of Him, a woman whose little daughter had
an unclean spirit immediately came and fell at His feet.
[26] Now the woman was a Gentile, of the Syrophoenician
race. And she kept asking Him to cast the demon out of her
daughter. [27] And He was saying to her, "Let the children be
satisfied first, for it is not good to take the children's bread
and throw it to the dogs." [28] But she answered and said to
Him, "Yes, Lord, but even the dogs under the table feed on
the children's crumbs." [29] And He said to her, "Because of
this answer go; the demon has gone out of your daughter."
[30] And going back to her home, she found the child lying
on the bed, the demon having left.

Jesus hoped He could go somewhere and not be noticed, but it didn't work out that way. When this Syrophoenician woman heard where Jesus was, she went to Him and asked Him repeatedly to attend to her daughter's need.

When she said, "Yes, Lord, but even the dogs under the table feed on the children's crumbs" (v. 28), she was saying that she could be helped with what was left after giving attention to the Jewish people first. She had such confidence in Jesus that she didn't need "a full course meal," but only the leftover crumbs. Her faith secured the answer to her urgent request.

Jesus Feeds 4,000 People (not including the women and children)

Matthew 15:32–39

[32] And Jesus called His disciples to Him, and said, "I feel compassion for the people, because they have remained with Me now three days and have nothing to eat; and I do not want to send them away hungry, for they might faint on the way." [33] The disciples said to Him, "Where would we get so many loaves in this desolate place to satisfy such a large crowd?" [34] And Jesus said to them, "How many loaves do you have?" And they said, "Seven, and a few small fish." [35] And He directed the people to sit down on the ground; [36] and He took the seven loaves and the fish; and giving thanks, He broke them and started giving them to the disciples, and the disciples gave them to the people. [37] And they all ate and were satisfied, and they picked up what was left over of the broken pieces, seven large baskets full. [38] And those who ate were four thousand men, besides women and children.

[39] And sending away the crowds, Jesus got into the boat and came to the region of Magadan.

Notice the expressed compassion of Jesus: "I feel compassion for the people, because they have remained with Me now three days and have nothing to eat; and I do not want to send them away hungry, for they might faint on the way" (v. 32). He not only cared about their spiritual needs, but their practical needs also.

When Jesus asked the disciples to check and see what they had for this urgent need, they sounded a little frustrated, as if too much was being asked of them. They were still learning that sometimes it seems Jesus asks more of His followers than we feel capable of giving, but in His strength we can do all that He has called us to do.

Four thousand men (not counting women and children) were miraculously fed. After Jesus had miraculously feed five thousand before, Mark wrote, "They had not gained any insight from the incident of the loaves, but their heart was hardened" (Mark 6:52). Perhaps this most recent incident softened their hearts and sharpened their insight.

Mark 8:1–9

1 *In those days, when there was again a large crowd and*
they had nothing to eat, Jesus called His disciples and
said to them, 2 *"I feel compassion for the people because*
they have remained with Me now three days and have
nothing to eat. 3 *If I send them away hungry to their*
homes, they will faint on the way; and some of them have
come from a great distance." 4 *And His disciples answered*
Him, "Where will anyone be able to find enough bread
here in this desolate place to satisfy these people?" 5 *And*
He was asking them, "How many loaves do you have?"
And they said, "Seven." 6 *And He directed the people to*
sit down on the ground; and taking the seven loaves, He
gave thanks and broke them, and started giving them
to His disciples to serve to them, and they served them
to the people. 7 *They also had a few small fish; and after*
He had blessed them, He ordered these to be served as
well. 8 *And they ate and were satisfied; and they picked up*
seven large baskets full of what was left over of the broken
pieces. 9 *About four thousand were there; and He sent*
them away.

We can assume that the disciples had been with Jesus long enough to know that when He made a statement about the people needing to be fed He was expecting them to do something about it. But they questioned how "anyone" could find "enough bread" in this "desolate place" (v. 4).

When they did look into their resources, they found seven

loaves and a few small fish. Jesus accepted what they had, though it wasn't much. He blessed it, and so multiplied it far beyond their expectations, directing the disciples to feed the people.

The crowd was fully satisfied with what Jesus provided for them. When we offer to Jesus what we have, He is able to multiply it beyond what we can imagine.

Confession of Deity

Matthew 16:13–20

*[13] Now when Jesus came into the district of Caesarea
Philippi, He was asking His disciples, "Who do people say
that the Son of Man is?" [14] And they said, "Some say John
the Baptist; and others, Elijah; but still others, Jeremiah,
or one of the prophets." [15] He said to them, "But who do
you say that I am?" [16] Simon Peter answered, "You are
the Christ, the Son of the living God." [17] And Jesus said
to him, "Blessed are you, Simon Barjona, because flesh
and blood did not reveal this to you, but My Father who
is in heaven. [18] I also say to you that you are Peter, and
upon this rock I will build My church; and the gates of
Hades will not overpower it. [19] I will give you the keys of
the kingdom of heaven; and whatever you bind on earth
shall have been bound in heaven, and whatever you loose
on earth shall have been loosed in heaven." [20] Then He
warned the disciples that they should tell no one that He
was the Christ.*

When Jesus asked who people were saying He was, the disciples told Him that people thought He was a prophet. After hearing what the public was thinking, Jesus focused on His disciples, asking, "Who do you say that I am?" (v. 15). Peter answered correctly, "You are the Christ, the Son of the living God" (v. 16). Jesus praised Peter for His answer and said this kind of knowledge comes only by spiritual revelation—the Father gave it to Peter. Similarly, 2 Corinthians 2:14 says, "But a natural man does not accept the things of the Spirit of God, for they are foolishness to him; and he cannot understand them, because they are spiritually appraised."

Jesus is the rock the church is built upon, and Peter and the disciples would play a key role in the establishment and growth of the early church. The apostle Paul wrote in 1 Corinthians 3:11, "For no man can lay a foundation other than the one which is laid, which is Jesus Christ." The church that Jesus is building is constructed upon the foundational truth that He is the Son of God and Savior of the world. He is committed to building something eternal out of finite, imperfect disciples.

Mark 8:27–30

> [27] *Jesus went out, along with His disciples, to the villages of Caesarea Philippi; and on the way He questioned His disciples, saying to them, "Who do people say that I am?"* [28] *They told Him, saying, "John the Baptist; and others say Elijah; but others, one of the prophets."* [29] *And He continued by questioning them, "But who do you say that I am?" Peter answered and said to Him, "You are the Christ."* [30] *And He warned them to tell no one about Him.*

Jesus warned the disciples against revealing who He was. There would be intense political pressure for Jesus to fulfill what the majority believed was the role of the Messiah—to bring about Israel's nationalistic hopes by military means. (We see this later in the triumphal entry.)

For much of His ministry, people didn't understand who Jesus was or why He came. Even His disciples were slow to get the message. It wasn't until after He had fulfilled the prophecies regarding the Messiah and had risen from the grave that they understood.

Luke 9:18–21

[18] And it happened that while He was praying alone, the disciples were with Him, and He questioned them, saying, "Who do the people say that I am?" [19] They answered and said, "John the Baptist, and others say Elijah; but others, that one of the prophets of old has risen again." [20] And He said to them, "But who do you say that I am?" And Peter answered and said, "The Christ of God." [21] But He warned them and instructed them not to tell this to anyone,

Jesus had just been praying. It could be that there was something about His recent conversation with His Father that prompted Him to ask His disciples who they thought He was. It was meant to advance their understanding of His identity.

Neither they nor we can fathom how it came to be that God became flesh, but we can accept by faith what we cannot fully understand. Gabriel's answer to Mary in Luke 1:35 takes us to the edge of a great mystery: "The Holy Spirit will come upon you, and the power of the Most High will overshadow you; and for that reason the holy Child shall be called the Son of God."

Jesus Foretells His Death

Matthew 16:21–26

[21] From that time Jesus began to show His disciples that He must go to Jerusalem, and suffer many things from the elders and chief priests and scribes, and be killed, and be raised up on the third day. [22] Peter took Him aside and began to rebuke Him, saying, "God forbid it, Lord! This shall never happen to You." [23] But He turned and said to Peter, "Get behind Me, Satan! You are a stumbling block to Me; for you are not setting your mind on God's interests, but man's."

> [24] *Then Jesus said to His disciples, "If anyone wishes to come after Me, he must deny himself, and take up his cross and follow Me.* [25] *For whoever wishes to save his life will lose it; but whoever loses his life for My sake will find it.* [26] *For what will it profit a man if he gains the whole world and forfeits his soul? Or what will a man give in exchange for his soul?*

Assured that the disciples had gained some understanding of His identity, Jesus began sharing more of His mission with them. Apparently, Jesus realized that they were not ready to get this information until now. Notice how Jesus said He "must go" (v. 21). This was not His choice; it was His assignment.

From Peter's statement, "This shall never happen to You" (v. 22), we realize that he didn't get the full picture yet.

Jesus reacted strongly to Peter's rebuke, calling Peter's statement a "stumbling block" to His mission. Some time later, Jesus would ask His disciples to "watch and pray" when they were in the Garden of Gethsemane. How hard it must have been for Him to fulfill His mission when His closest friends and followers didn't understand it.

In a classic "cost of discipleship" verse, Jesus challenged His disciples, saying, "If anyone wishes to come after Me, he must deny himself, and take up his cross and follow me" (v. 24). Every follower of Christ is called to surrender his or her will and do the will of the Father, just as Jesus did.

In verse 25, Jesus continued to challenge His disciples' understanding of what following Him meant: "For whoever wishes to save his life will lose it; but whoever loses his life for My sake will find it." The truth is, we are incapable of securing life on our own. We make a huge mess of things. Life is a gift to us. It is much too precious to be left to inept management. The way to secure and enhance the gift of life is to hand the management of it over to Jesus. He has a cross for us to bear, but it is purposeful and well worth it. We will lose the life intended for us if we neglect to commit our lives to wholeheartedly following Jesus.

Mark 8:31–37

31 And He began to teach them that the Son of Man
must suffer many things and be rejected by the elders
and the chief priests and the scribes, and be killed, and
after three days rise again. 32 And He was stating the
matter plainly. And Peter took Him aside and began to
rebuke Him. 33 But turning around and seeing His disciples,
He rebuked Peter and said, "Get behind Me, Satan; for
you are not setting your mind on God's interests, but
man's."

34 And He summoned the crowd with His disciples, and
said to them, "If anyone wishes to come after Me, he must
deny himself, and take up his cross and follow Me. 35 For
whoever wishes to save his life will lose it, but whoever
loses his life for My sake and the gospel's will save it. 36 For
what does it profit a man to gain the whole world, and
forfeit his soul? 37 For what will a man give in exchange
for his soul?

Jesus saw that Peter's misguided words were being overheard by the other followers, so He corrected Peter with the strongest language, saying Peter's plan was coming from Satan. Jesus recognized the deceit of Satan in Peter's rebuke. The idea of avoiding the cross may have been tempting to Jesus, but He knew it wasn't His Father's will.

Jesus modeled self-denial to His followers. In the Garden of Gethsemane, He prayed for God's will to be done, not His own. Philippians 2:8 says, "He humbled Himself by becoming obedient to the point of death, even death on a cross." Self-denial on earth results in eternal joy in heaven.

Luke 9:18–25

[18] *And it happened that while He was praying alone, the disciples were with Him, and He questioned them, saying, "Who do the people say that I am?"* [19] *They answered and said, "John the Baptist, and others say Elijah; but others, that one of the prophets of old has risen again."* [20] *And He said to them, "But who do you say that I am?" And Peter answered and said, "The Christ of God."* [21] *But He warned them and instructed them not to tell this to anyone,* [22] *saying, "The Son of Man must suffer many things and be rejected by the elders and chief priests and scribes, and be killed and be raised up on the third day."*

[23] *And He was saying to them all, "If anyone wishes to come after Me, he must deny himself, and take up his cross daily and follow Me.* [24] *For whoever wishes to save his life will lose it, but whoever loses his life for My sake, he is the one who will save it.* [25] *For what is a man profited if he gains the whole world, and loses or forfeits himself?*

It's interesting to consider where each of the Gospel writers sequenced this episode. Matthew placed it just after a discussion in which Jesus cautioned His disciples about the teaching (or "leaven") of the Pharisees and Sadducees (Matthew 16:6). The disciples thought He was talking about bread. They had seen Jesus miraculously feed five thousand and four thousand men, so maybe bread was still on their minds. They were often slow to understand.

Mark places it after the healing of a blind man. The man was obviously healed by the power of Jesus. It would seem that miracle would convince His followers that He was the Son of God and not just some powerful person (like John the Baptist or Elijah).

Luke puts his version just as the disciples are cleaning up

after the feeding of the five thousand. No one else was capable of doing what these followers had just seen Jesus do—not John the Baptist, or Elijah, or any of the other prophets.

In each of these three accounts, the disciples are fresh from a miraculous display of power. Would they be convinced that Jesus was, as declared by John the Baptist, the Lamb of God who takes away the sin of the world (John 1:29)? And how could He die?

The Transfiguration of Jesus

Matthew 17:1–13

1 Six days later Jesus took with Him Peter and James and John his brother, and led them up on a high mountain by themselves. 2 And He was transfigured before them; and His face shone like the sun, and His garments became as white as light. 3 And behold, Moses and Elijah appeared to them, talking with Him. 4 Peter said to Jesus, "Lord, it is good for us to be here; if You wish, I will make three tabernacles here, one for You, and one for Moses, and one for Elijah." 5 While he was still speaking, a bright cloud overshadowed them, and behold, a voice out of the cloud said, "This is My beloved Son, with whom I am well-pleased; listen to Him!" 6 When the disciples heard this, they fell face down to the ground and were terrified. 7 And Jesus came to them and touched them and said, "Get up, and do not be afraid." 8 And lifting up their eyes, they saw no one except Jesus Himself alone.

9 As they were coming down from the mountain, Jesus commanded them, saying, "Tell the vision to no one until the Son of Man has risen from the dead." 10 And His disciples asked Him, "Why then do the scribes say that Elijah must come first?" 11 And He answered and said, "Elijah is coming and will restore all things; 12 but I say to

> *you that Elijah already came, and they did not recognize him, but did to him whatever they wished. So also the Son of Man is going to suffer at their hands."* [13] *Then the disciples understood that He had spoken to them about John the Baptist.*

Only Peter, James, and John were on this mountain with Jesus. That means none of the three who recorded this event were there; each heard it from one of these eyewitnesses. Wouldn't you have loved to have been there to hear from Peter, James, or John about their experience on the mountain? It's not hard to imagine how their eyes beamed with renewed excitement and wonder as they recounted what they saw and experienced when Jesus was transfigured.

The Greek word translated as "transfigured" is *metamorphoo*, and can also be translated as "to change" or "to transform." We get a hint of the eternality of Christ in this passage. In a sense, Jesus transformed into what He was before the incarnation, and the disciples saw the glory He had before He became human.

The disciples also saw Elijah and Moses. How they were able to recognize Elijah and Moses is not explained to us. Maybe there is something in this experience that gives us some insight into life in heaven (where, according to 1 Corinthians 13:12, we will know as we are fully known).

Moses and Elijah being present at the Transfiguration is significant: Moses represented the Law, and Elijah represented the prophets—both of which bear witness to Jesus as the Messiah. When Peter offered to make three tents—one for Moses, one for Elijah, and one for Jesus—he was wanting to mark the significance of what he was witnessing. But before he could even finish what he was saying, a voice from a bright cloud said, "This is My beloved Son, with whom I am well-pleased; listen to Him" (v. 5).

Jesus' comforting word to the disciples to not be afraid

can help us to see that we really have nothing to fear in our relationship with God. Fear seems to be a normal reaction when we're stretched far beyond what we're comfortable with. As we mature in our faith, part of what God has in mind for us is to lead us deeper and deeper into a relationship with Him, which likely means taking us farther and farther away from our comfort zones.

As Jesus and the three disciples were descending the mountain, Jesus commanded them not to say anything about what they had seen until after His resurrection. The resurrection would be the final, indisputable proof that Jesus was (and is) who He claimed to be.

Mark 9:2–13

2 Six days later, Jesus took with Him Peter and James
and John, and brought them up on a high mountain by
themselves. And He was transfigured before them; 3 and
His garments became radiant and exceedingly white, as no
launderer on earth can whiten them. 4 Elijah appeared to
them along with Moses; and they were talking with Jesus.
5 Peter said to Jesus, "Rabbi, it is good for us to be here; let us
make three tabernacles, one for You, and one for Moses, and
one for Elijah." 6 For he did not know what to answer; for
they became terrified. 7 Then a cloud formed, overshadowing
them, and a voice came out of the cloud, "This is My beloved
Son, listen to Him!" 8 All at once they looked around and
saw no one with them anymore, except Jesus alone.

9 As they were coming down from the mountain, He gave
them orders not to relate to anyone what they had seen,
until the Son of Man rose from the dead. 10 They seized
upon that statement, discussing with one another what
rising from the dead meant. 11 They asked Him, saying,
"Why is it that the scribes say that Elijah must come first?"
12 And He said to them, "Elijah does first come and restore

all things. And yet how is it written of the Son of Man that He will suffer many things and be treated with contempt?
[13] *But I say to you that Elijah has indeed come, and they did to him whatever they wished, just as it is written of him."*

Mark notes that Jesus' clothes "became radiant and exceedingly white, as no launderer on earth can whiten them" (v. 3). Whoever was relating the experience to Mark was impressed with the sheer brightness and radiance of it all.

When Jesus and the disciples were coming down the mountain, Jesus told them not to share what they had seen with anyone "until the Son of Man rose from the dead" (v. 9). We might wonder why they didn't ask what Jesus meant by that. We know that they "seized upon that statement, discussing with one another what rising from the dead meant," but they never asked Jesus. This suggests that the disciples were still unclear about Jesus' mission. It wasn't to overthrow the government; it was to give His life as a sacrifice and to defeat death by rising from the dead.

The disciples then asked Jesus, "Why is it that the scribes say that Elijah must come first?" (v. 11), which comes from a prophecy in Malachi 4:5–6: "Behold, I am going to send you Elijah the prophet before the coming of the great and terrible day of the LORD. He will restore the hearts of the fathers to their children and the hearts of the children to their fathers, so that I will not come and smite the land with a curse." Jesus told the disciples that Elijah had already come, and the disciples understood that He was talking about John the Baptist.

Luke 9:28–36

[28] *Some eight days after these sayings, He took along Peter and John and James, and went up on the mountain to*
pray. [29] *And while He was praying, the appearance of His face became different, and His clothing became white*
and gleaming. [30] *And behold, two men were talking with*

Him; and they were Moses and Elijah, [31] who, appearing in glory, were speaking of His departure which He was about to accomplish at Jerusalem. [32] Now Peter and his companions had been overcome with sleep; but when they were fully awake, they saw His glory and the two men standing with Him. [33] And as these were leaving Him, Peter said to Jesus, "Master, it is good for us to be here; let us make three tabernacles: one for You, and one for Moses, and one for Elijah"—not realizing what he was saying. [34] While he was saying this, a cloud formed and began to overshadow them; and they were afraid as they entered the cloud. [35] Then a voice came out of the cloud, saying, "This is My Son, My Chosen One; listen to Him!" [36] And when the voice had spoken, Jesus was found alone. And they kept silent, and reported to no one in those days any of the things which they had seen.

According to Luke, the primary purpose of Jesus going up on the mountain was to pray. As He prayed, visible changes took place. "His face became different, and His clothing became white and gleaming" (v. 29).

Luke's source told him some of what he heard Moses and Elijah discussing with Jesus. Jesus, Moses, and Elijah were talking about Jesus' "departure," which refers to His death, resurrection, and ascension. Moses may have been talking about how these events were fulfilling the law. Elijah may have been talking about how this event would be the climax of what he and the other prophets had been preaching and what John the Baptist had come to announce.

Paying the Temple Tax

Matthew 17:24–27

[24] When they came to Capernaum, those who collected the two-drachma tax came to Peter and said, "Does

> *your teacher not pay the two-drachma tax?"* [25] *He said, "Yes." And when he came into the house, Jesus spoke to him first, saying, "What do you think, Simon? From whom do the kings of the earth collect customs or poll-tax, from their sons or from strangers?"* [26] *When Peter said, "From strangers," Jesus said to him, "Then the sons are exempt.* [27] *However, so that we do not offend them, go to the sea and throw in a hook, and take the first fish that comes up; and when you open its mouth, you will find a shekel. Take that and give it to them for you and Me."*

God's law concerning paying the temple tax is detailed in Exodus 30:11–16.

> [11] *The LORD also spoke to Moses, saying,* [12] *"When you take a census of the sons of Israel to number them, then each one of them shall give a ransom for himself to the LORD, when you number them, so that there will be no plague among them when you number them.* [13] *This is what everyone who is numbered shall give: half a shekel according to the shekel of the sanctuary (the shekel is twenty gerahs), half a shekel as a contribution to the LORD.* [14] *Everyone who is numbered, from twenty years old and over, shall give the contribution to the LORD.* [15] *The rich shall not pay more and the poor shall not pay less than the half shekel, when you give the contribution to the LORD to make atonement for yourselves.* [16] *You shall take the atonement money from the sons of Israel and shall give it for the service of the tent of meeting, that it may be a memorial for the sons of Israel before the LORD, to make atonement for yourselves.*

The temple tax, which was collected annually, was the same amount for everyone, regardless of economic standing—half a shekel. The money was used for the service of the tabernacle, and then later the temple. Every person who was 20-years-old or older was expected to pay it.

Matthew is the only one of the Gospel writers to record Jesus' miracle of the shekel in the fish's mouth used to pay the temple tax, and it may have been because of his previous vocation as a tax collector. But one thing is for sure: since Matthew wrote his Gospel to a Jewish Christian audience, they would've been familiar with the custom of paying the temple tax. And they would've understood that when Jesus said "sons are exempt" from paying the tax, He was claiming to be the Son of God.

As God's Son, Jesus didn't have to pay the tax, but He submitted to the law and paid it anyway so as not to be a stumbling block to others (1 Corinthians 8:9). And He did so in a miraculous way that further proved His relationship with His Father.

Chapter 7

THE LATER JUDEAN MINISTRY

Jesus at the Feast of Tabernacles

John 7:11–52

[11] So the Jews were seeking Him at the feast and were saying, "Where is He?" [12] There was much grumbling among the crowds concerning Him; some were saying, "He is a good man"; others were saying, "No, on the contrary, He leads the people astray." [13] Yet no one was speaking openly of Him for fear of the Jews.

[14] But when it was now the midst of the feast Jesus went up into the temple, and began to teach. [15] The Jews then were astonished, saying, "How has this man become learned, having never been educated?" [16] So Jesus answered them and said, "My teaching is not Mine, but His who sent Me. [17] If anyone is willing to do His will, he will know of the teaching, whether it is of God or whether I speak from Myself. [18] He who speaks from himself seeks his own glory; but He who is seeking the glory of the One who sent Him, He is true, and there is no unrighteousness in Him.

[19] "Did not Moses give you the Law, and yet none of you carries out the Law? Why do you seek to kill Me?" [20] The crowd answered, "You have a demon! Who seeks to kill You?" [21] Jesus answered them, "I did one deed, and you all marvel. [22] For this reason Moses has given you circumcision (not because it is from Moses, but from the fathers), and on the Sabbath you circumcise a man. [23] If a man receives

circumcision on the Sabbath so that the Law of Moses will not be broken, are you angry with Me because I made an entire man well on the Sabbath? 24 *Do not judge according to appearance, but judge with righteous judgment."*

25 *So some of the people of Jerusalem were saying, "Is this not the man whom they are seeking to kill?* 26 *Look, He is speaking publicly, and they are saying nothing to Him. The rulers do not really know that this is the Christ, do they?* 27 *However, we know where this man is from; but whenever the Christ may come, no one knows where He is from."* 28 *Then Jesus cried out in the temple, teaching and saying, "You both know Me and know where I am from; and I have not come of Myself, but He who sent Me is true, whom you do not know.* 29 *I know Him, because I am from Him, and He sent Me."* 30 *So they were seeking to seize Him; and no man laid his hand on Him, because His hour had not yet come.* 31 *But many of the crowd believed in Him; and they were saying, "When the Christ comes, He will not perform more signs than those which this man has, will He?"*

32 *The Pharisees heard the crowd muttering these things about Him, and the chief priests and the Pharisees sent officers to seize Him.* 33 *Therefore Jesus said, "For a little while longer I am with you, then I go to Him who sent Me.* 34 *You will seek Me, and will not find Me; and where I am, you cannot come."* 35 *The Jews then said to one another, "Where does this man intend to go that we will not find Him? He is not intending to go to the Dispersion among the Greeks, and teach the Greeks, is He?* 36 *What is this statement that He said, 'You will seek Me, and will not find Me; and where I am, you cannot come'?"*

37 *Now on the last day, the great day of the feast, Jesus stood and cried out, saying, "If anyone is thirsty, let him*

come to Me and drink. [38] *He who believes in Me, as the Scripture said, 'From his innermost being will flow rivers of living water.'"* [39] *But this He spoke of the Spirit, whom those who believed in Him were to receive; for the Spirit was not yet given, because Jesus was not yet glorified.*

[40] *Some of the people therefore, when they heard these words, were saying, "This certainly is the Prophet."* [41] *Others were saying, "This is the Christ." Still others were saying, "Surely the Christ is not going to come from Galilee, is He?* [42] *Has not the Scripture said that the Christ comes from the descendants of David, and from Bethlehem, the village where David was?"* [43] *So a division occurred in the crowd because of Him.* [44] *Some of them wanted to seize Him, but no one laid hands on Him.*

[45] *The officers then came to the chief priests and Pharisees, and they said to them, "Why did you not bring Him?"* [46] *The officers answered, "Never has a man spoken the way this man speaks."* [47] *The Pharisees then answered them, "You have not also been led astray, have you?* [48] *No one of the rulers or Pharisees has believed in Him, has he?* [49] *But this crowd which does not know the Law is accursed."* [50] *Nicodemus (he who came to Him before, being one of them) said to them,* [51] *"Our Law does not judge a man unless it first hears from him and knows what he is doing, does it?"* [52] *They answered him, "You are not also from Galilee, are you? Search, and see that no prophet arises out of Galilee."*

The Feast of Tabernacles was an annual seven-day festival that commemorated the 40 years the Hebrew people lived in booths or huts after their exodus from Egypt.

In John 7, hostility toward Jesus had begun to grow. In verse 11, we see that the Jews were searching for Jesus, asking, "Where is He?" because they wanted to kill Him (see 7:1). But

Jesus, being obedient to His Father, didn't hide from them; instead, in the middle of the feast, He went to the temple and started to preach. When He did, the people who heard Him were amazed because He didn't have any formal rabbinical training but knew the Scriptures so well! Jesus' authority came from His Father.

Jesus did not get distracted by vain questions. When the critics questioned where He received His education, He didn't try to defend Himself; rather, He answered that He had received His teaching from the One who had sent Him—His Father. His teaching should have convinced His critics that He was not just another rabbi.

Jesus did nothing wrong, yet some in the crowd wished to kill Him. We weren't there, but that doesn't mean we're innocent. Like the thief who died with Jesus, we admit our guilt, admit that "this man has done nothing wrong" (Luke 23:41), and plead for mercy.

When Jesus said, "Do not judge according to appearance, but judge with righteous judgment" (v. 24), He was challenging the people to not lose sight of the purpose of the law, instead of simply focusing on the letter of the law.

In this encounter there was gossip among the crowd about who Jesus was. Some thought the Christ would come from an unknown place, not Galilee. Jesus, knowing what they were thinking, said they may have known where He was from but they didn't know who sent Him. That was their trouble, they didn't really know—or seek to know—Jesus' Father.

The officers who were sent to arrest Jesus returned without Him. When questioned by the chief priests and Pharisees they replied, "Never has a man spoken the way this man speaks" (v. 46).

These religious leaders attempted to exert their power when they challenged the guards who had returned without Jesus. "No one of the rulers or Pharisees has believed in Him, has he?" (v. 48). They seemed to think that their views would squelch those of others. John tells us that Nicodemus was there, and He was a believer in Jesus. We might be tempted to criticize Nicodemus for not doing more, but we might have done the same thing if we were there.

The Healing of the Man Born Blind

John 9:1–41

*[1] As He passed by, He saw a man blind from birth. [2] And
His disciples asked Him, "Rabbi, who sinned, this man or
his parents, that he would be born blind?" [3] Jesus answered,
"It was neither that this man sinned, nor his parents; but
it was so that the works of God might be displayed in him.
[4] We must work the works of Him who sent Me as long as
it is day; night is coming when no one can work. [5] While I
am in the world, I am the Light of the world." [6] When He
had said this, He spat on the ground, and made clay of
the spittle, and applied the clay to his eyes, [7] and said to
him, "Go, wash in the pool of Siloam" (which is translated,
Sent). So he went away and washed, and came back seeing.
[8] Therefore the neighbors, and those who previously saw
him as a beggar, were saying, "Is not this the one who
used to sit and beg?" [9] Others were saying, "This is he,"
still others were saying, "No, but he is like him." He kept
saying, "I am the one." [10] So they were saying to him, "How
then were your eyes opened?" [11] He answered, "The man
who is called Jesus made clay, and anointed my eyes, and
said to me, 'Go to Siloam and wash'; so I went away and
washed, and I received sight." [12] They said to him, "Where
is He?" He said, "I do not know."*

*[13] They brought to the Pharisees the man who was formerly
blind. [14] Now it was a Sabbath on the day when Jesus
made the clay and opened his eyes. [15] Then the Pharisees
also were asking him again how he received his sight.*

And he said to them, "He applied clay to my eyes, and I washed, and I see." [16] *Therefore some of the Pharisees were saying, "This man is not from God, because He does not keep the Sabbath." But others were saying, "How can a man who is a sinner perform such signs?" And there was a division among them.* [17] *So they said to the blind man again, "What do you say about Him, since He opened your eyes?" And he said, "He is a prophet."*

[18] *The Jews then did not believe it of him, that he had been blind and had received sight, until they called the parents of the very one who had received his sight,* [19] *and questioned them, saying, "Is this your son, who you say was born blind? Then how does he now see?"* [20] *His parents answered them and said, "We know that this is our son, and that he was born blind;* [21] *but how he now sees, we do not know; or who opened his eyes, we do not know. Ask him; he is of age, he will speak for himself."* [22] *His parents said this because they were afraid of the Jews; for the Jews had already agreed that if anyone confessed Him to be Christ, he was to be put out of the synagogue.* [23] *For this reason his parents said, "He is of age; ask him."*

[24] *So a second time they called the man who had been blind, and said to him, "Give glory to God; we know that this man is a sinner."* [25] *He then answered, "Whether He is a sinner, I do not know; one thing I do know, that though I was blind, now I see."* [26] *So they said to him, "What did He do to you? How did He open your eyes?"* [27] *He answered them, "I told you already and you did not listen; why do you want to hear it again? You do not want to become His disciples too, do you?"* [28] *They reviled him and said, "You are His disciple, but we are disciples of Moses.* [29] *We know that God has spoken to Moses, but as for this man, we do not know where He is from."* [30] *The man answered and*

said to them, "Well, here is an amazing thing, that you do
not know where He is from, and yet He opened my eyes.
[31] We know that God does not hear sinners; but if anyone
is God-fearing and does His will, He hears him. [32] Since
the beginning of time it has never been heard that anyone
opened the eyes of a person born blind. [33] If this man were
not from God, He could do nothing." [34] They answered
him, "You were born entirely in sins, and are you teaching
us?" So they put him out.

[35] Jesus heard that they had put him out, and finding
him, He said, "Do you believe in the Son of Man?" [36] He
answered, "Who is He, Lord, that I may believe in Him?"
[37] Jesus said to him, "You have both seen Him, and He is
the one who is talking with you." [38] And he said, "Lord, I
believe." And he worshiped Him. [39] And Jesus said, "For
judgment I came into this world, so that those who do not
see may see, and that those who see may become blind."
[40] Those of the Pharisees who were with Him heard these
things and said to Him, "We are not blind too, are we?"
[41] Jesus said to them, "If you were blind, you would have
no sin; but since you say, 'We see,' your sin remains.

The disciples assumed the man was blind due to personal sin or the sin of his parents. Jesus corrected that notion, saying that the man's blindness was not a punishment for sin. Even so, we live in a world that is reeling from sin. When sin came into the world it brought with it the pain and problems that we now contend with. God assures us that in His future, when sin is no more, there will be no more sickness or pain. This man's blindness presented Jesus with the opportunity to reveal the power of God through the man's healing.

When Jesus said "must" (v. 4), He was emphasizing the urgency of His mission. He added, "While I am in the world, I am the light of the world" (v. 5). His presence dispels the darkness. We can go into dark places with the presence of Jesus and see the darkness retreat.

We can only speculate as to why Jesus used the clay to heal the man. The clay might have represented a creative act as it does elsewhere in Scripture (Genesis 2:7). Or perhaps using some type of symbolic, physical method was more meaningful to the blind man. Regardless, we have ample evidence of Jesus merely saying a word and healing occurring. There is also a lesson here that God is not limited by our expectations. He can use whatever means He knows is best for a particular situation.

As we might expect, the first to notice the change in this man were those who knew him best—his neighbors and family. Other people were less sure it was actually him. It's not every day that a blind man receives back his sight.

The formerly blind man knew Jesus by voice and by what Jesus did for him. He had not yet seen Jesus. We have something in common with this man. We have not yet seen Jesus, but, as 1 Peter 1:8 says, "though you have not seen Him, you love Him, and though you do not see Him now, but believe in Him, you greatly rejoice with joy inexpressible and full of glory."

Obviously, this miracle created quite a stir. Some of the Pharisees criticized Jesus for making clay on the Sabbath. Once again they had missed the point. Jesus had healed a blind man, changing the man's life. They should have been happy for the man, not resentful of Jesus.

Notice how obstinate the skeptics were. They had the witness of the man himself, backed up by the neighbors, and then restated by the parents, yet they held on to their unbelief.

The questioning by these leaders intimidated the parents. They had been threatened with expulsion from the synagogue if they made any statement that could be construed as recognizing Jesus as the Messiah. They reminded the leaders that their son was of responsible age, so they should direct their questions to him. If the leaders were really interested in what happened, they could go directly to the one to whom it had happened.

We have to admire this man. He refused to be intimidated by the leaders. He simply said, "I only know that I was blind; but, now I see" (v. 25). That's all a witness is required to do—to tell the truth.

The man Jesus healed didn't have a full understanding of who Jesus was, but he knew enough to know that Jesus wasn't an ordinary man. He readily affirmed his faith when he learned more about who Jesus is (v. 38).

When Jesus said, "If you were blind, you would have no sin; but since you say, 'We see,' your sin remains" (v. 41), He is warning against spiritual pride leading to ignorance. Here were people who had made their choice about Jesus despite evidence to the contrary.

Jesus Visits Martha and Mary

Luke 10:38–42

[38] *Now as they were traveling along, He entered a village;*
and a woman named Martha welcomed Him into her
home. [39] *She had a sister called Mary, who was seated at*
the Lord's feet, listening to His word. [40] *But Martha was*
distracted with all her preparations; and she came up to
Him and said, "Lord, do You not care that my sister has
left me to do all the serving alone? Then tell her to help
me." [41] *But the Lord answered and said to her, "Martha,*
Martha, you are worried and bothered about so many
things; [42] *but only one thing is necessary, for Mary has*
chosen the good part, which shall not be taken away from
her."

We are left to speculate as to how Jesus became acquainted with this home. When Jesus sent out His disciples on their first mission trip, He told them to find houses that were hospitable to their mission. Perhaps this home of Martha and Mary was one such home.

From the way Martha busied herself with hosting, she must have had an appreciation for the caliber of guests she was entertaining. Yet she was overly concerned with the preparations as well as the fact that her sister wasn't helping her. Mary sat at Jesus' feet, listening to Him. Jesus said this was the more important thing to focus on. Jesus was more interested in sharing His mission than the menu.

We can learn from the differences in their response to Jesus. Martha wasn't doing anything wrong, but she was distracted and overly busy. Mary put knowing the Lord before everything else.

Chapter 8

THE LATER PEREAN MINISTRY

Jesus Raises Lazarus from the Dead

John 11:1–46

1 *Now a certain man was sick, Lazarus of Bethany, the*
village of Mary and her sister Martha. 2 *It was the Mary*
who anointed the Lord with ointment, and wiped His feet
with her hair, whose brother Lazarus was sick. 3 *So the*
sisters sent word to Him, saying, "Lord, behold, he whom
You love is sick." 4 *But when Jesus heard this, He said,*
"This sickness is not to end in death, but for the glory of
God, so that the Son of God may be glorified by it." 5 *Now*
Jesus loved Martha and her sister and Lazarus. 6 *So when*
He heard that he was sick, He then stayed two days longer
in the place where He was. 7 *Then after this He said to the*
disciples, "Let us go to Judea again." 8 *The disciples said to*
Him, "Rabbi, the Jews were just now seeking to stone You,
and are You going there again?" 9 *Jesus answered, "Are there*
not twelve hours in the day? If anyone walks in the day, he
does not stumble, because he sees the light of this world.
10 *But if anyone walks in the night, he stumbles, because*
the light is not in him." 11 *This He said, and after that He*
said to them, "Our friend Lazarus has fallen asleep; but I
go, so that I may awaken him out of sleep." 12 *The disciples*
then said to Him, "Lord, if he has fallen asleep, he will
recover." 13 *Now Jesus had spoken of his death, but they*
thought that He was speaking of literal sleep. 14 *So Jesus*
then said to them plainly, "Lazarus is dead, 15 *and I am*
glad for your sakes that I was not there, so that you may

*believe; but let us go to him." [16] Therefore Thomas, who is
called Didymus, said to his fellow disciples, "Let us also
go, so that we may die with Him."*

*[17] So when Jesus came, He found that he had already been
in the tomb four days. [18] Now Bethany was near Jerusalem,
about two miles off; [19] and many of the Jews had come
to Martha and Mary, to console them concerning their
brother. [20] Martha therefore, when she heard that Jesus
was coming, went to meet Him, but Mary stayed at the
house. [21] Martha then said to Jesus, "Lord, if You had been
here, my brother would not have died. [22] Even now I know
that whatever You ask of God, God will give You." [23] Jesus
said to her, "Your brother will rise again." [24] Martha said
to Him, "I know that he will rise again in the resurrection
on the last day." [25] Jesus said to her, "I am the resurrection
and the life; he who believes in Me will live even if he dies,
[26] and everyone who lives and believes in Me will never
die. Do you believe this?" [27] She said to Him, "Yes, Lord;
I have believed that You are the Christ, the Son of God,
even He who comes into the world."*

*[28] When she had said this, she went away and called
Mary her sister, saying secretly, "The Teacher is here and
is calling for you." [29] And when she heard it, she got up
quickly and was coming to Him.*

*[30] Now Jesus had not yet come into the village, but was still
in the place where Martha met Him. [31] Then the Jews who
were with her in the house, and consoling her, when they
saw that Mary got up quickly and went out, they followed
her, supposing that she was going to the tomb to weep
there. [32] Therefore, when Mary came where Jesus was, she
saw Him, and fell at His feet, saying to Him, "Lord, if You
had been here, my brother would not have died." [33] When
Jesus therefore saw her weeping, and the Jews who came*

with her also weeping, He was deeply moved in spirit and
was troubled, [34] *and said, "Where have you laid him?"*
They said to Him, "Lord, come and see." [35] *Jesus wept.*
[36] *So the Jews were saying, "See how He loved him!"* [37] *But*
some of them said, "Could not this man, who opened
the eyes of the blind man, have kept this man also from
dying?"

[38] *So Jesus, again being deeply moved within, came to the*
tomb. Now it was a cave, and a stone was lying against
it. [39] *Jesus said, "Remove the stone." Martha, the sister of*
the deceased, said to Him, "Lord, by this time there will
be a stench, for he has been dead four days." [40] *Jesus said*
to her, "Did I not say to you that if you believe, you will
see the glory of God?" [41] *So they removed the stone. Then*
Jesus raised His eyes, and said, "Father, I thank You that
You have heard Me. [42] *I knew that You always hear Me;*
but because of the people standing around I said it, so that
they may believe that You sent Me." [43] *When He had said*
these things, He cried out with a loud voice, "Lazarus,
come forth." [44] *The man who had died came forth, bound*
hand and foot with wrappings, and his face was wrapped
around with a cloth. Jesus said to them, "Unbind him,
and let him go."

[45] *Therefore many of the Jews who came to Mary, and saw*
what He had done, believed in Him. [46] *But some of them*
went to the Pharisees and told them the things which Jesus
had done.

The phrase "he whom You love" (v. 3) that Martha used when messaging Jesus about Lazarus identifies Lazarus as beloved by Jesus. John repeated the assurance that Jesus loved this family when he noted, "Now Jesus loved Martha, and her sister and Lazarus" (v. 5). It's a good reminder that Jesus loves us personally, too.

When Jesus got the message He said, "The sickness is not to end in death, but for the glory of God, so that the Son of God may be glorified in it" (v. 4). The disciples likely heard Him say this. The one bearing the message might have heard it also. Jesus' word brought encouragement and assurance to everyone who heard it.

Jesus' disciples were concerned about returning to Judea because of the threats against Jesus. But Jesus knew that the timing was right to go to see Lazarus despite the risks. The healing of Lazarus was for the glory of God. Besides, Jesus knew that nothing would happen to Him before the appointed time.

A resigned Thomas said, "Let us also go, so that we may die with Him" (v. 16). He may have been prone to doubt, but he apparently had some courage too. If we were in his shoes, we might have responded as he did, fearing the worst. We need not fear following Jesus, though.

John tells us that there were many people at and around the house to offer their comfort to the sisters. Some of that crowd must have alerted Martha that Jesus was coming. The first words Martha spoke to Jesus were: "Lord, If You had been here, my brother would not have died" (v. 21). She followed that up with a faith-filled statement: "Even now I know that whatever You ask of God, God will give You" (v. 22).

Jesus assured Martha that Lazarus would rise from the dead, which Martha took to mean as some distant event in the future. Jesus corrected her, saying, "I am the resurrection and the life" (v. 25). Hope resides in a person of Jesus, now and in the future. Trust in Christ negates the power of death.

We are assured that Jesus grieves with us. John notes that He was "deeply moved in spirit and was troubled" (v. 33) by the sadness surrounding the death of Lazarus. Here were people He knew and loved. Their hurt became His hurt. Need there be any commentary on the poignant note, "Jesus wept" (v. 25)?

Jesus ordered them to remove the stone despite objections that there would be a terrible stench. He could have blasted the stone out Himself, but He had them move it. God has assigned to us the task of joining with Him to remove obstacles to redemption. He uses us to bring His life to others.

After Jesus called Lazarus out of the grave, Jesus instructed the crowd to "unbind him, and let him go" (v. 44). That service of "unbinding" and "letting go" is a task assigned to the church. People enter new life bound to a past that hinders them. The church helps set them free.

John says that "many" believed. How could there be any skeptics? They had all seen what happened. The reaction—"But some of them went to the Pharisees and told them the things which Jesus had done" (v. 46)—is hard to understand. Some opted to fortify their unbelief with a barrage of questions rather than follow the evidence. It is a sad testimony to the power of unbelief that we sometimes won't accept the truth.

Jesus Begins His Last Trip to Jerusalem

Luke 17:11

> 11 *While He was on the way to Jerusalem, He was passing between Samaria and Galilee.*

After raising Lazarus, Jesus took Himself out of the public eye. He knew of the plot to arrest Him. John 11:54 tells us, "Jesus no longer continued to walk publicly among the Jews, but went away from there to the country near the wilderness, into a city called Ephraim; and there He stayed with the disciples." There was wide-spread curiosity about whether or not Jesus would come to the next Passover celebration. Luke informs us here that Jesus did decide to go to Jerusalem, and that His route took Him through Samaria.

These next events are very compressed. Time is running short.

Jesus Blesses the Children

Matthew 19:13–15

> [13] *Then some children were brought to Him so that He*
> *might lay His hands on them and pray; and the disciples*
> *rebuked them.* [14] *But Jesus said, "Let the children alone,*
> *and do not hinder them from coming to Me; for the*
> *kingdom of heaven belongs to such as these."* [15] *After laying*
> *His hands on them, He departed from there.*

We don't know if the disciples were rebuking the parents or the children or both. In any event, the disciples showed they still had a lot to learn. We should all seek the childlike innocence that isn't intimidated by position.

Jesus' statement, "the kingdom of heaven belongs to such as these" (v. 14), speaks not of immaturity but of dependence. Children aren't self-sufficient, and they know it.

Mark 10:13–15

> [13] *And they were bringing children to Him so that He*
> *might touch them; but the disciples rebuked them.* [14] *But*
> *when Jesus saw this, He was indignant and said to them,*
> *"Permit the children to come to Me; do not hinder them;*
> *for the kingdom of God belongs to such as these.* [15] *Truly I*
> *say to you, whoever does not receive the kingdom of God*
> *like a child will not enter it at all."*

When Jesus said, "receive the kingdom like a child" (v. 15), He challenges us to come to God with humility and trust. The pure trust that a child has in a loving parent illustrates the kind of trust God is looking for in His children. When we trust God, we want to obey Him.

Luke 18:15–17

15 And they were bringing even their babies to Him so that He would touch them, but when the disciples saw it, they began rebuking them. 16 But Jesus called for them, saying, "Permit the children to come to Me, and do not hinder them, for the kingdom of God belongs to such as these. 17 Truly I say to you, whoever does not receive the kingdom of God like a child will not enter it at all."

Luke tells us that people "were bringing even their babies to Jesus" (v. 15). Babies are totally dependent on their parents, as we should be on God.

Jesus and The Rich Young Ruler

Matthew 19:16–30

16 And someone came to Him and said, "Teacher, what good thing shall I do that I may obtain eternal life?" 17 And He said to him, "Why are you asking Me about what is good? There is only One who is good; but if you wish to enter into life, keep the commandments." 18 Then he said to Him, "Which ones?" And Jesus said, "YOU SHALL NOT COMMIT MURDER; YOU SHALL NOT COMMIT ADULTERY; YOU SHALL NOT STEAL; YOU SHALL NOT BEAR FALSE WITNESS; 19 HONOR YOUR FATHER AND MOTHER; and YOU SHALL LOVE YOUR NEIGHBOR AS YOURSELF." 20 The young man said to Him, "All these things I have kept; what am I still lacking?" 21 Jesus said to him, "If you wish to be complete, go and sell your possessions and give to the poor, and you will have treasure in heaven; and come, follow Me." 22 But when the young man heard this statement, he went away grieving; for he was one who owned much property.

> 23 *And Jesus said to His disciples, "Truly I say to you, it*
> *is hard for a rich man to enter the kingdom of heaven.*
> 24 *Again I say to you, it is easier for a camel to go through*
> *the eye of a needle, than for a rich man to enter the*
> *kingdom of God."* 25 *When the disciples heard this, they*
> *were very astonished and said, "Then who can be saved?"*
> 26 *And looking at them Jesus said to them, "With people*
> *this is impossible, but with God all things are possible."*
>
> 27 *Then Peter said to Him, "Behold, we have left everything*
> *and followed You; what then will there be for us?"* 28 *And*
> *Jesus said to them, "Truly I say to you, that you who have*
> *followed Me, in the regeneration when the Son of Man*
> *will sit on His glorious throne, you also shall sit upon*
> *twelve thrones, judging the twelve tribes of Israel.* 29 *And*
> *everyone who has left houses or brothers or sisters or*
> *father or mother or children or farms for My name's sake,*
> *will receive many times as much, and will inherit eternal*
> *life.* 30 *But many who are first will be last; and the last,*
> *first.*

The identity of the person (Matthew refers to him as "someone") was not as important as the content of the message. The question, "What good thing shall I do that I may obtain eternal life?" (v. 16) shows confusion about how salvation occurs.

Jesus challenged this person at the point of common understanding—the need to keep the commandments to secure eternal life. Notice the commandments Jesus mentioned in response to the man's question. He didn't mention the very first commandment, "You shall have no other gods before Me." The ultimate response of this man indicated that he couldn't keep the first commandment.

The young man had been living a good moral life, but he wasn't satisfied. He knew he was missing something. Jesus asked him to do what He had asked the disciples to do—give up their personal ideas of life and follow Him. Specifically, Jesus said, "If you wish to be complete, go and sell all your possessions and give to the poor, and you will have treasure in heaven; and come, follow Me" (v. 21). The key phrase is "follow Me." If he accepted Jesus as his Lord, then doing whatever Jesus asked would be next. Peter, James, and John had given up their lives as professional fishermen. Matthew had given up his career as a tax collector. To them, what was given up was not that important. What was gained was what mattered.

This young man was not really willing to do a "good thing" in order to be saved. He would grieve, but ultimately he would not surrender his wealth. Because Matthew in his previous career knew about taxing, he may have known about the value of the properties this young man owned. Matthew says, "He went away grieving; for he was one who owned much property" (v. 22).

Jesus said to His disciples, "Truly I say to you, it is hard for a rich man to enter the kingdom of Heaven" (v. 23). What makes it so hard for a rich person to enter heaven? It might be an attitude that says, "Regular rules don't apply to me." It could be the absence of any real sense of dependency. It might be the mistaken idea that wealth provides more security than it really does.

Jesus says it's hard for a rich person to enter the kingdom because they tend to be so attached to their wealth. This surprised the disciples as wealth was generally viewed as evidence of God's favor. Jesus assured them that all things are possible with God, including a rich person surrendering his wealth for the sake of the kingdom. In fact, it's a wonderful thing when a wealthy person uses his wealth for God's purposes. Unfortunately, the rich young man in this story was unwilling to do that.

Peter asked what all who follow Jesus might want to ask:

"We have left everything and followed You; what then will there be for us?" (v. 27). Jesus answered: "Everyone who has left houses or brothers or sisters or father or mother or children or farms for My name's sake, will receive many times as much, and will inherit eternal life" (v. 29). Followers of Jesus receive far more than they ever give up. Disciples are empowered to live the abundant life later described in John 10:10. On top of that, disciples are assured of eternal life!

God's kingdom doesn't operate as the world does. The rich and famous aren't necessarily great in the kingdom. Jesus said that "many who are first will be last, and the last, first" (v. 30). Humble servants of Jesus are great in the kingdom.

Mark 10:17–31

17 *As He was setting out on a journey, a man ran up
to Him and knelt before Him, and asked Him, "Good
Teacher, what shall I do to inherit eternal life?"* 18 *And
Jesus said to him, "Why do you call Me good? No one is
good except God alone.* 19 *You know the commandments,
'DO NOT MURDER, DO NOT COMMIT ADULTERY,
DO NOT STEAL, DO NOT BEAR FALSE WITNESS,
Do not defraud, HONOR YOUR FATHER AND
MOTHER.'"* 20 *And he said to Him, "Teacher, I have
kept all these things from my youth up."* 21 *Looking
at him, Jesus felt a love for him and said to him, "One
thing you lack: go and sell all you possess and give to the
poor, and you will have treasure in heaven; and come,
follow Me."* 22 *But at these words he was saddened, and
he went away grieving, for he was one who owned much
property.*

23 *And Jesus, looking around, said to His disciples,
"How hard it will be for those who are wealthy to enter
the kingdom of God!"* 24 *The disciples were amazed at*

His words. But Jesus answered again and said to them, "Children, how hard it is to enter the kingdom of God! [25] *It is easier for a camel to go through the eye of a needle than for a rich man to enter the kingdom of God."* [26] *They were even more astonished and said to Him, "Then who can be saved?"* [27] *Looking at them, Jesus said, "With people it is impossible, but not with God; for all things are possible with God."*

[28] *Peter began to say to Him, "Behold, we have left everything and followed You."* [29] *Jesus said, "Truly I say to you, there is no one who has left house or brothers or sisters or mother or father or children or farms, for My sake and for the gospel's sake,* [30] *but that he will receive a hundred times as much now in the present age, houses and brothers and sisters and mothers and children and farms, along with persecutions; and in the age to come, eternal life.* [31] *But many who are first will be last, and the last, first."*

Jesus recognized that this man knew the commandments. It is interesting to note that he listed "do not defraud" (v. 19) and didn't list (as Matthew did) "Love your neighbor as yourself."

In saying that "Jesus felt a love for him" (v. 21), we see that Jesus took this questioning seriously and answered with compassion. He wasn't put off by the questioning, but was drawn in by it. Jesus didn't regard this man as merely a curiosity-seeker. Jesus was seeing what the future could be for this young man.

Jesus tells Peter that the cost of discipleship is worth every sacrifice. The blessings we receive are not only future, but also present—though that doesn't mean we get whatever we want in this life. What we do get right now is God's presence and power.

Luke 18:18–30

[18] A ruler questioned Him, saying, "Good Teacher, what shall I do to inherit eternal life?" [19] And Jesus said to him, "Why do you call Me good? No one is good except God alone. [20] You know the commandments, 'DO NOT COMMIT ADULTERY, DO NOT MURDER, DO NOT STEAL, DO NOT BEAR FALSE WITNESS, HONOR YOUR FATHER AND MOTHER.'" [21] And he said, "All these things I have kept from my youth." [22] When Jesus heard this, He said to him, "One thing you still lack; sell all that you possess and distribute it to the poor, and you shall have treasure in heaven; and come, follow Me." [23] But when he had heard these things, he became very sad, for he was extremely rich. [24] And Jesus looked at him and said, "How hard it is for those who are wealthy to enter the kingdom of God! [25] For it is easier for a camel to go through the eye of a needle than for a rich man to enter the kingdom of God." [26] They who heard it said, "Then who can be saved?" [27] But He said, "The things that are impossible with people are possible with God."

[28] Peter said, "Behold, we have left our own homes and followed You." [29] And He said to them, "Truly I say to you, there is no one who has left house or wife or brothers or parents or children, for the sake of the kingdom of God, [30] who will not receive many times as much at this time and in the age to come, eternal life."

Luke identifies this person as "a ruler" (v. 18). We know he was rich, and as a ruler, he was likely quite powerful, too. From a worldly perspective, there would be a big cost for this man to follow Jesus.

Jesus Reminds His Disciples of His Death and Resurrection

Matthew 20:17–19

> [17] *As Jesus was about to go up to Jerusalem, He took the twelve disciples aside by themselves, and on the way He said to them,* [18] *"Behold, we are going up to Jerusalem; and the Son of Man will be delivered to the chief priests and scribes, and they will condemn Him to death,* [19] *and will hand Him over to the Gentiles to mock and scourge and crucify Him, and on the third day He will be raised up."*

We're told that Jesus "took the twelve disciples aside by themselves" (v. 17), so they must have been traveling with a larger group. As they were walking, Jesus reminded them of what was going to happen in Jerusalem. What he had been discussing with them was about to take place.

They must have wondered just who would deliver Jesus to the religious authorities. It must have shocked these disciples (although we know that Judas was there) to be aware that men of such prestige and honor as the chief priests and scribes would press for execution. The Romans would have to carry out the execution, for occupied national law didn't allow the Jewish leaders to do it, but these leaders were certainly behind it.

Mark 10:32–34

> [32] *They were on the road going up to Jerusalem, and Jesus was walking on ahead of them; and they were amazed, and those who followed were fearful. And again He took the twelve aside and began to tell them what was going to happen to Him,* [33] *saying, "Behold, we are going up to Jerusalem, and the Son of Man will be delivered to the*

chief priests and the scribes; and they will condemn Him to death and will hand Him over to the Gentiles. [34] *They will mock Him and spit on Him, and scourge Him and kill Him, and three days later He will rise again."*

Jesus knew what was ahead of Him and was determined to face it. His disciples were amazed at what He shared with them, and others who were following were fearful of what could happen.

Luke 18:31–34

[31] *Then He took the twelve aside and said to them, "Behold, we are going up to Jerusalem, and all things which are written through the prophets about the Son of Man will be accomplished.* [32] *For He will be handed over to the Gentiles, and will be mocked and mistreated and spit upon,* [33] *and after they have scourged Him, they will kill Him; and the third day He will rise again."* [34] *But the disciples understood none of these things, and the meaning of this statement was hidden from them, and they did not comprehend the things that were said.*

When Jesus said the Scriptures would be fulfilled, the disciples would have known about the suffering servant in Isaiah. Despite their familiarity with the Old Testament depiction of the Messiah, they still didn't understand what Jesus was saying. Perhaps they didn't want to believe it, so they chose not to accept it.

Jesus Heals the Blind Men on the Jericho Road

Matthew 20:29–34

[29] *As they were leaving Jericho, a large crowd followed Him.* [30] *And two blind men sitting by the road, hearing that Jesus was passing by, cried out, "Lord, have mercy*

on us, Son of David!" [31] *The crowd sternly told them*
to be quiet, but they cried out all the more, "Lord, Son
of David, have mercy on us!" [32] *And Jesus stopped and*
called them, and said, "What do you want Me to do for
you?" [33] *They said to Him, "Lord, we want our eyes to be*
opened." [34] *Moved with compassion, Jesus touched their*
eyes; and immediately they regained their sight and
followed Him.

Even though Jesus was focused on His mission, He had time to stop for these men despite the crowd telling them to be quiet. He was not so much distracted as touched by their pleas. Unlike us, Jesus doesn't get compassion fatigue. He is not too busy for our pleas for help either.

Jesus stopped to grant the request of these desperate men. When Matthew notes that "they regained their sight" (v. 34), we might understand that to mean they had been able to see at one point before going blind. Once they could see again, they followed Jesus.

Mark 10:46–52

[46] *Then they came to Jericho. And as He was leaving Jericho*
with His disciples and a large crowd, a blind beggar
named Bartimaeus, the son of Timaeus, was sitting by the
road. [47] *When he heard that it was Jesus the Nazarene, he*
began to cry out and say, "Jesus, Son of David, have mercy
on me!" [48] *Many were sternly telling him to be quiet, but*
he kept crying out all the more, "Son of David, have mercy
on me!" [49] *And Jesus stopped and said, "Call him here." So*
they called the blind man, saying to him, "Take courage,
stand up! He is calling for you." [50] *Throwing aside his cloak,*
he jumped up and came to Jesus. [51] *And answering him,*
Jesus said, "What do you want Me to do for you?" And
the blind man said to Him, "Rabboni, I want to regain my
sight!" [52] *And Jesus said to him, "Go; your faith has made*

> *you well." Immediately he regained his sight and began following Him on the road.*

Mark may have had some personal knowledge of this man since he mentions him by name, even noting who his father was. Perhaps that's why he doesn't mention the other blind man.

Bartimaeus cried for help because he had heard about Jesus. While many in the crowd tried to quiet him down, Jesus called for him, and then some in the crowd encouraged him to get up and go to Jesus. Bartimaeus jumped up and went to Jesus. The fact that he was blind didn't seem to hold him back at all.

When Jesus asked, "What do you want Me to do for you?" He said, "Rabboni, I want to regain my sight" (v. 51). *Rabboni* means "my great master." Bartimaeus had either already made Jesus his great master or was confessing his faith in Jesus. It was that faith that led to the miracle.

Luke 18:35–43

> 35 *As Jesus was approaching Jericho, a blind man was*
> *sitting by the road begging.* 36 *Now hearing a crowd going*
> *by, he began to inquire what this was.* 37 *They told him*
> *that Jesus of Nazareth was passing by.* 38 *And he called out,*
> *saying, "Jesus, Son of David, have mercy on me!"* 39 *Those*
> *who led the way were sternly telling him to be quiet; but*
> *he kept crying out all the more, "Son of David, have mercy*
> *on me!"* 40 *And Jesus stopped and commanded that he be*
> *brought to Him; and when he came near, He questioned*
> *him,* 41 *"What do you want Me to do for you?" And he*
> *said, "Lord, I want to regain my sight!"* 42 *And Jesus said*
> *to him, "Receive your sight; your faith has made you well."*
> 43 *Immediately he regained his sight and began following*
> *Him, glorifying God; and when all the people saw it, they*
> *gave praise to God.*

Luke said that Jesus was approaching Jericho. Matthew and Mark said that He was leaving Jericho. Luke may have meant that Jesus was in the vicinity of Jericho when this took place.

Jesus asked the man, "What do you want me to do for you?" (v. 41), and the blind man gave an honest answer—he wanted to be able to see. God asks us what we want too. That doesn't mean He always gives us what we want, but He does invite us to ask. The Gospels repeatedly emphasize the importance of faith, and here's another instance where faith is rewarded.

Jesus Meets Zaccheus

Luke 19:1–10

> [1] *He entered Jericho and was passing through.* [2] *And there was a man called by the name of Zaccheus; he was a chief tax collector and he was rich.* [3] *Zaccheus was trying to see who Jesus was, and was unable because of the crowd, for he was small in stature.* [4] *So he ran on ahead and climbed up into a sycamore tree in order to see Him, for He was about to pass through that way.* [5] *When Jesus came to the place, He looked up and said to him, "Zaccheus, hurry and come down, for today I must stay at your house."* [6] *And he hurried and came down and received Him gladly.* [7] *When they saw it, they all began to grumble, saying, "He has gone to be the guest of a man who is a sinner."* [8] *Zaccheus stopped and said to the Lord, "Behold, Lord, half of my possessions I will give to the poor, and if I have defrauded anyone of anything, I will give back four times as much."*
> [9] *And Jesus said to him, "Today salvation has come to this house, because he, too, is a son of Abraham.* [10] *For the Son of Man has come to seek and to save that which was lost."*

Zaccheus was well-known locally. He might have known Matthew, since Matthew had been a tax collector, too. In fact, he may have heard about Jesus from Matthew and wanted to see Jesus in person.

We aren't told how Jesus knew who Zaccheus was, but He did. Note that Zaccheus climbed a tree in order to see Jesus, and yet Jesus saw him and asked him to come down. God is looking for us more than we're looking for Him.

Zaccheus's encounter with Jesus clearly changed him, for he promised to give away half of his wealth to the poor, and pay back those he had cheated. It's an amazing example of what grace can do. The generosity of Jesus produces gratitude and generosity in His followers, and Zaccheus had become one. "He too is a son of Abraham" (v. 9), said Jesus.

The kingdom is available to people whom society frowns upon. Zaccheus was an outsider before experiencing the welcoming grace of Jesus.

Chapter 9

THE LAST PUBLIC MINISTRY IN JERUSALEM

Christ's Return Visit with Mary and Martha

John 11:55–12:1

*55 Now the Passover of the Jews was near, and many went
up to Jerusalem out of the country before the Passover to
purify themselves. 56 So they were seeking for Jesus, and
were saying to one another as they stood in the temple,
"What do you think; that He will not come to the feast at
all?" 57 Now the chief priests and the Pharisees had given
orders that if anyone knew where He was, he was to report
it, so that they might seize Him.*

*12:1 Jesus, therefore, six days before the Passover, came to
Bethany where Lazarus was, whom Jesus had raised from
the dead.*

John was with Jesus. He must have visited with people at the Passover to get this information about the order for Jesus' arrest.

Earlier when Jesus went to Lazarus's grave he explained to His disciples that the timing was right. He always did things at the pace His Father set for Him. He knew that now was the time to go to Jerusalem.

The Triumphal Entry

Matthew 21:1–11

*1 When they had approached Jerusalem and had come to
Bethphage, at the Mount of Olives, then Jesus sent two*

disciples, [2] saying to them, "Go into the village opposite you, and immediately you will find a donkey tied there and a colt with her; untie them and bring them to Me. [3] If anyone says anything to you, you shall say, 'The Lord has need of them,' and immediately he will send them." [4] This took place to fulfill what was spoken through the prophet:

> *[5] "SAY TO THE DAUGHTER OF ZION,*
> *'BEHOLD YOUR KING IS COMING TO YOU,*
> *GENTLE, AND MOUNTED ON A DONKEY,*
> *EVEN ON A COLT, THE FOAL OF A BEAST OF BURDEN.'"*

[6] The disciples went and did just as Jesus had instructed them, [7] and brought the donkey and the colt, and laid their coats on them; and He sat on the coats. [8] Most of the crowd spread their coats in the road, and others were cutting branches from the trees and spreading them in the road. [9] The crowds going ahead of Him, and those who followed, were shouting,

"Hosanna to the Son of David;
BLESSED IS HE WHO COMES IN THE NAME OF THE LORD;
Hosanna in the highest!"

[10] When He had entered Jerusalem, all the city was stirred, saying, "Who is this?" [11] And the crowds were saying, "This is the prophet Jesus, from Nazareth in Galilee."

John tells us that the Jewish leaders had spread the word that if anyone knew of Jesus' whereabouts they were to report it to the authorities. They suspected Jesus would slip into town, if He came at all. They must have been shocked by this scene. Jesus didn't slip into town; He made a grand entrance!

The two disciples who were instructed to go into town and bring back a donkey and a colt must have had some doubt that they would be there exactly as Jesus said. Their faith must have grown after completing their mission. God often calls us to do things we don't completely understand. He grows our trust in Him that way.

Matthew wrote this after the fact. As he pondered it, he recognized that a prophecy for these events was recorded in Zechariah 9:9, which reads, "Rejoice greatly, O daughter of Zion! Shout in triumph, O daughter of Jerusalem! Behold, your king is coming to you; He is just and endowed with salvation, humble, and mounted on a donkey, even on a colt, the foal of a donkey."

Note that the "crowd" following Jesus on the trip to Jerusalem became "crowds." His entrance created quite a commotion. Everyone was asking who He was, and the answer came back as: "This is the prophet Jesus, from Nazareth in Galilee" (v. 11). Despite all they had seen, the crowds didn't really grasp that Jesus was the Messiah, the Son of God. To them, Jesus was just a powerful prophet.

Mark 11:1–10

1 *As they approached Jerusalem, at Bethphage and*
Bethany, near the Mount of Olives, He sent two of His
disciples, 2 *and said to them, "Go into the village opposite*
you, and immediately as you enter it, you will find a colt
tied there, on which no one yet has ever sat; untie it and
bring it here. 3 *If anyone says to you, 'Why are you doing*
this?' you say, 'The Lord has need of it'; and immediately
he will send it back here." 4 *They went away and found a*
colt tied at the door, outside in the street; and they untied
it. 5 *Some of the bystanders were saying to them, "What*
are you doing, untying the colt?" 6 *They spoke to them just*
as Jesus had told them, and they gave them permission.
7 *They brought the colt to Jesus and put their coats on it;*

and He sat on it. [8] *And many spread their coats in the road, and others spread leafy branches which they had cut from the fields.* [9] *Those who went in front and those who followed were shouting:*

"Hosanna!
BLESSED IS HE WHO COMES IN THE NAME OF THE LORD;

[10] *Blessed is the coming kingdom of our father David;*
Hosanna in the highest!"

No one had broken the colt to be ridden. Yet Jesus got on and rode into Jerusalem!

Those who had coats threw them on the road. Those who didn't have coats cut palm branches and covered the road ahead of Jesus. According to historians, it was a custom in the East to cover the path of a person deserving high honor. The shouts from the crowd show that they regarded Jesus as royalty from the lineage of David.

Luke 19:29–44

[29] *When He approached Bethphage and Bethany, near the*
mount that is called Olivet, He sent two of the disciples,
[30] *saying, "Go into the village ahead of you; there, as you*
enter, you will find a colt tied on which no one yet has ever
sat; untie it and bring it here. [31] *If anyone asks you, 'Why*
are you untying it?' you shall say, 'The Lord has need of
it.'" [32] *So those who were sent went away and found it just*
as He had told them. [33] *As they were untying the colt, its*
owners said to them, "Why are you untying the colt?"
[34] *They said, "The Lord has need of it."* [35] *They brought it*
to Jesus, and they threw their coats on the colt and put
Jesus on it. [36] *As He was going, they were spreading their*
coats on the road. [37] *As soon as He was approaching, near*

the descent of the Mount of Olives, the whole crowd of the disciples began to praise God joyfully with a loud voice for all the miracles which they had seen, [38] shouting:

> *"BLESSED IS THE KING WHO COMES IN THE NAME OF THE LORD;*
>
> *Peace in heaven and glory in the highest!"*

[39] Some of the Pharisees in the crowd said to Him, "Teacher, rebuke Your disciples." [40] But Jesus answered, "I tell you, if these become silent, the stones will cry out!"

[41] When He approached Jerusalem, He saw the city and wept over it, [42] saying, "If you had known in this day, even you, the things which make for peace! But now they have been hidden from your eyes. [43] For the days will come upon you when your enemies will throw up a barricade against you, and surround you and hem you in on every side, [44] and they will level you to the ground and your children within you, and they will not leave in you one stone upon another, because you did not recognize the time of your visitation."

Luke adds that the owners of the colt questioned why the two disciples were taking it. The disciples told them the Lord needed it, and apparently they were fine with that answer.

According to Luke, a "whole crowd" (v. 37) of disciples was praising God. We sometimes forget there were many followers of Jesus in addition to the twelve.

When the Pharisees chided Jesus about the cheers of the disciples, Jesus responded by saying, "I tell you, if these become silent, the stones will cry out" (v. 40). Jesus had created new life in these vocal disciples, and they were vocalizing their gratitude and excitement. Praise for Jesus cannot be muted! Should we, His disciples, go silent, witness will come forth from His creation! Romans 1:19–20 says, "That which is known about God is evident within them; for God made it evident to them. For since the creation of the world His invisible attributes, His eternal power and divine nature, have been clearly seen, being understood through what has been made." Creation speaks of the Creator.

When Jesus saw the city, He "wept over it" (v. 41). This is only the second time we read of Jesus weeping. The mourning over the death of Lazarus also revealed His deep compassion for the people and His love for Lazarus. Here he weeps not only because He loves the people of Israel, but because He knows that they will ultimately reject Him. They were still spiritually blind, and their opportunity to believe in Him was slipping away.

Jesus sadly forecasted that "the days will come upon you when your enemies will throw up a barricade against you, and surround you and hem you in on every side, and they will level you to the ground and your children within you, and they will not leave in you one stone upon another, because you did not recognize the time of your visitation" (vv. 43–44). This devastation would come because they had not been responsive to God's revelation to them. This all ended up taking place in A.D. 70 when the Roman army under Titus built a wall five miles in length to hold the city in, and then destroyed Jerusalem and the temple buildings.

The chief priests had schemed that if they could find a scapegoat in Jesus, the nation would be spared. They crucified Jesus in that political hope. History reveals their error.

John 12:12–19

12 *On the next day the large crowd who had come to the*
feast, when they heard that Jesus was coming to Jerusalem,
13 *took the branches of the palm trees and went out to*
meet Him, and began to shout, "Hosanna! BLESSED IS
HE WHO COMES IN THE NAME OF THE LORD, even
the King of Israel." 14 *Jesus, finding a young donkey, sat*
on it; as it is written, 15 *"FEAR NOT, DAUGHTER OF*

ZION; BEHOLD, YOUR KING IS COMING, SEATED ON A DONKEY'S COLT." [16] *These things His disciples did not understand at the first; but when Jesus was glorified, then they remembered that these things were written of Him, and that they had done these things to Him.* [17] *So the people, who were with Him when He called Lazarus out of the tomb and raised him from the dead, continued to testify about Him.* [18] *For this reason also the people went and met Him, because they heard that He had performed this sign.* [19] *So the Pharisees said to one another, "You see that you are not doing any good; look, the world has gone after Him."*

John says that the crowd that had come into town for the feast heard the procession announcing the arrival of Jesus. They went out to meet Him and joined the crowd coming from the Mount of Olives. It must have been some procession, filling the road from out of town into Jerusalem.

While these things were happening, the twelve couldn't grasp them. It was only afterward, as they remembered the events and related those events to what they knew from Scripture, that things started to make sense to them.

The Barren Fig Tree

Matthew 21:18–19

[18] *Now in the morning, when He was returning to the city, He became hungry.* [19] *Seeing a lone fig tree by the road, He came to it and found nothing on it except leaves only; and He said to it, "No longer shall there ever be any fruit from you." And at once the fig tree withered.*

Jesus didn't spend the night in the city. He went out to Bethany. He may have spent the night with Lazarus's family.

Jesus came across a barren fig tree and cursed it, causing

it to wither. Fig trees are supposed to bear fruit, but this one wasn't. The nature of the tree was that it would never bear any fruit. It was what tree experts call a "bull tree"—it used all of its nutrients for foliage (to make it look better), so that none was available for fruit. The tree represented something it was not!

Mark 11:12–14

[12] *On the next day, when they had left Bethany, He became*
hungry. [13] *Seeing at a distance a fig tree in leaf, He went to*
see if perhaps He would find anything on it; and when He
came to it, He found nothing but leaves, for it was not the
season for figs. [14] *He said to it, "May no one ever eat fruit*
from you again!" And His disciples were listening.

Jesus spotted a tree in leaf. Since Mark mentioned that "it was not the season for figs" (v. 13), perhaps this tree had come out a little earlier than any of the other fig trees. Since it would have leaves before fruit, and since it showed leaves, Jesus assumed that it might have fruit early also. When Jesus said to the tree, "May no one ever eat fruit from you again" (v. 14), He was eliminating the possibility that the tree would ever deceive someone again. It appeared to have something it didn't have. The parallel to the teaching of the Jewish religious leaders was unmistakable.

Jesus Cleanses the Temple

Matthew 21:12–13

[12] *And Jesus entered the temple and drove out all those who*
were buying and selling in the temple, and overturned
the tables of the money changers and the seats of those
who were selling doves. [13] *And He said to them, "It is*
written, 'MY HOUSE SHALL BE CALLED A HOUSE
OF PRAYER'; but you are making it a ROBBERS' DEN."

In order for the temple to function as a place of worship, Jesus had to drive out all the people buying and selling there. They had corrupted the purpose of the temple. God will not bless crass commercialization at the expense of true worship, then or now.

Mark 11:15–18

[15] Then they came to Jerusalem. And He entered the temple and began to drive out those who were buying and selling in the temple, and overturned the tables of the money changers and the seats of those who were selling doves; [16] and He would not permit anyone to carry merchandise through the temple. [17] And He began to teach and say to them, "Is it not written, 'MY HOUSE SHALL BE CALLED A HOUSE OF PRAYER FOR ALL THE NATIONS'? But you have made it a ROBBERS' DEN."
[18] The chief priests and the scribes heard this, and began seeking how to destroy Him; for they were afraid of Him, for the whole crowd was astonished at His teaching.

There would have been a lot of business taking place at the temple during this national holiday. Just as we can miss the point of Christmas amidst all the busyness and sales, the people had lost sight of the reason they were there. Jesus said the temple was supposed to be a place of prayer, not a marketplace. It's a reminder for us to make sure that our churches don't drift from their original purpose.

Skeptics Question Jesus' Authority

Matthew 21:23–27

[23] When He entered the temple, the chief priests and the elders of the people came to Him while He was teaching, and said, "By what authority are You doing these things, and who gave You this authority?" [24] Jesus said to them,

"I will also ask you one thing, which if you tell Me, I will also tell you by what authority I do these things. [25] The baptism of John was from what source, from heaven or from men?" And they began reasoning among themselves, saying, "If we say, 'From heaven,' He will say to us, 'Then why did you not believe him?' [26] But if we say, 'From men,' we fear the people; for they all regard John as a prophet." [27] And answering Jesus, they said, "We do not know." He also said to them, "Neither will I tell you by what authority I do these things.

The critics confronted Jesus about the issue of authority. They had not granted Him license to be so bold. Apparently, their question was intended to intimidate Jesus into silence. Because He recognized a higher authority than these religious and political leaders, Jesus wasn't intimidated, and He challenged them with a question about John the Baptist. Present-day disciples can expect to be increasingly faced with attempts at intimidation as our culture becomes more and more secular. We must, as Jesus did, recognize that God is our ultimate authority and remain faithful to Him.

The question Jesus asked them about John the Baptist caused them to be quiet. They had wished to quiet Jesus and lessen His influence, but Jesus turned the tables on them by asking them a question He knew they wouldn't answer. He was always in control during these confrontations with the religious leaders.

Mark 11:27–33

[27] They came again to Jerusalem. And as He was walking in the temple, the chief priests and the scribes and the elders came to Him, [28] and began saying to Him, "By what authority are You doing these things, or who gave You this authority to do these things?" [29] And Jesus said to them, "I will ask you one question, and you answer Me, and then I

will tell you by what authority I do these things. [30] *Was the baptism of John from heaven, or from men? Answer Me."* [31] *They began reasoning among themselves, saying, "If we say, 'From heaven,' He will say, 'Then why did you not believe him?'* [32] *But shall we say, 'From men'?"—they were afraid of the people, for everyone considered John to have been a real prophet.* [33] *Answering Jesus, they said, "We do not know." And Jesus said to them, "Nor will I tell you by what authority I do these things."*

The religious leaders' refusal to answer the question demonstrated that they were really more concerned about personal reputation than an honest answer. Fear of diminishing their public image forced them to deny the truth.

Luke 20:1–8

[1] *On one of the days while He was teaching the people in the temple and preaching the gospel, the chief priests and the scribes with the elders confronted Him,* [2] *and they spoke, saying to Him, "Tell us by what authority You are doing these things, or who is the one who gave You this authority?"* [3] *Jesus answered and said to them, "I will also ask you a question, and you tell Me:* [4] *Was the baptism of John from heaven or from men?"* [5] *They reasoned among themselves, saying, "If we say, 'From heaven,' He will say, 'Why did you not believe him?'* [6] *But if we say, 'From men,' all the people will stone us to death, for they are convinced that John was a prophet."* [7] *So they answered that they did not know where it came from.* [8] *And Jesus said to them, "Nor will I tell you by what authority I do these things."*

The religious leaders' confession of ignorance about the authority of John the Baptist meant they couldn't really question Jesus' authority either.

The Parable of the Two Sons

Matthew 21:28–32

28 "But what do you think? A man had two sons, and he came to the first and said, 'Son, go work today in the vineyard.' 29 And he answered, 'I will not'; but afterward he regretted it and went. 30 The man came to the second and said the same thing; and he answered, 'I will, sir'; but he did not go. 31 Which of the two did the will of his father?" They said, "The first." Jesus said to them, "Truly I say to you that the tax collectors and prostitutes will get into the kingdom of God before you. 32 For John came to you in the way of righteousness and you did not believe him; but the tax collectors and prostitutes did believe him; and you, seeing this, did not even feel remorse afterward so as to believe him."

In the parable of the two sons, the first son actually followed through despite his words, and that's what mattered. The people with the most knowledge of the Scriptures—the religious leaders—should have been the first to realize what God was doing in Jesus and put their faith in Him, but they didn't. Instead, Jesus was received by tax collectors and prostitutes. What counts with God is not just what you know (or say), but what you do with what you know.

The Parable of the Landowner

Matthew 21:33–46

33 "Listen to another parable. There was a landowner who PLANTED A VINEYARD AND PUT A WALL AROUND IT AND DUG A WINE PRESS IN IT, AND BUILT A TOWER, and rented it out to vine-growers and went on a journey. 34 When the harvest time approached, he sent his slaves to the vine-growers to receive his produce. 35 The vine-growers took his slaves and beat one, and killed another, and stoned a third. [36] Again he sent another group of slaves larger than the first; and they did the same thing to them. [37] But afterward he sent his son to them, saying, 'They will respect my son.' [38] But when the vine-growers saw the son, they said among themselves, 'This is the heir; come, let us kill him and seize his inheritance.' [39] They took him, and threw him out of the vineyard and killed him. [40] Therefore when the owner of the vineyard comes, what will he do to those vine-growers?" [41] They said to Him, "He will bring those wretches to a wretched end, and will rent out the vineyard to other vine-growers who will pay him the proceeds at the proper seasons."

[42] Jesus said to them, "Did you never read in the Scriptures,
> *'THE STONE WHICH THE BUILDERS REJECTED,*
> *THIS BECAME THE CHIEF CORNER stone;*
> *THIS CAME ABOUT FROM THE LORD,*
> *AND IT IS MARVELOUS IN OUR EYES'?*

[43] Therefore I say to you, the kingdom of God will be taken away from you and given to a people, producing the fruit of it. [44] And he who falls on this stone will be broken to pieces; but on whomever it falls, it will scatter him like dust."

[45] When the chief priests and the Pharisees heard His parables, they understood that He was speaking about them. [46] When they sought to seize Him, they feared the people, because they considered Him to be a prophet.

The owner of the vineyard rented it out to people he expected to take care of it. He then sent some of his slaves to the vineyard to collect the produce, and they were treated very badly. He then sent even more slaves, and the same thing happened. The listeners would have recognized the parallel between the way the slaves were mistreated in this story and the way the prophets of Israel were often mistreated. Jeremiah 35:15 says, "I have sent to you all My servants the prophets, sending them again and again."

As a final effort, the owner sends his son, and he too is thrown out and killed. The parallel to the Father sending the Son is clear, though it probably wasn't fully grasped by the religious leaders. They did understand, though, that Jesus was talking about them, and they wanted to arrest Him but couldn't because of the crowds.

The Parable of the Marriage Feast

Matthew 22:1–14

> 1 *Jesus spoke to them again in parables, saying,* 2 *"The kingdom of heaven may be compared to a king who gave a wedding feast for his son.* 3 *And he sent out his slaves to call those who had been invited to the wedding feast, and they were unwilling to come.* 4 *Again he sent out other slaves saying, 'Tell those who have been invited, "Behold, I have prepared my dinner; my oxen and my fattened livestock are all butchered and everything is ready; come to the wedding feast."'* 5 *But they paid no attention and went their way, one to his own farm, another to his business,* 6 *and the rest seized his slaves and mistreated them and killed them.* 7 *But the king was enraged, and he sent his armies and destroyed those murderers and set their city on fire.* 8 *Then he said to his slaves, 'The wedding is ready, but those who were invited were not worthy.* 9 *Go therefore to the main highways, and as many as you find there, invite to the wedding feast.'* 10 *Those slaves went out into the streets and gathered together all they found, both evil and good; and the wedding hall was filled with dinner guests.*

[11] "But when the king came in to look over the dinner guests, he saw a man there who was not dressed in wedding clothes, [12] and he said to him, 'Friend, how did you come in here without wedding clothes?' And the man was speechless. [13] Then the king said to the servants, 'Bind him hand and foot, and throw him into the outer darkness; in that place there will be weeping and gnashing of teeth.' [14] For many are called, but few are chosen."

A wedding was going to take place and invitations had been extended. The invitation could either be accepted or rejected, but to reject the invitation is to reject the king who extended it. Some who received the invitation were too busy to bother with it, and some mistreated the messengers. There were severe consequences for the latter.

The king decided to open up the wedding to everyone, good and bad people alike. One person crashed the wedding, refusing to accept the garment offered to each guest who responded to the wedding invitation. The invitation was gracious, but compliance with the host was mandatory. In other words, we enter the kingdom of God in the way God prescribes—through Jesus.

This parable shows the demise of the Jewish leaders and forecasts how the kingdom is available to all people, including the Gentiles. It also encourages the church to reach out to everyone with the gospel message, since no repentant sinner will be turned away from God's kingdom banquet.

Tribute to Caesar

Matthew 22:15–22

[15] Then the Pharisees went and plotted together how they might trap Him in what He said. [16] And they sent their disciples to Him, along with the Herodians, saying, "Teacher, we know that You are truthful and teach the

way of God in truth, and defer to no one; for You are not partial to any. [17] *Tell us then, what do You think? Is it lawful to give a poll-tax to Caesar, or not?"* [18] *But Jesus perceived their malice, and said, "Why are you testing Me, you hypocrites?* [19] *Show Me the coin used for the poll-tax." And they brought Him a denarius.* [20] *And He said to them, "Whose likeness and inscription is this?"* [21] *They said to Him, "Caesar's." Then He said to them, "Then render to Caesar the things that are Caesar's; and to God the things that are God's."* [22] *And hearing this, they were amazed, and leaving Him, they went away.*

The Pharisees wanted to get rid of Jesus. In order to accomplish this, they allied themselves with the Herodians, a group who supported the evil family of Herod. They were a strange ally for the Pharisees, who were strict adherents to the Law of Moses. They were willing to ally, despite their philosophical differences, in an attempt to trap Jesus.

Their effort was couched in flattery, but right away Jesus picked up on what they were trying to do when they asked Him about paying taxes to Caesar. After calling them hypocrites for trying to trap Him, Jesus offered them a brilliant reply: "Render to Caesar the things that are Caesars; and to God the things that are God's" (v. 21). We're told they were amazed by His response and walked away. This has to be one of the more entertaining exchanges Jesus had with the religious leaders. He was completely unafraid of them and always knew the right thing to say.

Marriage at the Resurrection

Matthew 22:23–33

[23] *On that day some Sadducees (who say there is no resurrection) came to Jesus and questioned Him,* [24] *asking, "Teacher, Moses said, 'IF A MAN DIES HAVING NO*

CHILDREN, HIS BROTHER AS NEXT OF KIN SHALL
MARRY HIS WIFE, AND RAISE UP CHILDREN FOR
HIS BROTHER.' [25] *Now there were seven brothers with us;*
and the first married and died, and having no children
left his wife to his brother; [26] *so also the second, and the*
third, down to the seventh. [27] *Last of all, the woman died.*
[28] *In the resurrection, therefore, whose wife of the seven*
will she be? For they all had married her."

[29] *But Jesus answered and said to them, "You are mistaken,*
not understanding the Scriptures nor the power of God.
[30] *For in the resurrection they neither marry nor are*
given in marriage, but are like angels in heaven. [31] *But*
regarding the resurrection of the dead, have you not read
what was spoken to you by God: [32] *'I AM THE GOD OF*
ABRAHAM, AND THE GOD OF ISAAC, AND THE
GOD OF JACOB'? He is not the God of the dead but
of the living." [33] *When the crowds heard this, they were*
astonished at His teaching.

The Sadducees did not believe in the resurrection of the dead, so they tried to trap Jesus in an absurdity by creating a hypothetical situation involving marriage. Jesus knew what they were trying to do, so He put them in their place and gave them a theology lesson about marriage and the resurrection. The lesson for us is to humbly seek to understand God's Word, submitting to what we don't completely understand.

The Greatest Commandment

Matthew 22:34–40

[34] *But when the Pharisees heard that Jesus had silenced*
the Sadducees, they gathered themselves together. [35] *One*
of them, a lawyer, asked Him a question, testing Him,

[36] "Teacher, which is the great commandment in the Law?"
[37] And He said to him, "'YOU SHALL LOVE THE LORD
YOUR GOD WITH ALL YOUR HEART, AND WITH
ALL YOUR SOUL, AND WITH ALL YOUR MIND.'
[38] This is the great and foremost commandment. [39] The
second is like it, 'YOU SHALL LOVE YOUR NEIGHBOR
AS YOURSELF.' [40] On these two commandments depend
the whole Law and the Prophets."

This was not a sincere question from the lawyer, but Jesus gave a valid answer, as though the questioner was asking from pure motives. We should follow His example when people ask us questions with less than pure motives. This lawyer was trying to test Jesus to see if he could catch Him in some inconsistency. Jesus told him that loving God and loving your neighbor sum up the Law. It seems He answered to their satisfaction because we're not told they reacted against Jesus after His reply. And He had clearly given them the correct answer, consistent with the Old Testament.

Whose Son Is the Christ?

Matthew 22:41–46

[41] Now while the Pharisees were gathered together, Jesus
asked them a question: [42] "What do you think about the
Christ, whose son is He?" They said to Him, "The son of
David." [43] He said to them, "Then how does David in the
Spirit call Him 'Lord,' saying,

[44] 'THE LORD SAID TO MY LORD,
"SIT AT MY RIGHT HAND,
UNTIL I PUT YOUR ENEMIES BENEATH YOUR FEET"'?

> 45 *If David then calls Him 'Lord,' how is He his son?"* 46 *No one was able to answer Him a word, nor did anyone dare from that day on to ask Him another question.*

Jesus posed a question to those intent upon discrediting Him, "What do you think about the Christ, whose son is He?" (v. 42). They were right to think the Christ would come from the line of David, but they didn't understand that He was superior to David. They didn't understand that the Christ was the Son of God, and He was standing before them.

A Warning Against Hypocrisy

> ***Matthew 23:1–12***
>
> 1 *Then Jesus spoke to the crowds and to His disciples,* 2 *saying: "The scribes and the Pharisees have seated themselves in the chair of Moses;* 3 *therefore all that they tell you, do and observe, but do not do according to their deeds; for they say things and do not do them.* 4 *They tie up heavy burdens and lay them on men's shoulders, but they themselves are unwilling to move them with so much as a finger.* 5 *But they do all their deeds to be noticed by men; for they broaden their phylacteries and lengthen the tassels of their garments.* 6 *They love the place of honor at banquets and the chief seats in the synagogues,* 7 *and respectful greetings in the market places, and being called Rabbi by men.* 8 *But do not be called Rabbi; for One is your Teacher, and you are all brothers.* 9 *Do not call anyone on earth your father; for One is your Father, He who is in heaven.* 10 *Do not be called leaders; for One is your Leader, that is, Christ.* 11 *But the greatest among you shall be your servant.* 12 *Whoever exalts himself shall be humbled; and whoever humbles himself shall be exalted.*

Jesus said the scribes and Pharisees say the right things but don't follow their own advice. Therefore, do as they say, but don't follow their example.

These religious leaders exhibited very little compassion. "They tie up heavy burdens and lay them on people's shoulders, but they themselves are unwilling to move them with so much as a finger" (v. 4), said Jesus. They were willing enough to "lay down the law," but weren't willing to lend a hand. Jesus had already said that the second great commandment is to "love your neighbor as yourself" (Matthew 22:39)—something the religious leaders were completely failing to do. They were missing the Spirit of God, who gave the law they were administering.

Basically, these religious leaders were doing everything for show. "They do all their deeds to be noticed by men" (v. 5), said Jesus. This included how they dressed, where they sat at banquets and at the synagogue, how they wanted to be greeted, and so on.

Jesus explained how true leadership is humble servanthood. The kingdom of God is a level playing field since we're all saved by grace. We're all brothers and sisters in Christ, sharing the same heavenly Father. There is no hierarchy in Christ's community.

Eight Woes to the Scribes and Pharisees

Matthew 23:13–36

13 *"But woe to you, scribes and Pharisees, hypocrites,*
because you shut off the kingdom of heaven from people;
for you do not enter in yourselves, nor do you allow those
who are entering to go in. 14 *[Woe to you, scribes and*
Pharisees, hypocrites, because you devour widows' houses,
and for a pretense you make long prayers; therefore you
will receive greater condemnation.]

15 *"Woe to you, scribes and Pharisees, hypocrites, because you travel around on sea and land to make one proselyte; and when he becomes one, you make him twice as much a son of hell as yourselves.*

16 *"Woe to you, blind guides, who say, 'Whoever swears by the temple, that is nothing; but whoever swears by the gold of the temple is obligated.'* 17 *You fools and blind men! Which is more important, the gold or the temple that sanctified the gold?* 18 *And, 'Whoever swears by the altar, that is nothing, but whoever swears by the offering on it, he is obligated.'* 19 *You blind men, which is more important, the offering, or the altar that sanctifies the offering?* 20 *Therefore, whoever swears by the altar, swears both by the altar and by everything on it.* 21 *And whoever swears by the temple, swears both by the temple and by Him who dwells within it.* 22 *And whoever swears by heaven, swears both by the throne of God and by Him who sits upon it.*

23 *"Woe to you, scribes and Pharisees, hypocrites! For you tithe mint and dill and cummin, and have neglected the weightier provisions of the law: justice and mercy and faithfulness; but these are the things you should have done without neglecting the others.* 24 *You blind guides, who strain out a gnat and swallow a camel!*

25 *"Woe to you, scribes and Pharisees, hypocrites! For you clean the outside of the cup and of the dish, but inside they are full of robbery and self-indulgence.* 26 *You blind Pharisee, first clean the inside of the cup and of the dish, so that the outside of it may become clean also.*

27 *"Woe to you, scribes and Pharisees, hypocrites! For you are like whitewashed tombs which on the outside appear beautiful, but inside they are full of dead men's bones and all uncleanness.* 28 *So you, too, outwardly appear*

righteous to men, but inwardly you are full of hypocrisy and lawlessness.

[29] *"Woe to you, scribes and Pharisees, hypocrites! For you build the tombs of the prophets and adorn the monuments of the righteous,* [30] *and say, 'If we had been living in the days of our fathers, we would not have been partners with them in shedding the blood of the prophets.'* [31] *So you testify against yourselves, that you are sons of those who murdered the prophets.* [32] *Fill up, then, the measure of the guilt of your fathers.* [33] *You serpents, you brood of vipers, how will you escape the sentence of hell?*

[34] *"Therefore, behold, I am sending you prophets and wise men and scribes; some of them you will kill and crucify, and some of them you will scourge in your synagogues, and persecute from city to city,* [35] *so that upon you may fall the guilt of all the righteous blood shed on earth, from the blood of righteous Abel to the blood of Zechariah, the son of Berechiah, whom you murdered between the temple and the altar.* [36] *Truly I say to you, all these things will come upon this generation.*

Jesus takes direct aim at the religious leaders in the "woes" He pronounces against them. We sometimes picture Him as always being "nice," but the Gospels show that He was strongly opposed to the religious hypocrisy that led God's people away from the truth.

Regarding tithing, it is not that it is unimportant; it is that it is not of more importance than practicing justice, mercy, and faithfulness. Focusing on tithing can mean focusing on doing the bare minimum—making sure to check off all the religious boxes. Their concern was how much—or little—they could give to stay inside the law.

It is a woeful condition to be more concerned about

appearance than integrity. "Woe to you, scribes and Pharisees, hypocrites! For you clean the outside of the cup and of the dish, but inside they are full of robbery and self-indulgence" (v. 26). It's possible to camouflage one's exterior so that what is inside is not readily seen. Jesus wants the light inside His followers to be seen, but this light comes from God and creates honesty and authenticity.

It is a woeful condition to fail to learn from past generations. These leaders were challenged to learn from the mistakes of past generations rather than simply repeat their errors, but they were blind to what they were doing. God had sent the Messiah and they were blind to Him. Worse, they were leading others astray.

Parable of the Vine-growers

Mark 12:1–12

1 And He began to speak to them in parables: "A man
PLANTED A VINEYARD AND PUT A WALL AROUND
IT, AND DUG A VAT UNDER THE WINE PRESS AND
BUILT A TOWER, and rented it out to vine-growers and
went on a journey. 2 At the harvest time he sent a slave to
the vine-growers, in order to receive some of the produce
of the vineyard from the vine-growers. 3 They took him,
and beat him and sent him away empty-handed. 4 Again
he sent them another slave, and they wounded him in the
head, and treated him shamefully. 5 And he sent another,
and that one they killed; and so with many others, beating
some and killing others. 6 He had one more to send, a
beloved son; he sent him last of all to them, saying, 'They
will respect my son.' 7 But those vine-growers said to one
another, 'This is the heir; come, let us kill him, and the
inheritance will be ours!' 8 They took him, and killed him
and threw him out of the vineyard. 9 What will the owner
of the vineyard do? He will come and destroy the vine-

growers, and will give the vineyard to others. [10] *Have you not even read this Scripture:*

'THE STONE WHICH THE BUILDERS REJECTED,
THIS BECAME THE CHIEF CORNER stone;
[11] *THIS CAME ABOUT FROM THE LORD,*
AND IT IS MARVELOUS IN OUR EYES'?"

[12] *And they were seeking to seize Him, and yet they feared the people, for they understood that He spoke the parable against them. And so they left Him and went away.*

Jesus told this parable to challenge the religious leaders, as they are represented by the wicked vine-growers in the story. The parables functioned as a judgment or warning to the hardhearted and unrepentant.

Jesus Answers the Pharisees, Sadducees, and Scribes

Mark 12:13–38

[13] *Then they sent some of the Pharisees and Herodians to*
Him in order to trap Him in a statement. [14] *They came*
and said to Him, "Teacher, we know that You are truthful
and defer to no one; for You are not partial to any, but
teach the way of God in truth. Is it lawful to pay a poll-
tax to Caesar, or not? [15] *Shall we pay or shall we not pay?"*
But He, knowing their hypocrisy, said to them, "Why are
you testing Me? Bring Me a denarius to look at." [16] *They*
brought one. And He said to them, "Whose likeness and
inscription is this?" And they said to Him, "Caesar's."
[17] *And Jesus said to them, "Render to Caesar the things*
that are Caesar's, and to God the things that are God's."
And they were amazed at Him.

[18] *Some Sadducees (who say that there is no resurrection)*
came to Jesus, and began questioning Him, saying,

19 *"Teacher, Moses wrote for us that IF A MAN'S
BROTHER DIES and leaves behind a wife AND LEAVES
NO CHILD, HIS BROTHER SHOULD MARRY THE
WIFE AND RAISE UP CHILDREN TO HIS BROTHER.*
20 *There were seven brothers; and the first took a wife, and
died leaving no children.* 21 *The second one married her,
and died leaving behind no children; and the third likewise;*
22 *and so all seven left no children. Last of all the woman
died also.* 23 *In the resurrection, when they rise again,
which one's wife will she be? For all seven had married
her."* 24 *Jesus said to them, "Is this not the reason you are
mistaken, that you do not understand the Scriptures or
the power of God?* 25 *For when they rise from the dead,
they neither marry nor are given in marriage, but are like
angels in heaven.* 26 *But regarding the fact that the dead
rise again, have you not read in the book of Moses, in the
passage about the burning bush, how God spoke to him,
saying, 'I AM THE GOD OF ABRAHAM, AND THE
GOD OF ISAAC, AND THE GOD OF JACOB'?* 27 *He is
not the God of the dead, but of the living; you are greatly
mistaken."*

28 *One of the scribes came and heard them arguing, and
recognizing that He had answered them well, asked
Him, "What commandment is the foremost of all?"*
29 *Jesus answered, "The foremost is, 'HEAR, O ISRAEL!
THE LORD OUR GOD IS ONE LORD;* 30 *AND YOU
SHALL LOVE THE LORD YOUR GOD WITH ALL
YOUR HEART, AND WITH ALL YOUR SOUL, AND
WITH ALL YOUR MIND, AND WITH ALL YOUR
STRENGTH.'* 31 *The second is this, 'YOU SHALL LOVE
YOUR NEIGHBOR AS YOURSELF.' There is no other
commandment greater than these."* 32 *The scribe said to
Him, "Right, Teacher; You have truly stated that HE IS
ONE, AND THERE IS NO ONE ELSE BESIDES HIM;*

[33] AND TO LOVE HIM WITH ALL THE HEART AND WITH ALL THE UNDERSTANDING AND WITH ALL THE STRENGTH, AND TO LOVE ONE'S NEIGHBOR AS HIMSELF, is much more than all burnt offerings and sacrifices." [34] When Jesus saw that he had answered intelligently, He said to him, "You are not far from the kingdom of God." After that, no one would venture to ask Him any more questions.

[35] And Jesus began to say, as He taught in the temple, "How is it that the scribes say that the Christ is the son of David? [36] David himself said in the Holy Spirit,

'THE LORD SAID TO MY LORD,
"SIT AT MY RIGHT HAND,
UNTIL I PUT YOUR ENEMIES BENEATH YOUR FEET."'

[37] David himself calls Him 'Lord'; so in what sense is He his son?" And the large crowd enjoyed listening to Him.

[38] In His teaching He was saying: "Beware of the scribes who like to walk around in long robes, and like respectful greetings in the market places, [39] and chief seats in the synagogues and places of honor at banquets, [40] who devour widows' houses, and for appearance's sake offer long prayers; these will receive greater condemnation."

This section shows Jesus' mastery over any potential obstacle to His mission. He was always in control of the confrontations He had with the religious leaders. They couldn't trap Him, trick Him, stump Him, intimidate Him, or get Him to stop preaching the gospel of the kingdom. He was utterly free from the fear of man.

The Widow's Mite

Mark 12:41–44

[41] And He sat down opposite the treasury, and began observing how the people were putting money into the treasury; and many rich people were putting in large sums. [42] A poor widow came and put in two small copper coins, which amount to a cent. [43] Calling His disciples to Him, He said to them, "Truly I say to you, this poor widow put in more than all the contributors to the treasury; [44] for they all put in out of their surplus, but she, out of her poverty, put in all she owned, all she had to live on."

Mark notes an incident where Jesus was observing worshippers putting their offerings in the receptacle. He was deeply impressed when He saw a lady make a sacrificial gift, while most others were giving out of their surplus. Jesus said to His followers that "she, out of her poverty, put in all she owned, all she had to live on" (v. 44). It's the heart behind our giving that matters.

Jesus' Authority Questioned

Luke 20:1–8

[1] On one of the days while He was teaching the people in the temple and preaching the gospel, the chief priests and the scribes with the elders confronted Him, [2] and they spoke, saying to Him, "Tell us by what authority You are doing these things, or who is the one who gave You this authority?" [3] Jesus answered and said to them, "I will also ask you a question, and you tell Me: [4] Was the baptism of John from heaven or from men?" [5] They reasoned among themselves, saying, "If we say, 'From heaven,' He will say, 'Why did you not believe him?' [6] But if we say, 'From men,'

all the people will stone us to death, for they are convinced
that John was a prophet." 7 *So they answered that they did*
not know where it came from. 8 *And Jesus said to them,*
"Nor will I tell you by what authority I do these things."

While Jesus was completely free of the fear of man, this incident shows that the chief priests and scribes certainly were not.

Parable of the Vine-growers

Luke 20:9–18

9 *And He began to tell the people this parable: "A man*
planted a vineyard and rented it out to vine-growers, and
went on a journey for a long time. 10 *At the harvest time*
he sent a slave to the vine-growers, so that they would
give him some of the produce of the vineyard; but the
vine-growers beat him and sent him away empty-handed.
11 *And he proceeded to send another slave; and they beat*
him also and treated him shamefully and sent him away
empty-handed. 12 *And he proceeded to send a third; and*
this one also they wounded and cast out. 13 *The owner of*
the vineyard said, 'What shall I do? I will send my beloved
son; perhaps they will respect him.' 14 *But when the vine-*
growers saw him, they reasoned with one another, saying,
'This is the heir; let us kill him so that the inheritance
will be ours.' 15 *So they threw him out of the vineyard and*
killed him. What, then, will the owner of the vineyard do
to them? 16 *He will come and destroy these vine-growers*
and will give the vineyard to others." When they heard it,
they said, "May it never be!" 17 *But Jesus looked at them*
and said, "What then is this that is written:

'THE STONE WHICH THE BUILDERS REJECTED,
THIS BECAME THE CHIEF CORNER stone'?

[18] *Everyone who falls on that stone will be broken to pieces; but on whomever it falls, it will scatter him like dust."*

The rejected Son of God would become the head of the church. Verse 17 is quoted from Psalm 118:22 and also repeated in 1 Peter 2:7.

Tribute to Caesar

Luke 20:19–26

[19] The scribes and the chief priests tried to lay hands on Him that very hour, and they feared the people; for they understood that He spoke this parable against them. [20] So they watched Him, and sent spies who pretended to be righteous, in order that they might catch Him in some statement, so that they could deliver Him to the rule and the authority of the governor. [21] They questioned Him, saying, "Teacher, we know that You speak and teach correctly, and You are not partial to any, but teach the way of God in truth. [22] Is it lawful for us to pay taxes to Caesar, or not?" [23] But He detected their trickery and said to them, [24] "Show Me a denarius. Whose likeness and inscription does it have?" They said, "Caesar's." [25] And He said to them, "Then render to Caesar the things that are Caesar's, and to God the things that are God's." [26] And they were unable to catch Him in a saying in the presence of the people; and being amazed at His answer, they became silent.

Luke makes a significant note about authority when he says, "So they watched Him, and sent spies who pretended to be righteous, in order that they might catch Him in some statement, so that they could deliver Him to the rule and the authority of the governor" (20:20). The governor, of course, was Pontius Pilate. So even while these religious leaders were questioning Jesus' authority, they were under the authority of the Romans. And while they didn't know it, all these earthly leaders were under God's authority. They were in their place of authority because God allowed it; and, they would be held accountable for how they used that authority.

Is There a Resurrection?

Luke 20:27–47

27 *Now there came to Him some of the Sadducees (who say that there is no resurrection),* 28 *and they questioned Him, saying, "Teacher, Moses wrote for us that IF A MAN'S BROTHER DIES, having a wife, AND HE IS CHILDLESS, HIS BROTHER SHOULD MARRY THE WIFE AND RAISE UP CHILDREN TO HIS BROTHER.* 29 *Now there were seven brothers; and the first took a wife and died childless;* 30 *and the second* 31 *and the third married her; and in the same way all seven died, leaving no children.* 32 *Finally the woman died also.* 33 *In the resurrection therefore, which one's wife will she be? For all seven had married her."*

34 *Jesus said to them, "The sons of this age marry and are given in marriage,* 35 *but those who are considered worthy to attain to that age and the resurrection from the dead, neither marry nor are given in marriage;* 36 *for they cannot even die anymore, because they are like angels, and are sons of God, being sons of the resurrection.* 37 *But that the dead are raised, even Moses showed, in the passage about the burning bush, where he calls the Lord THE GOD OF ABRAHAM, AND THE GOD OF ISAAC, AND THE GOD OF JACOB.* 38 *Now He is not the God of the dead but of the living; for all live to Him."* 39 *Some of the scribes answered and said, "Teacher, You have spoken well."* 40 *For*

they did not have courage to question Him any longer about anything.

[41] *Then He said to them, "How is it that they say the Christ is David's son?* [42] *For David himself says in the book of Psalms,*

'THE LORD SAID TO MY LORD,
"SIT AT MY RIGHT HAND,

[43] *UNTIL I MAKE YOUR ENEMIES A FOOTSTOOL FOR YOUR FEET."'*

[44] *Therefore David calls Him 'Lord,' and how is He his son?"*

[45] *And while all the people were listening, He said to the disciples,* [46] *"Beware of the scribes, who like to walk around in long robes, and love respectful greetings in the market places, and chief seats in the synagogues and places of honor at banquets,* [47] *who devour widows' houses, and for appearance's sake offer long prayers. These will receive greater condemnation."*

Jesus talked a lot about the hypocrisy of the religious leaders. They wanted others to think they were righteous and worthy of honor, but their outside didn't match their hearts. He said these would "receive greater condemnation" (v. 47).

The Widow's Gift

Luke 21:1–4

[1] *And He looked up and saw the rich putting their gifts into the treasury.* [2] *And He saw a poor widow putting in two small copper coins.* [3] *And He said, "Truly I say to you,*

> *this poor widow put in more than all of them;* [4] *for they all out of their surplus put into the offering; but she out of her poverty put in all that she had to live on."*

Jesus is always looking at the heart. Generosity is a matter of the heart, not the size of your bank account.

Chapter 10

IN THE SHADOW WITH JESUS

Jesus Anointed with Costly Perfume

Matthew 26:6–13

[6] Now when Jesus was in Bethany, at the home of Simon the leper, [7] a woman came to Him with an alabaster vial of very costly perfume, and she poured it on His head as He reclined at the table. [8] But the disciples were indignant when they saw this, and said, "Why this waste? [9] For this perfume might have been sold for a high price and the money given to the poor." [10] But Jesus, aware of this, said to them, "Why do you bother the woman? For she has done a good deed to Me. [11] For you always have the poor with you; but you do not always have Me. [12] For when she poured this perfume on My body, she did it to prepare Me for burial. [13] Truly I say to you, wherever this gospel is preached in the whole world, what this woman has done will also be spoken of in memory of her."

Simon, the host, is referred to as "the leper," but it's safe to assume that he wasn't suffering from the skin disease anymore, likely because Jesus had healed him. Simon may have been doing as Matthew had done earlier—hosting a dinner for his friends in order to introduce them to Jesus.

Matthew doesn't identify the woman who came to anoint Jesus, but it was likely Mary, Lazarus's sister, as John's Gospel indicates. Simon's house was in her hometown of Bethany, and we know the devotion Mary had to Jesus.

Jesus was deeply moved by this woman anointing Him. He

told everyone who was there that her selfless act of devotion would be spoken of wherever the gospel was proclaimed. She probably didn't realize the impact of what she had done, but she didn't do it for impact or show. And how many people have been touched by her story?

We might wonder (though we will never know this side of heaven) how many people we have touched through our obedience to the Lord's command to love others.

Mark 14:3–9

3 While He was in Bethany at the home of Simon the leper,
and reclining at the table, there came a woman with an
alabaster vial of very costly perfume of pure nard; and
she broke the vial and poured it over His head. 4 But some
were indignantly remarking to one another, "Why has this
perfume been wasted? 5 For this perfume might have been
sold for over three hundred denarii, and the money given
to the poor." And they were scolding her. 6 But Jesus said,
"Let her alone; why do you bother her? She has done a
good deed to Me. 7 For you always have the poor with you,
and whenever you wish you can do good to them; but you
do not always have Me. 8 She has done what she could; she
has anointed My body beforehand for the burial. 9 Truly
I say to you, wherever the gospel is preached in the whole
world, what this woman has done will also be spoken of
in memory of her."

When the disciples saw this woman's extravagant act of love, they were annoyed and angry and asked each other why she didn't instead put her costly perfume to better use. They thought she should have sold it and then given the money to the poor.

Perhaps at first glance we might think the same thing. The perfume, after all, was very expensive, and we can see why the disciples thought she was being wasteful in breaking the jar and pouring it over Jesus' head. But in her extravagant act of devotion to her Savior, this woman showed Jesus that He was worth more to her than anything else, and she would gladly sacrifice her most costly possessions for His sake.

John 12:1–8

> [1] *Jesus, therefore, six days before the Passover, came to Bethany where Lazarus was, whom Jesus had raised from the dead.* [2] *So they made Him a supper there, and Martha was serving; but Lazarus was one of those reclining at the table with Him.* [3] *Mary then took a pound of very costly perfume of pure nard, and anointed the feet of Jesus and wiped His feet with her hair; and the house was filled with the fragrance of the perfume.* [4] *But Judas Iscariot, one of His disciples, who was intending to betray Him, said,* [5] *"Why was this perfume not sold for three hundred denarii and given to poor people?"* [6] *Now he said this, not because he was concerned about the poor, but because he was a thief, and as he had the money box, he used to pilfer what was put into it.* [7] *Therefore Jesus said, "Let her alone, so that she may keep it for the day of My burial.* [8] *For you always have the poor with you, but you do not always have Me."*

According to both Matthew and Mark, this supper was at Simon the leper's house. How interesting that, according to John's Gospel, Lazarus was one of the guests, and that his sister Martha was serving at the meal. Can you imagine the atmosphere, with resurrected Lazarus at the table?

According to John, Judas was the disciple who scolded the woman, whom John identifies as Mary, Lazarus' sister, for wasting her costly perfume. John paints a stark contrast between Judas' greed (he was a thief and had been taking money from the fund Jesus and His disciples used to support themselves) and Mary's generosity, giving all she had to Jesus.

We can see very clearly Jesus' words in Matthew 6:24 acted out here: "No one can serve two masters; for either he will hate the one and love the other, or he will be devoted to one and despise the other. You cannot serve God and wealth." Money was Judas's master, and God was Mary's.

The Plot Against Jesus

Matthew 26:14–16

[14] Then one of the twelve, named Judas Iscariot, went to the chief priests [15] and said, "What are you willing to give me to betray Him to you?" And they weighed out thirty pieces of silver to him. [16] From then on he began looking for a good opportunity to betray Jesus.

On one level it's hard to imagine how Judas could betray Jesus after being chosen by Jesus and spending so much time with Him. But sin doesn't make sense. And Judas was captive to the sin of greed. Mary's extravagant act of love toward Jesus at Simon's house might have been the last straw. He might have felt that Jesus was too careless with money. Jesus, we recall, had chided the disciples when they complained about the extravagance of Mary's offering. The way Matthew describes it, Judas's objection was motivated by greed.

The actual betrayal came some time later, so we know it wasn't a spur of the moment decision. Judas, says Matthew, "began looking for a good opportunity to betray Jesus" (v. 16).

Mark 14:10–11

[10] Then Judas Iscariot, who was one of the twelve, went off to the chief priests in order to betray Him to them. [11] They were glad when they heard this, and promised to give him money. And he began seeking how to betray Him at an opportune time.

They may have been looking for a time to arrest Jesus when the public reaction would be minimized. We know that the priests were concerned about arresting Jesus publicly because they feared the reaction from the crowds.

Luke 22:1–6

[1] *Now the Feast of Unleavened Bread, which is called the Passover, was approaching.* [2] *The chief priests and the scribes were seeking how they might put Him to death; for they were afraid of the people.*

[3] *And Satan entered into Judas who was called Iscariot, belonging to the number of the twelve.* [4] *And he went away and discussed with the chief priests and officers how he might betray Him to them.* [5] *They were glad and agreed to give him money.* [6] *So he consented, and began seeking a good opportunity to betray Him to them apart from the crowd.*

According to Luke, Satan entered into Judas, and he began following Satan's bidding. It could have happened because Judas had let his guard down. He had a smoldering discontent that he refused to deal with. An unguarded mind is an opportunity for Satan. Judas didn't resist this entry and acted upon the impulse Satan gave him.

Luke confirms that they were looking for the right time to arrest Jesus because they were concerned about the reaction of the crowd.

The Last Supper

Matthew 26:17–30

[17] *Now on the first day of Unleavened Bread the disciples came to Jesus and asked, "Where do You want us to prepare for You to eat the Passover?"* [18] *And He said,*

> *"Go into the city to a certain man, and say to him, 'The Teacher says, "My time is near; I am to keep the Passover at your house with My disciples."'" 19 The disciples did as Jesus had directed them; and they prepared the Passover.*
>
> *20 Now when evening came, Jesus was reclining at the table with the twelve disciples. 21 As they were eating, He said, "Truly I say to you that one of you will betray Me." 22 Being deeply grieved, they each one began to say to Him, "Surely not I, Lord?" 23 And He answered, "He who dipped his hand with Me in the bowl is the one who will betray Me. 24 The Son of Man is to go, just as it is written of Him; but woe to that man by whom the Son of Man is betrayed! It would have been good for that man if he had not been born." 25 And Judas, who was betraying Him, said, "Surely it is not I, Rabbi?" Jesus said to him, "You have said it yourself."*
>
> *26 While they were eating, Jesus took some bread, and after a blessing, He broke it and gave it to the disciples, and said, "Take, eat; this is My body." 27 And when He had taken a cup and given thanks, He gave it to them, saying, "Drink from it, all of you; 28 for this is My blood of the covenant, which is poured out for many for forgiveness of sins. 29 But I say to you, I will not drink of this fruit of the vine from now on until that day when I drink it new with you in My Father's kingdom."*
>
> *30 After singing a hymn, they went out to the Mount of Olives.*

It's possible Jesus made arrangements with friends in Jerusalem, or He had divine knowledge of how things would unfold. Matthew doesn't mention the name of the man the disciples met. Perhaps they knew him.

The disciples were shocked and dismayed at the news Jesus gave them that He would be betrayed by one of them. We can only imagine how Judas must have felt when he realized that Jesus knew what he had done.

The observance of the Passover meal took on a new and deeper meaning in the presence of Jesus. The bread that normally represented the dough that didn't have time to rise before the Exodus came to represent the body of Christ. When Jesus broke the loaf, they didn't fully understand that His body would be broken by the consequences of sin. They didn't grasp that God was at work in providing another deliverance that would be for the whole world and not just for the people of Israel. The wine represented His very life, which would be poured out for them. He had become the true and final Passover Lamb.

Jesus said He wouldn't drink with them again until His Father's kingdom, pointing to the great end-time banquet still to come.

Mark 14:12–26

[12] *On the first day of Unleavened Bread, when the Passover*
lamb was being sacrificed, His disciples said to Him,
"Where do You want us to go and prepare for You to eat
the Passover?" [13] *And He sent two of His disciples and*
said to them, "Go into the city, and a man will meet you
carrying a pitcher of water; follow him; [14] *and wherever he*
enters, say to the owner of the house, 'The Teacher says,
"Where is My guest room in which I may eat the Passover
with My disciples?"' [15] *And he himself will show you a large*
upper room furnished and ready; prepare for us there."
[16] *The disciples went out and came to the city, and found it*
just as He had told them; and they prepared the Passover.

[17] *When it was evening He came with the twelve.* [18] *As they*
were reclining at the table and eating, Jesus said, "Truly

I say to you that one of you will betray Me—one who is
eating with Me." 19 *They began to be grieved and to say to*
Him one by one, "Surely not I?" 20 *And He said to them,*
"It is one of the twelve, one who dips with Me in the bowl.
21 *For the Son of Man is to go just as it is written of Him;*
but woe to that man by whom the Son of Man is betrayed!
It would have been good for that man if he had not been
born."

22 *While they were eating, He took some bread, and after*
a blessing He broke it, and gave it to them, and said,
"Take it; this is My body." 23 *And when He had taken a cup*
and given thanks, He gave it to them, and they all drank
from it. 24 *And He said to them, "This is My blood of the*
covenant, which is poured out for many. 25 *Truly I say to*
you, I will never again drink of the fruit of the vine until
that day when I drink it new in the kingdom of God."

26 *After singing a hymn, they went out to the Mount of*
Olives.

Matthew said "a certain man" would direct them to the place where they would observe the Passover. Mark adds some additional details about this man leading them to the house and then the owner showing them to the room.

The mood turned sober when Jesus announced that one of them would betray Him. Given how they questioned Jesus, it might be that they all knew they were capable of wavering faith and possibly even betrayal.

Luke 22:7–23

7 *Then came the first day of Unleavened Bread on which*
the Passover lamb had to be sacrificed. 8 *And Jesus sent*
Peter and John, saying, "Go and prepare the Passover for
us, so that we may eat it." 9 *They said to Him, "Where*

do You want us to prepare it?" [10] *And He said to them,*
"When you have entered the city, a man will meet you
carrying a pitcher of water; follow him into the house that
he enters. [11] *And you shall say to the owner of the house,*
'The Teacher says to you, "Where is the guest room in
which I may eat the Passover with My disciples?"' [12] *And*
he will show you a large, furnished upper room; prepare
it there." [13] *And they left and found everything just as He*
had told them; and they prepared the Passover.

[14] *When the hour had come, He reclined at the table, and*
the apostles with Him. [15] *And He said to them, "I have*
earnestly desired to eat this Passover with you before I
suffer; [16] *for I say to you, I shall never again eat it until it is*
fulfilled in the kingdom of God." [17] *And when He had taken*
a cup and given thanks, He said, "Take this and share it
among yourselves; [18] *for I say to you, I will not drink of the*
fruit of the vine from now on until the kingdom of God
comes." [19] *And when He had taken some bread and given*
thanks, He broke it and gave it to them, saying, "This is
My body which is given for you; do this in remembrance
of Me." [20] *And in the same way He took the cup after they*
had eaten, saying, "This cup which is poured out for you
is the new covenant in My blood. [21] *But behold, the hand*
of the one betraying Me is with Mine on the table. [22] *For*
indeed, the Son of Man is going as it has been determined;
but woe to that man by whom He is betrayed!" [23] *And they*
began to discuss among themselves which one of them it
might be who was going to do this thing.

Luke identifies Peter and John as the two Jesus sent to make arrangements for observing the Passover meal. As Mark noted, they identified a man carrying a pitcher and followed him to the house where they found the upper room already arranged for them.

Jesus shared a cup of wine with His disciples for the last time before He would taste the bitter cup of suffering. He would not be able to share that with them. He would soon become the sacrificial lamb symbolized by the Passover meal.

Luke says that there was a discussion among His disciples about who would betray Jesus. They might have become suspicious of one another.

John 13:1–38

[1] Now before the Feast of the Passover, Jesus knowing that His hour had come that He would depart out of this world to the Father, having loved His own who were in the world, He loved them to the end. [2] During supper, the devil having already put into the heart of Judas Iscariot, the son of Simon, to betray Him, [3] Jesus, knowing that the Father had given all things into His hands, and that He had come forth from God and was going back to God, [4] got up from supper, and laid aside His garments; and taking a towel, He girded Himself.

[5] Then He poured water into the basin, and began to wash the disciples' feet and to wipe them with the towel with which He was girded. [6] So He came to Simon Peter. He said to Him, "Lord, do You wash my feet?" [7] Jesus answered and said to him, "What I do you do not realize now, but you will understand hereafter." [8] Peter said to Him, "Never shall You wash my feet!" Jesus answered him, "If I do not wash you, you have no part with Me." [9] Simon Peter said to Him, "Lord, then wash not only my feet, but also my hands and my head." [10] Jesus said to him, "He who has bathed needs only to wash his feet, but is completely clean; and you are clean, but not all of you." [11] For He knew the one who was betraying Him; for this reason He said, "Not all of you are clean."

[12] So when He had washed their feet, and taken His
garments and reclined at the table again, He said to them,
"Do you know what I have done to you? [13] You call Me
Teacher and Lord; and you are right, for so I am. [14] If I
then, the Lord and the Teacher, washed your feet, you
also ought to wash one another's feet. [15] For I gave you an
example that you also should do as I did to you. [16] Truly,
truly, I say to you, a slave is not greater than his master,
nor is one who is sent greater than the one who sent him.
[17] If you know these things, you are blessed if you do them.
[18] I do not speak of all of you. I know the ones I have
chosen; but it is that the Scripture may be fulfilled, 'HE
WHO EATS MY BREAD HAS LIFTED UP HIS HEEL
AGAINST ME.' [19] From now on I am telling you before it
comes to pass, so that when it does occur, you may believe
that I am He. [20] Truly, truly, I say to you, he who receives
whomever I send receives Me; and he who receives Me
receives Him who sent Me."

[21] When Jesus had said this, He became troubled in spirit,
and testified and said, "Truly, truly, I say to you, that
one of you will betray Me." [22] The disciples began looking
at one another, at a loss to know of which one He was
speaking. [23] There was reclining on Jesus' bosom one of His
disciples, whom Jesus loved. [24] So Simon Peter gestured to
him, and said to him, "Tell us who it is of whom He is
speaking." [25] He, leaning back thus on Jesus' bosom, said
to Him, "Lord, who is it?" [26] Jesus then answered, "That is
the one for whom I shall dip the morsel and give it to him."
So when He had dipped the morsel, He took and gave it to
Judas, the son of Simon Iscariot. [27] After the morsel, Satan
then entered into him. Therefore Jesus said to him, "What
you do, do quickly." [28] Now no one of those reclining at
the table knew for what purpose He had said this to him.
[29] For some were supposing, because Judas had the money

> *box, that Jesus was saying to him, "Buy the things we have need of for the feast"; or else, that he should give something to the poor.* [30] *So after receiving the morsel he went out immediately; and it was night.*
>
> [31] *Therefore when he had gone out, Jesus said, "Now is the Son of Man glorified, and God is glorified in Him;* [32] *if God is glorified in Him, God will also glorify Him in Himself, and will glorify Him immediately.* [33] *Little children, I am with you a little while longer. You will seek Me; and as I said to the Jews, now I also say to you, 'Where I am going, you cannot come.'* [34] *A new commandment I give to you, that you love one another, even as I have loved you, that you also love one another.* [35] *By this all men will know that you are My disciples, if you have love for one another."*
>
> [36] *Simon Peter said to Him, "Lord, where are You going?" Jesus answered, "Where I go, you cannot follow Me now; but you will follow later."* [37] *Peter said to Him, "Lord, why can I not follow You right now? I will lay down my life for You."* [38] *Jesus answered, "Will you lay down your life for Me? Truly, truly, I say to you, a rooster will not crow until you deny Me three times.*

John's gospel adds some additional details, including Jesus washing the disciples' feet. Washing another person's feet was normally assigned to servants or slaves, not teachers or leaders. It was a matter of status. That's why Peter objected to it. Jesus assured Peter that he would understand later what he couldn't understand now and that He needed to do this for Peter. He was teaching the disciples about servant leadership and urging them to follow in His footsteps by living a life of sacrificial love.

John notes that Jesus became troubled when He had to inform His disciples that one of them at the table would betray

Him. Jesus said He told them ahead of time so that they would understand that He was the Messiah (v. 19).

John says Judas's betrayal was influenced by Satan. That did not let Judas off the hook, though. He was still responsible for his actions. Constant vigilance against the lies and temptations of the enemy is necessary for every follower of Christ.

Jesus said to them, "A new commandment I give to you, that you love one another, even as I have loved you, that you also love one another" (v. 34). This new commandment exceeded the 10 Commandments and even the commandment to "love your neighbor as yourself" (Mark 12:31) since Jesus qualified it by saying, "even as I have loved you." What does it mean to love as Jesus loves? Just from the short time He was with them, we see unconditional love (calling Matthew, the tax collector), we see patient love (the disciples were often slow to understand), and we see serving love (washing the disciples' feet). Basically, we see self-sacrificing love, as Jesus was committing Himself to what was best for them.

How little we know of what we are capable of doing. Peter offered to lay down his life for Jesus. Jesus, however, knew that Peter would fold under pressure. He hadn't yet developed the spiritual strength he would need for the long run. While we know so little about ourselves, we can take hope in the realization that Jesus knows all about us and still loves us!

Jesus Comforts His Disciples

John 14:1–6

1 "Do not let your heart be troubled; believe in God,
believe also in Me. 2 In My Father's house are many
dwelling places; if it were not so, I would have told you;
for I go to prepare a place for you. 3 If I go and prepare
a place for you, I will come again and receive you to
Myself, that where I am, there you may be also. 4 And you
know the way where I am going." 5 Thomas said to Him,

"Lord, we do not know where You are going, how do we know the way?" [6] Jesus said to him, "I am the way, and the truth, and the life; no one comes to the Father but through Me.

Jesus reminds us that we do have some control over our thoughts and feelings. We don't have to give in to fear and worry. Instead, we can choose to believe in God and in Jesus, just as He said. Worry dissipates when we understand that God is in control. And we can trust that Jesus will lead us into a relationship with God that lasts forever.

Oneness with the Father

John 14:7–15

[7] If you had known Me, you would have known My Father also; from now on you know Him, and have seen Him."

[8] Philip said to Him, "Lord, show us the Father, and it is
enough for us." [9] Jesus said to him, "Have I been so long
with you, and yet you have not come to know Me, Philip?
He who has seen Me has seen the Father; how can you say,
'Show us the Father'? [10] Do you not believe that I am in
the Father, and the Father is in Me? The words that I say
to you I do not speak on My own initiative, but the Father
abiding in Me does His works. [11] Believe Me that I am
in the Father and the Father is in Me; otherwise believe
because of the works themselves. [12] Truly, truly, I say to
you, he who believes in Me, the works that I do, he will do
also; and greater works than these he will do; because I go
to the Father. [13] Whatever you ask in My name, that will I
do, so that the Father may be glorified in the Son. [14] If you
ask Me anything in My name, I will do it.

[15] "If you love Me, you will keep My commandments.

Jesus shows us what the abiding life looks like—constant communion with the Father and obedience to His will. He said the words He spoke and the works He performed were at the Father's initiative.

We are given a demanding challenge when Jesus says, "The person who believes in Me, the works that I do, he will do also; and greater works than these will he do; because I go to The Father" (v. 12). The effects of Jesus' ministry will be magnified in the multiplied lives of His followers.

Role of the Spirit

John 14:16–31

[16] *I will ask the Father, and He will give you another Helper,*
that He may be with you forever; [17] *that is the Spirit of*
truth, whom the world cannot receive, because it does not
see Him or know Him, but you know Him because He
abides with you and will be in you.

[18] *"I will not leave you as orphans; I will come to you.*
[19] *After a little while the world will no longer see Me, but*
you will see Me; because I live, you will live also. [20] *In that*
day you will know that I am in My Father, and you in
Me, and I in you. [21] *He who has My commandments and*
keeps them is the one who loves Me; and he who loves
Me will be loved by My Father, and I will love him and
will disclose Myself to him." [22] *Judas (not Iscariot) said*
to Him, "Lord, what then has happened that You are
going to disclose Yourself to us and not to the world?"
[23] *Jesus answered and said to him, "If anyone loves Me,*
he will keep My word; and My Father will love him, and
We will come to him and make Our abode with him. [24] *He*
who does not love Me does not keep My words; and the
word which you hear is not Mine, but the Father's who
sent Me.

> *[25] "These things I have spoken to you while abiding with you. [26] But the Helper, the Holy Spirit, whom the Father will send in My name, He will teach you all things, and bring to your remembrance all that I said to you. [27] Peace I leave with you; My peace I give to you; not as the world gives do I give to you. Do not let your heart be troubled, nor let it be fearful. [28] You heard that I said to you, 'I go away, and I will come to you.' If you loved Me, you would have rejoiced because I go to the Father, for the Father is greater than I. [29] Now I have told you before it happens, so that when it happens, you may believe. [30] I will not speak much more with you, for the ruler of the world is coming, and he has nothing in Me; [31] but so that the world may know that I love the Father, I do exactly as the Father commanded Me. Get up, let us go from here.*

Jesus assures His disciples of the uninterrupted fellowship they will enjoy with Him through the Holy Spirit that He will send. We are never out of the presence of Jesus because the Holy Spirit is here to empower and comfort us.

Jesus' statement, "Because I live, you will live also" (v. 19), assures us of eternal life.

Jesus promises that He will disclose Himself to the person who loves Him as evidenced by obedience to His commands.

We are assured of a Helper who will "teach you all things, and bring to your remembrance all that I have said to you" (v. 26). It's like we are provided with a personal tutor who patiently explains and reminds us of the things Jesus taught.

Jesus said that He was leaving His peace with the disciples. They didn't need to be afraid or worried. His peace is a gift, and it is different from the kind of peace the world offers, which is based on circumstances. Jesus illustrated this peace as He stood before Pilate and didn't say anything in His defense. The apostle Paul would later say that this peace "surpasses all comprehension" (Philippians 4:7).

Jesus recognized that the disciples would have times when they would be tempted to doubt that He was really the Messiah, so He said to them, "I have told you before this happens, so that when it happens, you may believe" (v. 29). When we're tempted to doubt we can return to His words in the Bible and be reminded that He really is who He said He is.

Because we know the end of the story, we know that Jesus fully obeyed His Father's will all the way to the cross. Obedience to the Lord is the measure of our discipleship and our love. John also wrote: "For this is the love of God, that we keep His commandments; and His commandments are not burdensome" (1 John 5:3). We mustn't think of obedience as a burdensome duty, but as an opportunity to join with God in doing good in the world for the benefit of others.

What a lot of information Jesus was hoping these followers would take in! They had been told, again, that what Jesus was doing was an extension of the Father's will. Jesus was the tangible, visible agent sent by the Father.

Jesus used another analogy to get them to grasp this lesson.

Jesus Is the Vine—Followers Are Branches

John 15:1–11

1 "I am the true vine, and My Father is the vinedresser.
2 Every branch in Me that does not bear fruit, He takes
away; and every branch that bears fruit, He prunes it
so that it may bear more fruit. 3 You are already clean
because of the word which I have spoken to you. 4 Abide in
Me, and I in you. As the branch cannot bear fruit of itself
unless it abides in the vine, so neither can you unless you
abide in Me. 5 I am the vine, you are the branches; he who
abides in Me and I in him, he bears much fruit, for apart
from Me you can do nothing. 6 If anyone does not abide
in Me, he is thrown away as a branch and dries up; and
they gather them, and cast them into the fire and they are

> *burned.* [7] *If you abide in Me, and My words abide in you, ask whatever you wish, and it will be done for you.* [8] *My Father is glorified by this, that you bear much fruit, and so prove to be My disciples.* [9] *Just as the Father has loved Me, I have also loved you; abide in My love.* [10] *If you keep My commandments, you will abide in My love; just as I have kept My Father's commandments and abide in His love.* [11] *These things I have spoken to you so that My joy may be in you, and that your joy may be made full.*

Jesus is the true vine. The Father is the vinedresser. The Father's desire is that His true vine will be bear much fruit. For the vine to produce lots of fruit, it has to grow branches. The vine supports and supplies the branches. The life that vitalizes the vine also vitalizes the branches. What is in the vine is also in the branch. When a branch bears fruit, the vinedresser prunes it so that even more fruit can be produced by it.

The secret to a productive life is to be vitally attached to the vine—to actually grow out of the vine. It is not at all possible for a branch to produce any fruit if not attached to the vine, and it is not possible for a disciple of Jesus to bear fruit apart from abiding in Christ. The way to do something *for* Christ is to do something *with* Christ. We can do nothing without Christ. Anything we do with Christ is something! Potential and possibility are wasted if a person refuses to abide in Christ.

Jesus explains how abiding shapes our prayers. "If you abide in Me, and My words abide in you, ask whatsoever you wish, and it will be done for you" (v. 7). Because of this abiding relationship, our prayers will be in line with God's will.

When Jesus said, "Just as the Father has loved Me, I have also loved you; abide in My love" (v. 9), He explained that love is caught and taught. Jesus experienced the love of the Father, He loved His followers, and now His followers are called to love others.

Love is demonstrated by attitude and action. We want to

obey, and we follow through. Our obedience is from the heart. Jesus said, "If you keep My commandments, you will abide in My love; just as I have kept My Father's commandments and abide in His love" (v. 10). Abiding in love produces obedience, and obedience adds to the experience of abiding in His love.

Disciples' Relation to Each Other

John 15:12–17

> [12] *"This is My commandment, that you love one another, just as I have loved you.* [13] *Greater love has no one than this, that one lay down his life for his friends.* [14] *You are My friends if you do what I command you.* [15] *No longer do I call you slaves, for the slave does not know what his master is doing; but I have called you friends, for all things that I have heard from My Father I have made known to you.* [16] *You did not choose Me but I chose you, and appointed you that you would go and bear fruit, and that your fruit would remain, so that whatever you ask of the Father in My name He may give to you.* [17] *This I command you, that you love one another.*

Jesus called His disciples friends, not slaves. A slave doesn't have to know why he is doing something. He just does what he is ordered to do, without question. A friend is given an explanation. Jesus shared with His disciples what the Father had told Him. He counted them as friends.

We can take great joy in the fact that God has chosen us! In the view of much of the world, the disciples were not that special; but God choosing them made them special. God choosing us makes us special, too. It's not that we're in an exclusive club—all are welcome—but being a son or daughter of God is a great privilege.

Love is a command, not an option. Perhaps Jesus made "love one another" a command because it's not always easy to love, and He earlier said that keeping His commands is one of the ways we prove that we love Him.

Disciples' Relation to the World

John 15:18–27

[18] "If the world hates you, you know that it has hated Me before it hated you. [19] If you were of the world, the world would love its own; but because you are not of the world, but I chose you out of the world, because of this the world hates you. [20] Remember the word that I said to you, 'A slave is not greater than his master.' If they persecuted Me, they will also persecute you; if they kept My word, they will keep yours also. [21] But all these things they will do to you for My name's sake, because they do not know the One who sent Me. [22] If I had not come and spoken to them, they would not have sin, but now they have no excuse for their sin. [23] He who hates Me hates My Father also. [24] If I had not done among them the works which no one else did, they would not have sin; but now they have both seen and hated Me and My Father as well. [25] But they have done this to fulfill the word that is written in their Law, 'THEY HATED ME WITHOUT A CAUSE.'

[26] "When the Helper comes, whom I will send to you from the Father, that is the Spirit of truth who proceeds from the Father, He will testify about Me, [27] and you will testify also, because you have been with Me from the beginning.

Jesus talks of "the world" as if it were a competing system. "If the world hates you, you know that it has hated Me before it hated you" (v. 18). The world has another set of values, different allegiances, different expectations.

It seems that Jesus didn't oppose the world so much as it opposed Him. He came into the world to bring forgiveness and redemption, but the world hated the One who came to save it. No one likes to see their sin, and pride further blinds.

Jesus warned His followers that they would be persecuted just as He was. We should not expect the world to roll out a welcome mat to the gospel message. Some will receive it. Some will reject it.

Jesus said people must respond to the light they've received. "If I had not come and spoken to them, they would not have sin, but now they have no excuse for their sin" (v. 22). There's no excuse for ignoring the truth.

According to Jesus, people can't hate Him and love God: "He who hates Me hates My Father also" (v. 23). Jesus is the only way to know God. Earlier, He said, "I am the way, and the truth, and the life; no one comes to the Father but through Me" (John 14:6).

Jesus promised to send the Holy Spirit to testify about Him and to teach, lead, and encourage the disciples as they testified about Him as well. The church is powerless without the Holy Spirit.

Jesus' Warning

John 16:1–4

> [1] *"These things I have spoken to you so that you may be kept from stumbling.* [2] *They will make you outcasts from the synagogue, but an hour is coming for everyone who kills you to think that he is offering service to God.* [3] *These things they will do because they have not known the Father or Me.* [4] *But these things I have spoken to you, so that when their hour comes, you may remember that I told you of them. These things I did not say to you at the beginning, because I was with you.*

The upcoming events would strongly challenge the disciples, and Jesus sought to prepare them. Their faith did waiver, but they didn't fall away. We experience events that challenge us. Thank God, we have His Word to steady us. Throughout the centuries, the church has experienced persecution and continues to do so today.

The Holy Spirit Promised

John 16:5–15

5 *"But now I am going to Him who sent Me; and none of*
you asks Me, 'Where are You going?' 6 *But because I have*
said these things to you, sorrow has filled your heart. 7 *But*
I tell you the truth, it is to your advantage that I go away;
for if I do not go away, the Helper will not come to you; but
if I go, I will send Him to you. 8 *And He, when He comes,*
will convict the world concerning sin and righteousness
and judgment; 9 *concerning sin, because they do*
not believe in Me; 10 *and concerning righteousness,*
because I go to the Father and you no longer see Me; 11 *and*
concerning judgment, because the ruler of this world has
been judged.

12 *"I have many more things to say to you, but you cannot*
bear them now. 13 *But when He, the Spirit of truth,*
comes, He will guide you into all the truth; for He will
not speak on His own initiative, but whatever He hears,
He will speak; and He will disclose to you what is to
come. 14 *He will glorify Me, for He will take of Mine and*
will disclose it to you. 15 *All things that the Father has*
are Mine; therefore I said that He takes of Mine and will
disclose it to you.

The disciples were saddened when Jesus said He would be leaving them. They couldn't understand that they would be better off when the Holy Spirit came to live among them and in them.

Jesus said the Holy Spirit would bring conviction of sin over the refusal to believe in Him. The Spirit also would bring conviction of Christ's righteousness over against the worthless pursuit of self-righteousness. Christ's resurrection and ascension to the Father vindicates Jesus' righteousness and His claim to be the Son of God. Finally, the Spirit would convict the world that Satan was defeated at the cross. At Calvary, Satan did his very best to defeat Jesus but was utterly defeated himself.

Jesus told the disciples, "I have many more things to say to you, but you cannot bear them now" (v. 12). As Jesus illustrates here, there is a time and a place to say things. The disciples weren't ready to hear any more than He had already told them. We need God's wisdom to know what to say and when to say it.

Jesus assured the disciples that the Holy Spirit would continue to teach them in His absence. "But when He, The Spirit of Truth, comes, He will guide you into all the truth; for He will not speak on His own initiative, but, whatever He hears, He will speak; and He will disclose to you what is to come" (v. 13). They would be hearing a consistent message originating from the same Source. The Spirit is one with the Father and the Son.

The sending of the Spirit would be a great blessing to the disciples and, later, to the church. God's presence would be among them in an intensified, continuous way. And He would remind them of the things Jesus said.

Jesus' Death and Resurrection Foretold

John 16:16–22

16 "A little while, and you will no longer see Me; and again
a little while, and you will see Me." 17 Some of His disciples
then said to one another, "What is this thing He is telling
us, 'A little while, and you will not see Me; and again a

> *little while, and you will see Me'; and, 'because I go to the Father'?"* [18] *So they were saying, "What is this that He says, 'A little while'? We do not know what He is talking about."* [19] *Jesus knew that they wished to question Him, and He said to them, "Are you deliberating together about this, that I said, 'A little while, and you will not see Me, and again a little while, and you will see Me'?* [20] *Truly, truly, I say to you, that you will weep and lament, but the world will rejoice; you will grieve, but your grief will be turned into joy.* [21] *Whenever a woman is in labor she has pain, because her hour has come; but when she gives birth to the child, she no longer remembers the anguish because of the joy that a child has been born into the world.* [22] *Therefore you too have grief now; but I will see you again, and your heart will rejoice, and no one will take your joy away from you.*

The disciples wondered what Jesus meant when He said they wouldn't see Him for a little while and then they would see Him again, but they were hesitant to ask about it. They may have thought their questions were below Jesus' consideration, or they might not have wanted to reveal their lack of understanding, or perhaps they were unsure about how to put their questions into words. In any case, Jesus knew they were confused and gave them further explanation. In the same way, Jesus perceives our concerns and questions and invites us to come to Him and His Word for further explanation.

Jesus used the illustration of childbirth to explain how a painful process can yield a beautiful result and make all the pain worthwhile. In the Christian life, we are often called to wait on God during painful seasons, knowing that He will deliver us in the right way and at the right time.

Prayer Promises

John 16:23–33

[23] *In that day you will not question Me about anything. Truly, truly, I say to you, if you ask the Father for anything in My name, He will give it to you.* [24] *Until now you have asked for nothing in My name; ask and you will receive, so that your joy may be made full.*

[25] *"These things I have spoken to you in figurative language; an hour is coming when I will no longer speak to you in figurative language, but will tell you plainly of the Father.* [26] *In that day you will ask in My name, and I do not say to you that I will request of the Father on your behalf;* [27] *for the Father Himself loves you, because you have loved Me and have believed that I came forth from the Father.* [28] *I came forth from the Father and have come into the world; I am leaving the world again and going to the Father."*

[29] *His disciples said, "Lo, now You are speaking plainly and are not using a figure of speech.* [30] *Now we know that You know all things, and have no need for anyone to question You; by this we believe that You came from God."* [31] *Jesus answered them, "Do you now believe?* [32] *Behold, an hour is coming, and has already come, for you to be scattered, each to his own home, and to leave Me alone; and yet I am not alone, because the Father is with Me.* [33] *These things I have spoken to you, so that in Me you may have peace. In the world you have tribulation, but take courage; I have overcome the world."*

There may have been some remaining confusion in the minds of the disciples about God, the Father, and Jesus, the Son of God. They knew how Jesus felt about them; they may have been uncertain if God felt that same way. Note the assuring and comforting words of Jesus, "The Father Himself loves you" (v. 27). Jesus came so that they (and we) might know the Father's love.

Future events would shake their faith (v. 33), but they could still find peace in Jesus. It's the same for us. We can have peace when we are sure that Christ has overcome the world on our behalf.

The Ordeal in Gethsemane

Matthew 26:36–46

36 Then Jesus came with them to a place called Gethsemane, and said to His disciples, "Sit here while I go over there and pray." 37 And He took with Him Peter and the two sons of Zebedee, and began to be grieved and distressed. 38 Then He said to them, "My soul is deeply grieved, to the point of death; remain here and keep watch with Me."

39 And He went a little beyond them, and fell on His face and prayed, saying, "My Father, if it is possible, let this cup pass from Me; yet not as I will, but as You will." 40 And He came to the disciples and found them sleeping, and said to Peter, "So, you men could not keep watch with Me for one hour? 41 Keep watching and praying that you may not enter into temptation; the spirit is willing, but the flesh is weak."

42 He went away again a second time and prayed, saying, "My Father, if this cannot pass away unless I drink it, Your will be done." 43 Again He came and found them sleeping, for their eyes were heavy. 44 And He left them again, and went away and prayed a third time, saying the same thing once more. 45 Then He came to the disciples and said to them, "Are you still sleeping and resting? Behold, the hour is at hand and the Son of Man is being betrayed into the hands of sinners. [46] *Get up, let us be going; behold, the one who betrays Me is at hand!"*

Jesus was in deep agony in the garden. The weight of what was before Him was absolutely crushing. We can't even imagine the suffering He went through.

The disciples could not stay awake to pray with Jesus, but we shouldn't judge them too harshly. They were weak and tired, fallible humans like us. The disciples certainly needed Jesus, but this was a time when He needed them. He was human and looked for the support of His friends during His darkest hour. Jesus was probably beyond weary Himself, but He stayed focused on doing the Father's will no matter what the cost.

Matthew tells us that Jesus found His disciples sleeping a second time but didn't bother to wake them. He must have felt completely alone other than whatever solace He could find in His prayers to His Father.

We're like the disciples in that we often fail Jesus. Even so, He continues to pick us up and give us grace to continue on the journey.

Mark 14:32–42

[32] *They came to a place named Gethsemane; and He said*
to His disciples, "Sit here until I have prayed." [33] *And He*
took with Him Peter and James and John, and began to
be very distressed and troubled. [34] *And He said to them,*
"My soul is deeply grieved to the point of death; remain
here and keep watch." [35] *And He went a little beyond*
them, and fell to the ground and began to pray that if
it were possible, the hour might pass Him by. [36] *And He*
was saying, "Abba! Father! All things are possible for You;
remove this cup from Me; yet not what I will, but what
You will." [37] *And He came and found them sleeping, and*
said to Peter, "Simon, are you asleep? Could you not keep

watch for one hour? [38] *Keep watching and praying that you may not come into temptation; the spirit is willing, but the flesh is weak."* [39] *Again He went away and prayed, saying the same words.* [40] *And again He came and found them sleeping, for their eyes were very heavy; and they did not know what to answer Him.* [41] *And He came the third time, and said to them, "Are you still sleeping and resting? It is enough; the hour has come; behold, the Son of Man is being betrayed into the hands of sinners.* [42] *Get up, let us be going; behold, the one who betrays Me is at hand!"*

When Jesus said, "Sit here until I have prayed" (v. 32), He was asking for some support from His friends while He prepared to do what He must do alone. Sometimes we might ask a friend to go with us to an important doctor's appointment for company and support. Our friend can't see the doctor with us, but he or she can be there to support us.

This was not the first time these followers had been with Jesus in prayer, but it was the first time they had seen such heaviness in Him.

The intensity and the agony of Jesus' praying is seen when He prays, "Abba! Father! All things are possible for You; remove this cup from Me; yet not what I will, but what You will" (v. 36). We know this prayer was excruciating for Jesus, but it must have been terribly painful for His Father also. Had there been any other way to accomplish redemption, they would have taken it. With humble submission to the Father's will, the Son accepted what He must do.

Jesus returned to His disciples to find them asleep on the job. It had been a long day, and they were tired. Jesus had to be exhausted too. For Him, the burden of His mission was stronger than the pull of rest though. These followers had yet to learn that spiritual necessity can override fatigue.

The disciples were given a second chance to stay awake and

pray with Jesus, but they once again fell asleep. Mark notes that these sleepy men didn't have an answer for Jesus. They were probably ashamed. Jesus must have been disappointed at having to wake them again at a time when He needed them the most.

Jesus told the disciples, "Let us be going, behold, the one who betrays Me is at hand" (v. 42). They were not escaping. They were going wherever God's will would lead them. What they had been dreading was about to take place.

Luke 22:40–46

> 40 *When He arrived at the place, He said to them, "Pray*
> *that you may not enter into temptation."* 41 *And He*
> *withdrew from them about a stone's throw, and He knelt*
> *down and began to pray,* 42 *saying, "Father, if You are*
> *willing, remove this cup from Me; yet not My will, but*
> *Yours be done."* 43 *Now an angel from heaven appeared to*
> *Him, strengthening Him.* 44 *And being in agony He was*
> *praying very fervently; and His sweat became like drops*
> *of blood, falling down upon the ground.* 45 *When He rose*
> *from prayer, He came to the disciples and found them*
> *sleeping from sorrow,* 46 *and said to them, "Why are you*
> *sleeping? Get up and pray that you may not enter into*
> *temptation."*

Jesus expected that His disciples would pray as He was praying. They couldn't pray with the same intensity, for they weren't carrying the same burden He was. He urged them to pray against the temptation to give in to the desire to sleep, but they were unable to stay awake and keep praying.

We can make temptation more of a threat if we leave ourselves unguarded. They may have allowed their emotions to influence them, since we read that they were "sleeping from sorrow" (v. 45). Emotions can strongly influence our ability to withstand temptation.

The burden Jesus was carrying was so heavy that His "sweat became like drops of blood" (v. 44). An angel came to minister to Jesus because of His prayers and the intensity of His pain.

Chapter 11

THE ARREST, TRIAL, CRUCIFIXION, AND BURIAL OF JESUS

Jesus' Betrayal and Arrest

Matthew 26:47–56

*47 While He was still speaking, behold, Judas, one of the
twelve, came up accompanied by a large crowd with
swords and clubs, who came from the chief priests and
elders of the people. 48 Now he who was betraying Him
gave them a sign, saying, "Whomever I kiss, He is the one;
seize Him." 49 Immediately Judas went to Jesus and said,
"Hail, Rabbi!" and kissed Him. 50 And Jesus said to him,
"Friend, do what you have come for." Then they came and
laid hands on Jesus and seized Him.*

*51 And behold, one of those who were with Jesus reached
and drew out his sword, and struck the slave of the high
priest and cut off his ear. 52 Then Jesus said to him, "Put
your sword back into its place; for all those who take up
the sword shall perish by the sword. 53 Or do you think
that I cannot appeal to My Father, and He will at once put
at My disposal more than twelve legions of angels? 54 How
then will the Scriptures be fulfilled, which say that it must
happen this way?"*

*55 At that time Jesus said to the crowds, "Have you come
out with swords and clubs to arrest Me as you would
against a robber? Every day I used to sit in the temple
teaching and you did not seize Me. 56 But all this has taken
place to fulfill the Scriptures of the prophets." Then all the
disciples left Him and fled.*

Judas must have felt uneasy when Jesus addressed him as "friend" (v. 50). Toward the end of this episode, we learn that Judas was overcome with remorse, but the deed could not be undone. Regret is tough to live with, and it doesn't change things.

The disciples had been concerned and confused about which of them would be the betrayer. They were on edge. Perhaps that's why one of them took his sword and cut off the ear of the high priest's slave when the religious leaders came to arrest Jesus. Given the size of the crowd, there was hardly a chance that this arrest could be defeated by force. Maybe it was a valiant effort to not go down without a fight.

Jesus actually didn't need protection. As He said, He had at his disposal twelve legions of angels! The Scriptures had predicted the events now taking place, and Jesus said they must be fulfilled.

Jesus questioned the crowd about the use of force since He hadn't done anything wrong. At the same time, He knew that this is how things had to happen. There's a sense in which He was at the mercy of the crowd, but behind it all was God's sovereign plan.

Jesus had asked some of His disciples to stay alert with Him in Gethsemane, and they had failed Him. This time they abandoned Him (v. 56). After the resurrection, Jesus graciously restored these faltering disciples. God's faithfulness to us is not dependent upon our faithfulness to Him.

Jesus Before Caiaphas

Matthew 26:57–68

57 Those who had seized Jesus led Him away to Caiaphas, the high priest, where the scribes and the elders were gathered together. 58 But Peter was following Him at a

distance as far as the courtyard of the high priest, and
entered in, and sat down with the officers to see the
outcome.

[59] *Now the chief priests and the whole Council kept trying*
to obtain false testimony against Jesus, so that they might
put Him to death. [60] *They did not find any, even though*
many false witnesses came forward. But later on two
came forward, [61] *and said, "This man stated, 'I am able*
to destroy the temple of God and to rebuild it in three
days.'" [62] *The high priest stood up and said to Him, "Do*
You not answer? What is it that these men are testifying
against You?" [63] *But Jesus kept silent. And the high priest*
said to Him, "I adjure You by the living God, that You tell
us whether You are the Christ, the Son of God." [64] *Jesus*
said to him, "You have said it yourself; nevertheless I tell
you, hereafter you will see THE SON OF MAN SITTING
AT THE RIGHT HAND OF POWER, and COMING ON
THE CLOUDS OF HEAVEN."

[65] *Then the high priest tore his robes and said, "He has*
blasphemed! What further need do we have of witnesses?
Behold, you have now heard the blasphemy; [66] *what do*
you think?" They answered, "He deserves death!"

[67] *Then they spat in His face and beat Him with their fists;*
and others slapped Him, [68] *and said, "Prophesy to us, You*
Christ; who is the one who hit You?"

What happened when Jesus was brought before the high priest could hardly be called a trial. It was an effort to justify what they had already purposed to do—call for Jesus' death. As with all of His interactions with the religious leaders, Jesus was not at all intimidated. He simply spoke the truth and let the chips fall where they may.

Peter's Denials

Matthew 26:69–75

[69] Now Peter was sitting outside in the courtyard, and a servant-girl came to him and said, "You too were with Jesus the Galilean." [70] But he denied it before them all, saying, "I do not know what you are talking about." [71] When he had gone out to the gateway, another servant-girl saw him and said to those who were there, "This man was with Jesus of Nazareth." [72] And again he denied it with an oath, "I do not know the man." [73] A little later the bystanders came up and said to Peter, "Surely you too are one of them; for even the way you talk gives you away." [74] Then he began to curse and swear, "I do not know the man!" And immediately a rooster crowed. [75] And Peter remembered the word which Jesus had said, "Before a rooster crows, you will deny Me three times." And he went out and wept bitterly.

Peter's denial was not his best moment, but we shouldn't judge Him too harshly. In spite of Peter's denial, Jesus restored him and launched him into a life of ministry. We are all capable of failing our Lord, and He knows that about us and still loves us. It's His grace that gives us the courage to keep going despite our failures.

Judas' Remorse

Matthew 27:1–10

[1] Now when morning came, all the chief priests and the elders of the people conferred together against Jesus to put Him to death; [2] and they bound Him, and led Him away and delivered Him to Pilate the governor.

[3] Then when Judas, who had betrayed Him, saw that He had been condemned, he felt remorse and returned

> *the thirty pieces of silver to the chief priests and elders,*
> [4] *saying, "I have sinned by betraying innocent blood." But*
> *they said, "What is that to us? See to that yourself!"* [5] *And*
> *he threw the pieces of silver into the temple sanctuary*
> *and departed; and he went away and hanged himself.*
> [6] *The chief priests took the pieces of silver and said, "It*
> *is not lawful to put them into the temple treasury, since*
> *it is the price of blood."* [7] *And they conferred together*
> *and with the money bought the Potter's Field as a burial*
> *place for strangers.* [8] *For this reason that field has been*
> *called the Field of Blood to this day.* [9] *Then that which*
> *was spoken through Jeremiah the prophet was fulfilled:*
> *"AND THEY TOOK THE THIRTY PIECES OF SILVER,*
> *THE PRICE OF THE ONE WHOSE PRICE HAD*
> *BEEN SET by the sons of Israel;* [10] *AND THEY GAVE*
> *THEM FOR THE POTTER'S FIELD, AS THE LORD*
> *DIRECTED ME."*

Judas regretted what he had done, but he couldn't change it or make up for it. His bad choices had dire consequences. We can make choices without thinking through the consequences, too. We must be on guard against temptation and drifting.

When Judas tried to fix what he had done by giving back the money, the chief priests said, "It is not lawful to put them into the temple treasury, since it is the price of blood" (v. 6). Here are murderers attempting to uphold the law. They could justify taking an innocent man's life, but they wouldn't accept tainted money!

The chief priests decided to use the betrayal fee that Judas returned to purchase a field as was prophesied in Zechariah 11:12–13: "And they took the thirty pieces of silver, the price of the one whose price had been set by the sons of Israel; and they gave them for the Potter's Field" (v. 9).

Jesus Before Pilate

Matthew 27:11–26

11 *Now Jesus stood before the governor, and the governor
questioned Him, saying, "Are You the King of the Jews?"
And Jesus said to him, "It is as you say."* 12 *And while He
was being accused by the chief priests and elders, He did
not answer.* 13 *Then Pilate said to Him, "Do You not hear
how many things they testify against You?"* 14 *And He did
not answer him with regard to even a single charge, so the
governor was quite amazed.*

15 *Now at the feast the governor was accustomed to release
for the people any one prisoner whom they wanted.* 16 *At
that time they were holding a notorious prisoner, called
Barabbas.* 17 *So when the people gathered together, Pilate
said to them, "Whom do you want me to release for you?
Barabbas, or Jesus who is called Christ?"* 18 *For he knew
that because of envy they had handed Him over.*

19 *While he was sitting on the judgment seat, his wife sent
him a message, saying, "Have nothing to do with that
righteous Man; for last night I suffered greatly in a dream
because of Him."* 20 *But the chief priests and the elders
persuaded the crowds to ask for Barabbas and to put Jesus
to death.* 21 *But the governor said to them, "Which of the
two do you want me to release for you?" And they said,
"Barabbas."* 22 *Pilate said to them, "Then what shall I do
with Jesus who is called Christ?" They all said, "Crucify
Him!"* 23 *And he said, "Why, what evil has He done?" But
they kept shouting all the more, saying, "Crucify Him!"*

24 *When Pilate saw that he was accomplishing nothing,
but rather that a riot was starting, he took water and
washed his hands in front of the crowd, saying, "I am
innocent of this Man's blood; see to that yourselves."* 25 *And*

all the people said, "His blood shall be on us and on our children!" 26 Then he released Barabbas for them; but after having Jesus scourged, he handed Him over to be crucified.

Pilate, the governor, was amazed that Jesus was so calm. He might have wondered if Jesus fully understood what was happening. Pilate didn't know that Jesus had already fought the battle on the inside and was prepared for the worst.

Pilate knew Jesus was innocent and was willing to release Him, but the crowd demanded they release a notorious criminal instead. Unwilling to take a real stand for justice, Pilate caved in to the crowd's demands to have Jesus crucified.

Betrayal and Arrest

Mark 14:43–52

43 Immediately while He was still speaking, Judas, one of
the twelve, came up accompanied by a crowd with swords
and clubs, who were from the chief priests and the scribes
and the elders. 44 Now he who was betraying Him had
given them a signal, saying, "Whomever I kiss, He is the
one; seize Him and lead Him away under guard." 45 After
coming, Judas immediately went to Him, saying, "Rabbi!"
and kissed Him. 46 They laid hands on Him and seized
Him. 47 But one of those who stood by drew his sword, and
struck the slave of the high priest and cut off his ear. 48 And
Jesus said to them, "Have you come out with swords and
clubs to arrest Me, as you would against a robber? 49 Every
day I was with you in the temple teaching, and you did not
seize Me; but this has taken place to fulfill the Scriptures."
50 And they all left Him and fled.

51 A young man was following Him, wearing nothing but
a linen sheet over his naked body; and they seized him.
52 But he pulled free of the linen sheet and escaped naked.

When Judas instructed them to take Jesus away "under guard" (v. 44), he was apparently afraid that Jesus would not submit to arrest. He may have feared some kind of retaliation from Jesus.

The disciples "all left Him and fled" (v. 50). Perhaps they had expected that Jesus would not submit to this arrest. They had not understood that this must happen. More likely, they were fearful that they too might be arrested.

Jesus Before His Accusers

Mark 14:53–65

53 *They led Jesus away to the high priest; and all the chief*
priests and the elders and the scribes gathered together.
54 *Peter had followed Him at a distance, right into the*
courtyard of the high priest; and he was sitting with
the officers and warming himself at the fire. 55 *Now the*
chief priests and the whole Council kept trying to obtain
testimony against Jesus to put Him to death, and they were
not finding any. 56 *For many were giving false testimony*
against Him, but their testimony was not consistent.
57 *Some stood up and began to give false testimony against*
Him, saying, 58 *"We heard Him say, 'I will destroy this*
temple made with hands, and in three days I will build
another made without hands.'" 59 *Not even in this respect*
was their testimony consistent. 60 *The high priest stood*
up and came forward and questioned Jesus, saying, "Do
You not answer? What is it that these men are testifying
against You?" 61 *But He kept silent and did not answer.*
Again the high priest was questioning Him, and saying
to Him, "Are You the Christ, the Son of the Blessed One?"
62 *And Jesus said, "I am; and you shall see THE SON OF*
MAN SITTING AT THE RIGHT HAND OF POWER,
and COMING WITH THE CLOUDS OF HEAVEN."

[63] Tearing his clothes, the high priest said, "What further
need do we have of witnesses? [64] You have heard the
blasphemy; how does it seem to you?" And they all
condemned Him to be deserving of death. [65] Some began
to spit at Him, and to blindfold Him, and to beat Him
with their fists, and to say to Him, "Prophesy!" And the
officers received Him with slaps in the face.

After agreeing to ask for Jesus to be put to death, the chief priests and others "began to spit at Him, and to blindfold Him, and to beat Him with their fists, and to say to Him, 'Prophesy!' And the officers received Him with slaps in the face" (v. 65). For all the world, it seemed that these hypocrites had won. They had Jesus in their grasp. What they didn't know was that their unrestrained sin led to Jesus' sacrificial death for the sins of the world. The worst possible event would lead to the greatest possible outcome.

Peter's Denials

Mark 14:66–72

[66] As Peter was below in the courtyard, one of the servant-
girls of the high priest came, [67] and seeing Peter warming
himself, she looked at him and said, "You also were with
Jesus the Nazarene." [68] But he denied it, saying, "I neither
know nor understand what you are talking about." And
he went out onto the porch. [69] The servant-girl saw him,
and began once more to say to the bystanders, "This is one
of them!" [70] But again he denied it. And after a little while
the bystanders were again saying to Peter, "Surely you are
one of them, for you are a Galilean too." [71] But he began to
curse and swear, "I do not know this man you are talking
about!" [72] Immediately a rooster crowed a second time.
And Peter remembered how Jesus had made the remark

to him, "Before a rooster crows twice, you will deny Me three times." And he began to weep.

Notice Peter's regret: "Immediately a rooster crowed a second time. And Peter remembered how Jesus had made the remark to him, 'Before a rooster crows twice, you will deny Me three times.' And he began to weep" (v. 72). There is a line in a hymn based on Jeremiah 17:5 that says, "The arm of flesh will fail you." That's what happened with Peter. He made bold claims about not denying Jesus, but that is exactly what he did. Our confidence must be in the Lord, not in ourselves.

Jesus Before Pilate

Mark 15:1–15

[1] Early in the morning the chief priests with the elders and scribes and the whole Council, immediately held a consultation; and binding Jesus, they led Him away and delivered Him to Pilate. [2] Pilate questioned Him, "Are You the King of the Jews?" And He answered him, "It is as you say." [3] The chief priests began to accuse Him harshly. [4] Then Pilate questioned Him again, saying, "Do You not answer? See how many charges they bring against You!" [5] But Jesus made no further answer; so Pilate was amazed.

[6] Now at the feast he used to release for them any one prisoner whom they requested. [7] The man named Barabbas had been imprisoned with the insurrectionists who had committed murder in the insurrection. [8] The crowd went up and began asking him to do as he had been accustomed to do for them. [9] Pilate answered them, saying, "Do you want me to release for you the King of the Jews?" [10] For he was aware that the chief priests had handed Him over because of envy. [11] But the chief priests

stirred up the crowd to ask him to release Barabbas for them instead. [12] *Answering again, Pilate said to them, "Then what shall I do with Him whom you call the King of the Jews?"* [13] *They shouted back, "Crucify Him!"* [14] *But Pilate said to them, "Why, what evil has He done?" But they shouted all the more, "Crucify Him!"* [15] *Wishing to satisfy the crowd, Pilate released Barabbas for them, and after having Jesus scourged, he handed Him over to be crucified.*

Pilate was "amazed" when Jesus gave no further answers to his questions. Pilate marveled that a man could remain so composed and calm in the middle of such chaos. The accusers were so adamant in their demands. Perhaps Pilate knew it was a desperate attempt to get done what they wanted done, even if they couldn't make a valid case. For Pilate, it became a matter of political expediency.

As was his custom, Pilate gave the accusers an option to release one of the prisoners, either Jesus or Barabbas. The accusers shouted for Barabbas. They had created a mob mentality among the crowd. "Wishing to satisfy the crowd, Pilate released Barabbas for them, and after having Jesus scourged, he handed Him over to be crucified" (v. 15). As is so often the case, fear of man leads to selfish, sinful choices. Pilate wanted to satisfy the crowd so he wouldn't have to deal with any problems resulting from an unpopular decision. Basically, he caved in to their demands.

Jesus Betrayed by Judas

Luke 22:47–53

[47] *While He was still speaking, behold, a crowd came, and the one called Judas, one of the twelve, was preceding them; and he approached Jesus to kiss Him.* [48] *But Jesus said to him, "Judas, are you betraying the Son of Man*

with a kiss?" [49] When those who were around Him saw what was going to happen, they said, "Lord, shall we strike with the sword?" [50] And one of them struck the slave of the high priest and cut off his right ear. [51] But Jesus answered and said, "Stop! No more of this." And He touched his ear and healed him. [52] Then Jesus said to the chief priests and officers of the temple and elders who had come against Him, "Have you come out with swords and clubs as you would against a robber? [53] While I was with you daily in the temple, you did not lay hands on Me; but this hour and the power of darkness are yours."

The betraying kiss clued in these sleepy disciples that something bad was about to happen. They felt the need to do something, so they asked Jesus, "Lord, shall we strike with the sword?" (v. 49). Before He could answer, one of them cut off the ear of the high priest's slave. Jesus quickly put an end to this futile resistance, and even healed the ear of the slave. If any of that crowd had been seeking the truth—proof of Jesus' deity—they could have found it in this healing. It seems their hearts were hardened though.

There was no need for such a show of force by the religious leaders. Jesus pointed out that He taught daily in the temple and no one did anything. But Jesus understood that these men's ignorance and malice had been accounted for in God's plan. They had been given over to the power of darkness (v. 53).

Jesus' Arrest

Luke 22:54–65

[54] Having arrested Him, they led Him away and brought Him to the house of the high priest; but Peter was following at a distance. [55] After they had kindled a fire in the middle of the courtyard and had sat down together, Peter was sitting among them. [56] And a servant-girl, seeing him as

he sat in the firelight and looking intently at him, said, "This man was with Him too." [57] *But he denied it, saying, "Woman, I do not know Him."* [58] *A little later, another saw him and said, "You are one of them too!" But Peter said, "Man, I am not!"* [59] *After about an hour had passed, another man began to insist, saying, "Certainly this man also was with Him, for he is a Galilean too."* [60] *But Peter said, "Man, I do not know what you are talking about." Immediately, while he was still speaking, a rooster crowed.* [61] *The Lord turned and looked at Peter. And Peter remembered the word of the Lord, how He had told him, "Before a rooster crows today, you will deny Me three times."* [62] *And he went out and wept bitterly.*

[63] *Now the men who were holding Jesus in custody were mocking Him and beating Him,* [64] *and they blindfolded Him and were asking Him, saying, "Prophesy, who is the one who hit You?"* [65] *And they were saying many other things against Him, blaspheming.*

Peter followed the mob that arrested Jesus to the house of the high priest, where Jesus would be questioned. A fire was kindled there, and Peter sat down among them. Three different people recognized Peter as being one of Jesus' disciples and three times Peter denied it, even denying that He knew Jesus at all.

We don't know how large the crowd there was, but Jesus was able to catch Peter's eye after the rooster crowed. Peter remembered that Jesus had told him, "Before a rooster crows today, you will deny Me three times" (v. 61), and "he went out and wept bitterly" (v. 62). Peter must have felt tremendous guilt and shame after such a big failure.

Jesus was subjected to abuse by the authorities. The perfect Son of God was mocked and beaten by sinful people under the sway of the evil one.

Jesus Before the Sanhedrin

Luke 22:66–71

66 When it was day, the Council of elders of the people assembled, both chief priests and scribes, and they led Him away to their council chamber, saying, 67 "If You are the Christ, tell us." But He said to them, "If I tell you, you will not believe; 68 and if I ask a question, you will not answer. 69 But from now on THE SON OF MAN WILL BE SEATED AT THE RIGHT HAND of the power OF GOD." 70 And they all said, "Are You the Son of God, then?" And He said to them, "Yes, I am." 71 Then they said, "What further need do we have of testimony? For we have heard it ourselves from His own mouth."

Jesus' accusers got what they wanted, what they would consider a confession, when they questioned: "'Are You the Son of God, then?' And He said to them, 'Yes, I am'" (v. 70). Though true, they considered His answer blasphemy.

Jesus Before Pilate

Luke 23:1–7

1 Then the whole body of them got up and brought Him before Pilate. 2 And they began to accuse Him, saying, "We found this man misleading our nation and forbidding to pay taxes to Caesar, and saying that He Himself is Christ, a King." 3 So Pilate asked Him, saying, "Are You the King of the Jews?" And He answered him and said, "It is as you say." 4 Then Pilate said to the chief priests and the crowds, "I find no guilt in this man." 5 But they kept on insisting, saying, "He stirs up the people, teaching all over Judea, starting from Galilee even as far as this place."

> [6] *When Pilate heard it, he asked whether the man was a Galilean.* [7] *And when he learned that He belonged to Herod's jurisdiction, he sent Him to Herod, who himself also was in Jerusalem at that time.*

These accusers had no problem twisting the truth: "They began to accuse Him, saying, 'We found this man misleading our nation and forbidding to pay taxes to Caesar, and saying that He Himself is Christ, a King'" (v. 2). The charges they presented before Pilate were completely unfounded other than the one about Jesus saying He was the Christ, which, of course, was true. But the truth didn't matter to the accusers.

Pilate wasn't ready to go along with the false charges. He flatly stated, "I find no guilt in this man" (v. 4). The accusers wouldn't be put off easily, though. When they mentioned Galilee, Pilate found an excuse to send the matter to Herod, which he did.

Jesus Before Herod

> ***Luke 23:8–12***
>
> [8] *Now Herod was very glad when he saw Jesus; for he had wanted to see Him for a long time, because he had been hearing about Him and was hoping to see some sign performed by Him.* [9] *And he questioned Him at some length; but He answered him nothing.* [10] *And the chief priests and the scribes were standing there, accusing Him vehemently.* [11] *And Herod with his soldiers, after treating Him with contempt and mocking Him, dressed Him in a gorgeous robe and sent Him back to Pilate.* [12] *Now Herod and Pilate became friends with one another that very day; for before they had been enemies with each other.*

Another Herod had executed John the Baptist—the man who announced the coming of the Messiah. Now, this Herod had his chance to see the man John had announced.

After Jesus refused to do some tricks for Herod's amusement, Jesus was mocked and sent back to Pilate—an act that settled the animosity between the two politicians.

Pilate Seeks Jesus' Release

Luke 23:13–25

[13] Pilate summoned the chief priests and the rulers and
the people, [14] and said to them, "You brought this man to
me as one who incites the people to rebellion, and behold,
having examined Him before you, I have found no guilt
in this man regarding the charges which you make against
Him. [15] No, nor has Herod, for he sent Him back to us; and
behold, nothing deserving death has been done by Him.
[16] Therefore I will punish Him and release Him." [17] [Now
he was obliged to release to them at the feast one prisoner.]

[18] But they cried out all together, saying, "Away with this
man, and release for us Barabbas!" [19] (He was one who
had been thrown into prison for an insurrection made
in the city, and for murder.) [20] Pilate, wanting to release
Jesus, addressed them again, [21] but they kept on calling
out, saying, "Crucify, crucify Him!" [22] And he said to them
the third time, "Why, what evil has this man done? I have
found in Him no guilt demanding death; therefore I will
punish Him and release Him." [23] But they were insistent,
with loud voices asking that He be crucified. And their
voices began to prevail. [24] And Pilate pronounced sentence
that their demand be granted. [25] And he released the man
they were asking for who had been thrown into prison for
insurrection and murder, but he delivered Jesus to their
will.

Pilate was pressured by the ceaseless barrage of accusations against Jesus. He was worn down to the place that he was ready to make some concession to the crowd. After asking three times what Jesus had done that deserved death and receiving no good answer, Pilate released a notorious criminal, Barabbas, into society in order to fulfill his obligation while surrendering to the demands of the Jewish leaders.

Judas Betrays Jesus

John 18:1–11

> [1] *Now Judas also, who was betraying Him, knew the place,*
> *for Jesus had often met there with His disciples.* [3] *Judas*
> *then, having received the Roman cohort and officers*
> *from the chief priests and the Pharisees, came there with*
> *lanterns and torches and weapons.* [4] *So Jesus, knowing all*
> *the things that were coming upon Him, went forth and*
> *said to them, "Whom do you seek?"* [5] *They answered Him,*
> *"Jesus the Nazarene." He said to them, "I am He." And*
> *Judas also, who was betraying Him, was standing with*
> *them.* [6] *So when He said to them, "I am He," they drew*
> *back and fell to the ground.* [7] *Therefore He again asked*
> *them, "Whom do you seek?" And they said, "Jesus the*
> *Nazarene."* [8] *Jesus answered, "I told you that I am He; so*
> *if you seek Me, let these go their way,"* [9] *to fulfill the word*
> *which He spoke, "Of those whom You have given Me I lost*
> *not one."* [10] *Simon Peter then, having a sword, drew it and*
> *struck the high priest's slave, and cut off his right ear; and*
> *the slave's name was Malchus.* [11] *So Jesus said to Peter,*
> *"Put the sword into the sheath; the cup which the Father*
> *has given Me, shall I not drink it?"*

Judas must have expected Jesus to resist arrest since he had a host of Roman soldiers and temple guards with him who were heavily armed. He was likely surprised, then, when he and his army arrived at the olive grove and Jesus didn't hide or fight but rather *approached them*, asking, "Whom do you seek?" (v. 4).

Judas and his cohort thought they were going to arrest Jesus. What they didn't understand was that Jesus was willingly laying down His life. As Jesus said earlier in the Gospel of John, "No one has taken [my life] away from Me, but I lay it down on My own initiative. I have authority to lay it down, and I have authority to take it up again. This commandment I received from My Father" (10:18).

Jesus was surrendering Himself to what He knew was the will of God. His readiness and His sheer majesty made the men fall to the ground—a preview of the day when every knee (both those of Jesus' followers and enemies) will bow before Jesus Christ.

Even though Jesus expressed His willingness to be arrested, Peter still tried to defend Jesus through the use of force. He took his sword and cut off the ear of the high priest's slave. But Jesus rebuked Peter, saying, "The cup which the Father has given Me, shall I not drink it?" (v. 11). The cup was a reference to the suffering Jesus was about to endure to pay the penalty for sin. The Son received the cup willingly, demonstrating faith in His Father's will.

Jesus Before the Priests

John 18:12–24

[12] So the Roman cohort and the commander and the officers of the Jews, arrested Jesus and bound Him, [13] and led Him to Annas first; for he was father-in-law of Caiaphas, who was high priest that year. [14] Now Caiaphas was the one who had advised the Jews that it was expedient for one man to die on behalf of the people.

[15] Simon Peter was following Jesus, and so was another disciple. Now that disciple was known to the high priest, and entered with Jesus into the court of the high priest, [16] but Peter was standing at the door outside. So the other disciple, who was known to the high priest, went out and spoke to the doorkeeper, and brought Peter in. [17] Then the slave-girl who kept the door said to Peter, "You are not also one of this man's disciples, are you?" He said, "I am not." [18] Now the slaves and the officers were standing there, having made a charcoal fire, for it was cold and they were warming themselves; and Peter was also with them, standing and warming himself.

[19] The high priest then questioned Jesus about His disciples, and about His teaching. [20] Jesus answered him, "I have spoken openly to the world; I always taught in synagogues and in the temple, where all the Jews come together; and I spoke nothing in secret. [21] Why do you question Me? Question those who have heard what I spoke to them; they know what I said." [22] When He had said this, one of the officers standing nearby struck Jesus, saying, "Is that the way You answer the high priest?" [23] Jesus answered him, "If I have spoken wrongly, testify of the wrong; but if rightly, why do you strike Me?" [24] So Annas sent Him bound to Caiaphas the high priest.

When Jesus was arrested He was taken first to Annas, the former high priest, who was highly respected among the Jewish people. Annas was also the father-in-law of Caiaphas, the high priest at that time. Peter and "another disciple," whom most scholars believe was John, followed Jesus to the court of the high priest. John went inside with Jesus, making his account of Jesus speaking with Annas an eyewitness one, but Peter stayed outside by the door.

While Jesus was inside being questioned by Annas, Peter

was outside being questioned by a slave-girl: "You are not also one of this man's disciples, are you?" Probably terrified of what would happen if he admitted to being a follower of Jesus, Peter replied, "I am not" (v. 17). This marks the first of three times that Peter denied Jesus (which Jesus predicted in John 13:38).

Inside, Annas was trying to trick Jesus into incriminating himself as a false prophet or a false teacher, but Jesus didn't allow Himself to be trapped. He told Annas that everything He taught, He taught openly. He then told Annas to speak with those who had heard His teachings; surely they would answer his questions.

The fact that Jesus wasn't afraid and wouldn't back down or incriminate Himself probably made Annas very anxious and angry. Perhaps seeing Annas's heightening angst, a court official hit Jesus and said, "Is that the way You answer the high priest?" (v. 22). Jesus answered, "If I have spoken wrongly, testify of the wrong; but if rightly, why do you strike Me?" (v. 23). Not knowing what else to do, Annas sent Jesus to Caiaphas.

Peter's Denial of Jesus

John 18:25–27

*[25] Now Simon Peter was standing and warming himself.
So they said to him, "You are not also one of His disciples,
are you?" He denied it, and said, "I am not." [26] One of the
slaves of the high priest, being a relative of the one whose
ear Peter cut off, said, "Did I not see you in the garden
with Him?" [27] Peter then denied it again, and immediately
a rooster crowed.*

Peter had already denied Jesus once to the slave girl at the door of the court of the high priest. After that, he moved away from her and warmed himself by the fire with slaves and officers. There, they asked Peter if he was one of Jesus' disciples. He denied it a second time.

Then, one of the slaves who was related to the man whose ear Peter had cut off, asked Peter, "Did I not see you in the garden with Him?" (v. 26). How could Peter deny it? But he did, a third time. And when he heard the rooster crow, he was immediately reminded of what the Lord had said about him denying association with Him.

John doesn't give us any of the details about the interaction between Caiaphas and Jesus. All we know is that they sent Jesus from Caiaphas to Pilate, the Roman governor of Judea.

Jesus Before Pilate

John 18:28–40

[28] Then they led Jesus from Caiaphas into the Praetorium,
and it was early; and they themselves did not enter into
the Praetorium so that they would not be defiled, but
might eat the Passover. [29] Therefore Pilate went out to
them and said, "What accusation do you bring against
this Man?" [30] They answered and said to him, "If this Man
were not an evildoer, we would not have delivered Him to
you." [31] So Pilate said to them, "Take Him yourselves, and
judge Him according to your law." The Jews said to him,
"We are not permitted to put anyone to death," [32] to fulfill
the word of Jesus which He spoke, signifying by what kind
of death He was about to die.

[33] Therefore Pilate entered again into the Praetorium, and
summoned Jesus and said to Him, "Are You the King of
the Jews?" [34] Jesus answered, "Are you saying this on your
own initiative, or did others tell you about Me?" [35] Pilate
answered, "I am not a Jew, am I? Your own nation and the
chief priests delivered You to me; what have You done?"

> [36] *Jesus answered, "My kingdom is not of this world. If My kingdom were of this world, then My servants would be fighting so that I would not be handed over to the Jews; but as it is, My kingdom is not of this realm."* [37] *Therefore Pilate said to Him, "So You are a king?" Jesus answered, "You say correctly that I am a king. For this I have been born, and for this I have come into the world, to testify to the truth. Everyone who is of the truth hears My voice."*
> [38] *Pilate said to Him, "What is truth?"*
>
> *And when he had said this, he went out again to the Jews and said to them, "I find no guilt in Him.* [39] *But you have a custom that I release someone for you at the Passover; do you wish then that I release for you the King of the Jews?"* [40] *So they cried out again, saying, "Not this Man, but Barabbas." Now Barabbas was a robber.*

John notes that the Jewish accusers would not enter Pilate's court because they wanted to remain ceremonially clean so they could observe Passover. The irony is not lost on John. They were trying to avoid defilement while they helped to bring about the death of the pure Son of God who took away the sins of the world!

Pilate was convinced that Jesus' accusers needed to try Him in their own court according to their own laws. But they said to Pilate, "We are not permitted to put anyone to death," and that's precisely what they wanted for Jesus (v. 31). But again, it's important to remember that it was the Father's will for Jesus to give His life. Even the circumstances leading up to Jesus' death were part of God's sovereign plan.

After Pilate questioned Jesus and listened closely to His responses, He went out to the Jews and told them that he found no guilt in Jesus. But to appease them, Pilate reminded them that it was customary for him to release a Jewish prisoner every year at Passover. When he recommended that they release Jesus, the Jews cried out, "Not this Man, but Barabbas," who was a convicted robber (v. 40).

Pilate must have been mystified by their decision. He was giving them a choice between letting an innocent man go free or a guilty man, and they chose the guilty man.

The Crown of Thorns

John 19:1–16

[1] Pilate then took Jesus and scourged Him. [2] And the soldiers twisted together a crown of thorns and put it on His head, and put a purple robe on Him; [3] and they began to come up to Him and say, "Hail, King of the Jews!" and to give Him slaps in the face. [4] Pilate came out again and said to them, "Behold, I am bringing Him out to you so that you may know that I find no guilt in Him." [5] Jesus then came out, wearing the crown of thorns and the purple robe. Pilate said to them, "Behold, the Man!" [6] So when the chief priests and the officers saw Him, they cried out saying, "Crucify, crucify!" Pilate said to them, "Take Him yourselves and crucify Him, for I find no guilt in Him." [7] The Jews answered him, "We have a law, and by that law He ought to die because He made Himself out to be the Son of God."

[8] Therefore when Pilate heard this statement, he was even more afraid; [9] and he entered into the Praetorium again and said to Jesus, "Where are You from?" But Jesus gave him no answer. [10] So Pilate said to Him, "You do not speak to me? Do You not know that I have authority to release You, and I have authority to crucify You?" [11] Jesus answered, "You would have no authority over Me, unless it had been given you from above; for this reason he who delivered Me to you has the greater sin." [12] As a result of this Pilate made efforts to release Him, but the Jews cried

out saying, "If you release this Man, you are no friend of Caesar; everyone who makes himself out to be a king opposes Caesar."

[13] *Therefore when Pilate heard these words, he brought Jesus out, and sat down on the judgment seat at a place called The Pavement, but in Hebrew, Gabbatha.* [14] *Now it was the day of preparation for the Passover; it was about the sixth hour. And he said to the Jews, "Behold, your King!"* [15] *So they cried out, "Away with Him, away with Him, crucify Him!" Pilate said to them, "Shall I crucify your King?" The chief priests answered, "We have no king but Caesar."* [16] *So he then handed Him over to them to be crucified.*

Even though Pilate was convinced of Jesus' innocence, he gave in to the demands of the Jews, and he ordered Jesus to be beaten. Then the soldiers fashioned a crown of thorns, likely made out of date palms with spikes several inches long, and placed it on Jesus' head. They also put a purple robe around Him, which was the color of royalty. And mocking Him, they presented Him to the Jews and said, "Hail, King of the Jews!" (v. 3).

Still convinced of Jesus' innocence, Pilate gave the Jews one more chance to let Jesus go free. But when the accusers said that Jesus called Himself the Son of God, "Pilate was even more afraid" (v. 8). It's interesting that John said "even more afraid." Pilate probably started to fear Jesus when he couldn't intimidate Him. The fear likely deepened when he heard Jesus say that He was a king, and then climaxed when the Jewish accusers said He claimed to be the Son of God.

When Pilate heard that Jesus claimed He was the Son of God, He went back in and asked Jesus where He was from, but Jesus gave no answer. Pilate couldn't understand such quiet confidence. He had the power to determine whether or not Jesus was going to be crucified, yet that didn't matter to Jesus.

He told Pilate that he had no authority over Him other than what the Father had given him.

Pilate made every effort to release Jesus, but the Jews weren't having it. In fact, they trapped Pilate by saying that they only had one king, and that king was Caesar. If Pilate released this so-called king of the Jews, wouldn't he make himself an enemy of Caesar? So Pilate gave in to the wishes of the crowd, and he handed Jesus over to be crucified.

The Crucifixion

Matthew 27:27–56

27 Then the soldiers of the governor took Jesus into the
Praetorium and gathered the whole Roman cohort
around Him. 28 They stripped Him and put a scarlet robe
on Him. 29 And after twisting together a crown of thorns,
they put it on His head, and a reed in His right hand; and
they knelt down before Him and mocked Him, saying,
"Hail, King of the Jews!" 30 They spat on Him, and took
the reed and began to beat Him on the head. 31 After they
had mocked Him, they took the scarlet robe off Him and
put His own garments back on Him, and led Him away
to crucify Him.

32 As they were coming out, they found a man of Cyrene named Simon, whom they pressed into service to bear His cross.

33 And when they came to a place called Golgotha, which
means Place of a Skull, 34 they gave Him wine to drink
mixed with gall; and after tasting it, He was unwilling to
drink.

35 And when they had crucified Him, they divided up His
garments among themselves by casting lots. 36 And sitting

down, they began to keep watch over Him there. [37] *And*
above His head they put up the charge against Him which
read, "THIS IS JESUS THE KING OF THE JEWS."

[38] *At that time two robbers were crucified with Him, one*
on the right and one on the left. [39] *And those passing by*
were hurling abuse at Him, wagging their heads [40] *and*
saying, "You who are going to destroy the temple and
rebuild it in three days, save Yourself! If You are the Son
of God, come down from the cross." [41] *In the same way the*
chief priests also, along with the scribes and elders, were
mocking Him and saying, [42] *"He saved others; He cannot*
save Himself. He is the King of Israel; let Him now come
down from the cross, and we will believe in Him. [43] *HE*
TRUSTS IN GOD; LET GOD RESCUE Him now, IF HE
DELIGHTS IN HIM; for He said, 'I am the Son of God.'"
[44] *The robbers who had been crucified with Him were also*
insulting Him with the same words.

[45] *Now from the sixth hour darkness fell upon all the*
land until the ninth hour. [46] *About the ninth hour Jesus*
cried out with a loud voice, saying, "ELI, ELI, LAMA
SABACHTHANI?" that is, "MY GOD, MY GOD, WHY
HAVE YOU FORSAKEN ME?" [47] *And some of those who*
were standing there, when they heard it, began saying,
"This man is calling for Elijah." [48] *Immediately one of them*
ran, and taking a sponge, he filled it with sour wine and put
it on a reed, and gave Him a drink. [49] *But the rest of them*
said, "Let us see whether Elijah will come to save Him."
[50] *And Jesus cried out again with a loud voice, and yielded*
up His spirit. [51] *And behold, the veil of the temple was*
torn in two from top to bottom; and the earth shook and
the rocks were split. [52] *The tombs were opened, and many*
bodies of the saints who had fallen asleep were raised;
[53] *and coming out of the tombs after His resurrection they*

entered the holy city and appeared to many. [54] *Now the centurion, and those who were with him keeping guard over Jesus, when they saw the earthquake and the things that were happening, became very frightened and said, "Truly this was the Son of God!"*

[55] *Many women were there looking on from a distance, who had followed Jesus from Galilee while ministering to Him.* [56] *Among them was Mary Magdalene, and Mary the mother of James and Joseph, and the mother of the sons of Zebedee.*

Matthew gives us some detail about the way Jesus was handled by the soldiers. They stripped Him of whatever He was wearing and put a scarlet robe on Him—mocking His claim to be the King of the Jews—and then they put a crown of thorns on His head and a reed in His right hand, which represented the sepulcher a king would hold. They mocked His royalty in brutal ignorance. Then they spit on Him and beat Him over the head with the reed from His right hand.

The familiarity of the story of Jesus' arrest and crucifixion might lead to Christians glossing over the horrific nature of what happened. But we must never forget the reality of the gospel message—God Himself, in the person of Jesus Christ, became a human and subjected Himself to humiliation and pain that we will never experience. And He did all of this to save us. May we never let this message become dull or boring!

Simon the Cyrene was chosen to carry Jesus' cross to Golgotha. When they got to the execution site and nailed Jesus to the cross, they offered Jesus a drink that was designed to somewhat dull the pain He would endure. But Jesus refused to drink it, choosing instead to fully experience the harsh brutality of unchecked sin so He could complete the work He had come to do.

Crucifixion was not instant death. It was a prolonged, humiliating ordeal. Jesus had no clothes to cover His exposed body. After gambling over Jesus' clothes, the Roman guards sat down to watch Him die a slow and painful death.

The mocking didn't stop when Jesus was on the cross. People were hurling insults at Him, telling Him to save Himself if He was indeed the Son of God. Even the robbers hanging on either side of Him mocked Him.

From noon to 3:00 p.m. darkness covered the earth, and then at 3:00 Jesus cried out, "My God, My God, why have You forsaken Me?" (v. 46). Jesus experienced in the Garden of Gethsemane a taste of just how difficult it would be for Him to endure this agony. His cry here expresses how deeply He was feeling the pain of separation from His Father that was necessary for our atonement.

The moment Jesus breathed His last breath, the veil in the temple was torn. In the Old Testament we learn that the veil separated the Holy of Holies—where the very presence of God dwelled in the Ark of the Covenant—from the rest of the temple. Only the high priest could enter the Holy of Holies, and he could only do so once a year on the Day of Atonement. But when Jesus died, all that changed. The torn veil represents our access to the Father through Jesus Christ, our High Priest.

The very earth reacted to the death of its Creator. Many saints were resurrected from their graves and, later, after Jesus was resurrected, they went into the city where many people saw them. The centurions and the guards watching over Jesus also saw instantly that He was who He said He was—the very Son of God.

Mark 15:16–41

16 The soldiers took Him away into the palace (that is, the
Praetorium), and they called together the whole Roman
cohort. 17 They dressed Him up in purple, and after
twisting a crown of thorns, they put it on Him; 18 and they

began to acclaim Him, "Hail, King of the Jews!" [19] *They kept beating His head with a reed, and spitting on Him, and kneeling and bowing before Him.* [20] *After they had mocked Him, they took the purple robe off Him and put His own garments on Him. And they led Him out to crucify Him.*

[21] *They pressed into service a passer-by coming from the country, Simon of Cyrene (the father of Alexander and Rufus), to bear His cross.*

[22] *Then they brought Him to the place Golgotha, which is translated, Place of a Skull.* [23] *They tried to give Him wine mixed with myrrh; but He did not take it.* [24] *And they crucified Him, and divided up His garments among themselves, casting lots for them to decide what each man should take.* [25] *It was the third hour when they crucified Him.* [26] *The inscription of the charge against Him read, "THE KING OF THE JEWS."*

[27] *They crucified two robbers with Him, one on His right and one on His left.* [28] *[And the Scripture was fulfilled which says, "And He was numbered with transgressors."]*
[29] *Those passing by were hurling abuse at Him, wagging their heads, and saying, "Ha! You who are going to destroy the temple and rebuild it in three days,* [30] *save Yourself, and come down from the cross!"* [31] *In the same way the chief priests also, along with the scribes, were mocking Him among themselves and saying, "He saved others; He cannot save Himself.* [32] *Let this Christ, the King of Israel, now come down from the cross, so that we may see and believe!" Those who were crucified with Him were also insulting Him.*

[33] *When the sixth hour came, darkness fell over the whole land until the ninth hour.* [34] *At the ninth hour*

Jesus cried out with a loud voice, "ELOI, ELOI, LAMA SABACHTHANI?" which is translated, "MY GOD, MY GOD, WHY HAVE YOU FORSAKEN ME?" [35] *When some of the bystanders heard it, they began saying, "Behold, He is calling for Elijah."* [36] *Someone ran and filled a sponge with sour wine, put it on a reed, and gave Him a drink, saying, "Let us see whether Elijah will come to take Him down."* [37] *And Jesus uttered a loud cry, and breathed His last.* [38] *And the veil of the temple was torn in two from top to bottom.* [39] *When the centurion, who was standing right in front of Him, saw the way He breathed His last, he said, "Truly this man was the Son of God!"*

[40] *There were also some women looking on from a distance, among whom were Mary Magdalene, and Mary the mother of James the Less and Joses, and Salome.* [41] *When He was in Galilee, they used to follow Him and minister to Him; and there were many other women who came up with Him to Jerusalem.*

Mark gives us a picture of the brutal treatment of Jesus by the soldiers of the Roman cohort. Mark says that all the troops were called in to heap abuse upon this innocent man. To them, Jesus was a mock king, and they took out their cruelty on Him.

Mark gives us some biographical information about Simon the Cyrene, the man who carried Jesus' cross, to further prove that he wasn't a fictional character. He was the father of two sons, Alexander and Rufus, which reinforces the validity of this event.

Two thieves were crucified with Jesus, which fulfilled the prophecy in Isaiah 53:12: "Because He poured out Himself to death, *And was numbered with the transgressors;* Yet He Himself bore the sin of many, And interceded for the transgressors" (emphasis added).

At the ninth hour, when Jesus had been hanging on the cross for three hours, He cried out in His native tongue, "MY GOD, MY GOD, WHY HAVE YOU FORSAKEN ME?" (v. 34). Then He surrendered Himself into the hands of His Father and breathed His last breath.

Luke 23:26–49

26 When they led Him away, they seized a man, Simon of
Cyrene, coming in from the country, and placed on him
the cross to carry behind Jesus.

27 And following Him was a large crowd of the people, and
of women who were mourning and lamenting Him. 28 But
Jesus turning to them said, "Daughters of Jerusalem, stop
weeping for Me, but weep for yourselves and for your
children. 29 For behold, the days are coming when they will
say, 'Blessed are the barren, and the wombs that never
bore, and the breasts that never nursed.' 30 Then they will
begin TO SAY TO THE MOUNTAINS, 'FALL ON US,'
AND TO THE HILLS, 'COVER US.' 31 For if they do these
things when the tree is green, what will happen when it
is dry?"

32 Two others also, who were criminals, were being led
away to be put to death with Him.

33 When they came to the place called The Skull, there
they crucified Him and the criminals, one on the right
and the other on the left. 34 But Jesus was saying, "Father,
forgive them; for they do not know what they are doing."
And they cast lots, dividing up His garments among
themselves. 35 And the people stood by, looking on. And
even the rulers were sneering at Him, saying, "He saved
others; let Him save Himself if this is the Christ of God,
His Chosen One." 36 The soldiers also mocked Him, coming

> *up to Him, offering Him sour wine,* [37] *and saying, "If You*
> *are the King of the Jews, save Yourself!"* [38] *Now there was*
> *also an inscription above Him, "THIS IS THE KING OF*
> *THE JEWS."*
>
> [39] *One of the criminals who were hanged there was hurling*
> *abuse at Him, saying, "Are You not the Christ? Save*
> *Yourself and us!"* [40] *But the other answered, and rebuking*
> *him said, "Do you not even fear God, since you are under*
> *the same sentence of condemnation?* [41] *And we indeed are*
> *suffering justly, for we are receiving what we deserve for*
> *our deeds; but this man has done nothing wrong."* [42] *And*
> *he was saying, "Jesus, remember me when You come in*
> *Your kingdom!"* [43] *And He said to him, "Truly I say to you,*
> *today you shall be with Me in Paradise."*
>
> [44] *It was now about the sixth hour, and darkness fell over*
> *the whole land until the ninth hour,* [45] *because the sun*
> *was obscured; and the veil of the temple was torn in two.*
> [46] *And Jesus, crying out with a loud voice, said, "Father,*
> *INTO YOUR HANDS I COMMIT MY SPIRIT." Having*
> *said this, He breathed His last.* [47] *Now when the centurion*
> *saw what had happened, he began praising God, saying,*
> *"Certainly this man was innocent."* [48] *And all the crowds*
> *who came together for this spectacle, when they observed*
> *what had happened, began to return, beating their*
> *breasts.* [49] *And all His acquaintances and the women*
> *who accompanied Him from Galilee were standing at a*
> *distance, seeing these things.*

Luke mentions something unique in his account, and that's the fact that Jesus spoke to the women who were following Him to the cross. His words were a warning to the "daughters of Jerusalem," to His people who had turned Him over to be crucified. Because they had a hand in slaying the promised One, they would experience judgment. And in the days of judgment, blessings would become curses, and curses blessings (e.g., those who are barren [considered a curse] would be considered blessed).

Luke is the only Gospel writer who quotes Jesus as praying, "Father, forgive them; for they do not know what they are doing" (v. 34). He prayed this in the middle of terrible mocking and abuse from the soldiers and onlookers as He hung on the cross. But in the middle of the horror, Luke shares a story of redemption. Jesus was hanging in between two thieves. While one was heaping abuse on Jesus, the other asked Jesus for inclusion in His kingdom! Jesus assured him, "Today, you shall be with Me in Paradise" (v. 43). Even as He was dying, Jesus was attending to the business God had sent Him to earth to accomplish.

Luke notes the reactions of those who watched Jesus die. The centurion immediately recognized Jesus' innocence and started praising God, and the other onlookers "beat their breast," a sign of regret. They were wrong about Jesus, and the magnitude of what they had done began to set in.

John 19:17–30

17 They took Jesus, therefore, and He went out, bearing His own cross, to the place called the Place of a Skull, which is called in Hebrew, Golgotha. 18 There they crucified Him, and with Him two other men, one on either side, and Jesus in between. 19 Pilate also wrote an inscription and put it on the cross. It was written, "JESUS THE NAZARENE, THE KING OF THE JEWS." 20 Therefore many of the Jews read this inscription, for the place where Jesus was crucified was near the city; and it was written in Hebrew, Latin and in Greek. 21 So the chief priests of the Jews were saying to Pilate, "Do not write, 'The King of the Jews'; but that He said, 'I am King of the Jews.'" 22 Pilate answered, "What I have written I have written."

23 Then the soldiers, when they had crucified Jesus, took His outer garments and made four parts, a part to every soldier and also the tunic; now the tunic was seamless, woven in one piece. 24 So they said to one another, "Let us not tear it, but cast lots for it, to decide whose it shall be"; this was to fulfill the Scripture: "THEY DIVIDED MY OUTER GARMENTS AMONG THEM, AND FOR MY CLOTHING THEY CAST LOTS." 25 Therefore the soldiers did these things.

But standing by the cross of Jesus were His mother, and His mother's sister, Mary the wife of Clopas, and Mary Magdalene. 26 When Jesus then saw His mother, and the disciple whom He loved standing nearby, He said to His mother, "Woman, behold, your son!" 27 Then He said to the disciple, "Behold, your mother!" From that hour the disciple took her into his own household.

28 After this, Jesus, knowing that all things had already been accomplished, to fulfill the Scripture, said, "I am thirsty." 29 A jar full of sour wine was standing there; so they put a sponge full of the sour wine upon a branch of hyssop and brought it up to His mouth. 30 Therefore when Jesus had received the sour wine, He said, "It is finished!" And He bowed His head and gave up His spirit.

31 Then the Jews, because it was the day of preparation, so that the bodies would not remain on the cross on the Sabbath (for that Sabbath was a high day), asked Pilate that their legs might be broken, and that they might be taken away. 32 So the soldiers came, and broke the legs of the first man and of the other who was crucified with Him; 33 but coming to Jesus, when they saw that He was already dead, they did not break His legs. 34 But one of the soldiers pierced His side with a spear, and immediately

> *blood and water came out.* [35] *And he who has seen has testified, and his testimony is true; and he knows that he is telling the truth, so that you also may believe.* [36] *For these things came to pass to fulfill the Scripture, "NOT A BONE OF HIM SHALL BE BROKEN."* [37] *And again another Scripture says, "THEY SHALL LOOK ON HIM WHOM THEY PIERCED."*

It was Roman custom to put a placard over the cross of the accused to let the onlookers know what the person was guilty of. The inscription over Jesus' cross was written in Greek, Latin, and Hebrew, which were the common languages at the time. Pilate had these words inscribed on it: "JESUS THE NAZARENE, THE KING OF THE JEWS." The Jewish leaders prevailed upon Pilate to change the caption to read, "*He said*, 'I am King of the Jews.'" There's an important distinction there. Pilate likely believed that Jesus was who He said He was—the King of the Jews—but thought His people wanted to crucify Him anyway. The Jewish leaders, though, wanted Him crucified because *He claimed to be* their king.

As in the other Gospels, John notes that the soldiers divided up Jesus' things. It must have been customary for the execution squad to do so. However, in dividing up His possessions, they noted that Jesus' tunic was seamless and too valuable to cut up. So they gambled to see who would win this prize, fulfilling the prophecy in Psalm 22:18: "They divide my garments among them, and for my clothing they cast lots."

Even while in agony on the cross, Jesus asked John to care for His mother. Most scholars agree that Jesus' earthly father, Joseph, died before the start of His ministry, leaving Mary a widow. Jesus wanted to make sure that Mary was well cared for when He was gone.

When Jesus knew that the Scripture had been fulfilled, He said from the cross, "It is finished," and surrendered His life to the Father (v. 30). Jesus held on to His life until everything required had been accomplished.

In John 19:31, the Jewish leaders asked for the legs of the men on the cross to be broken, so that they'd die before the Sabbath day. Breaking their legs meant they could no longer extend themselves in order to breathe. Suffocation would hasten their death.

The executioners may have been surprised to find that Jesus was already dead, so His legs didn't need to be broken, which was a fulfillment of prophecy: "He keeps all His bones, not one of them is broken" (Psalm 34:20). Instead of breaking His legs, one of the soldiers pierced His side and blood and water came pouring out, indicating that the spear pierced Jesus' heart. They didn't break His legs; they had broken His heart.

The Burial

Matthew 27:57–66

57 When it was evening, there came a rich man from
Arimathea, named Joseph, who himself had also become
a disciple of Jesus. 58 This man went to Pilate and asked
for the body of Jesus. Then Pilate ordered it to be given
to him. 59 And Joseph took the body and wrapped it in a
clean linen cloth, 60 and laid it in his own new tomb, which
he had hewn out in the rock; and he rolled a large stone
against the entrance of the tomb and went away. 61 And
Mary Magdalene was there, and the other Mary, sitting
opposite the grave.

62 Now on the next day, the day after the preparation, the
chief priests and the Pharisees gathered together with
Pilate, 63 and said, "Sir, we remember that when He was
still alive that deceiver said, 'After three days I am to rise
again.' 64 Therefore, give orders for the grave to be made

secure until the third day, otherwise His disciples may come and steal Him away and say to the people, 'He has risen from the dead,' and the last deception will be worse than the first." [65] *Pilate said to them, "You have a guard; go, make it as secure as you know how."* [66] *And they went and made the grave secure, and along with the guard they set a seal on the stone.*

We don't know how Joseph became a follower of Jesus. It would be interesting to know how Matthew knew him. Joseph was a wealthy man, and he must have been well known in political circles since he approached Pilate and asked for the body of Jesus. Pilate agreed, and Joseph took the body, prepared it for burial, and then laid it in his own tomb. Finally, he rolled a large stone in front of it to prevent wild animals from devouring it or a thief from stealing it.

All the while, Mary Magdalene and Mary the mother of Jesus were at the site, sitting across from the tomb.

The Jewish leaders must have been uneasy, because they went to Pilate and asked for guards to stand watch over the tomb. They remembered that Jesus had said He would rise from the grave after three days, and they didn't want His disciples stealing the body and then telling everyone that Jesus had in fact come back from the dead. They had no idea that nothing that could keep that grave secure! Their best efforts were so puny in comparison to God's power.

Mark 15:42–47

[42] *When evening had already come, because it was the preparation day, that is, the day before the Sabbath,*
[43] *Joseph of Arimathea came, a prominent member of the Council, who himself was waiting for the kingdom of God; and he gathered up courage and went in before Pilate, and asked for the body of Jesus.* [44] *Pilate wondered if He was dead by this time, and summoning the centurion, he*

questioned him as to whether He was already dead. [45] *And ascertaining this from the centurion, he granted the body to Joseph.* [46] *Joseph bought a linen cloth, took Him down, wrapped Him in the linen cloth and laid Him in a tomb which had been hewn out in the rock; and he rolled a stone against the entrance of the tomb.* [47] *Mary Magdalene and Mary the mother of Joses were looking on to see where He was laid.*

Mark notes that Joseph had to gather up the courage to ask Pilate for the body of Jesus. Joseph may have expected that he would catch some grief from the Jewish leadership, since he himself was a member of the Sanhedrin. But he asked anyway, and his courage helps us to see that there are necessary things we must do in life that won't come easy. But God will give us the courage to do whatever it is He has called us to do.

Luke 23:50–56

[50] *And a man named Joseph, who was a member of the Council, a good and righteous man* [51] *(he had not consented to their plan and action), a man from Arimathea, a city of the Jews, who was waiting for the kingdom of God;* [52] *this man went to Pilate and asked for the body of Jesus.* [53] *And he took it down and wrapped it in a linen cloth, and laid Him in a tomb cut into the rock, where no one had ever lain.* [54] *It was the preparation day, and the Sabbath was about to begin.* [55] *Now the women who had come with Him out of Galilee followed, and saw the tomb and how His body was laid.* [56] *Then they returned and prepared spices and perfumes. And on the Sabbath they rested according to the commandment.*

Mark mentions that Joseph had to gather up courage before coming to Pilate with his request. Luke adds that even though

Joseph was a member of the Jewish council who had ordered Jesus' death, he himself did not agree to it. The women who had come from Galilee and stayed for the crucifixion followed Joseph to the gravesite. Then they went to prepare spices, which they would use to anoint the body following Sabbath observance.

John 19:38–42

> [38] *After these things Joseph of Arimathea, being a disciple*
> *of Jesus, but a secret one for fear of the Jews, asked Pilate*
> *that he might take away the body of Jesus; and Pilate*
> *granted permission. So he came and took away His body.*
> [39] *Nicodemus, who had first come to Him by night, also*
> *came, bringing a mixture of myrrh and aloes, about a*
> *hundred pounds weight.* [40] *So they took the body of Jesus*
> *and bound it in linen wrappings with the spices, as is the*
> *burial custom of the Jews.* [41] *Now in the place where He*
> *was crucified there was a garden, and in the garden a*
> *new tomb in which no one had yet been laid.* [42] *Therefore*
> *because of the Jewish day of preparation, since the tomb*
> *was nearby, they laid Jesus there.*

According to John, Joseph had kept his allegiance to Jesus a secret "for fear of the Jews," which is a common phrase in the Gospel of John.

Did Joseph know that Nicodemus was also a follower of Christ? It may have been a surprise to Joseph when Nicodemus showed up to help him take down the body of Christ and prepare Him for burial. Nicodemus brought with him about one hundred pounds of myrrh and aloes for the preparation, which John tells us was "the burial custom of the Jews" (v. 40).

John's is the only Gospel account that locates the tomb in a garden near the execution site. John does not identify Joseph as the owner of that tomb, though he does state that no one had previously been laid there. The day of preparation necessitated the religious community to care for the body before dark, which is when the Sabbath would begin and all work had to be put on hold.

Chapter 12

THE RESURRECTION, APPEARANCES, AND ASCENSION OF CHRIST

The Resurrection

Matthew 28:1–10

[1] *Now after the Sabbath, as it began to dawn toward the
first day of the week, Mary Magdalene and the other
Mary came to look at the grave.* [2] *And behold, a severe
earthquake had occurred, for an angel of the Lord
descended from heaven and came and rolled away the
stone and sat upon it.* [3] *And his appearance was like
lightning, and his clothing as white as snow.* [4] *The guards
shook for fear of him and became like dead men.* [5] *The
angel said to the women, "Do not be afraid; for I know
that you are looking for Jesus who has been crucified.* [6] *He
is not here, for He has risen, just as He said. Come, see
the place where He was lying.* [7] *Go quickly and tell His
disciples that He has risen from the dead; and behold, He
is going ahead of you into Galilee, there you will see Him;
behold, I have told you."*

[8] *And they left the tomb quickly with fear and great joy
and ran to report it to His disciples.* [9] *And behold, Jesus
met them and greeted them. And they came up and took
hold of His feet and worshiped Him.* [10] *Then Jesus said to
them, "Do not be afraid; go and take word to My brethren
to leave for Galilee, and there they will see Me."*

On the first day of the week, after the Sabbath had ended, Mary Magdalene and "the other Mary," whom most scholars believe to be Mary the mother of Jesus, went to visit the tomb of Jesus, surely expecting to see His dead body. But they were surprised to find a great earthquake had occurred, and an angel of the Lord had rolled the massive stone away and was now sitting on it! The guards seemed to have passed out in fear, but the angel spoke to the women and told them not to be afraid, for Jesus had risen. Then he told them to go tell the disciples what they had seen—namely, the empty tomb.

Filled with great joy, and even some fear, the women ran to share the news with the disciples and met Jesus on the way! They grabbed His feet and worshipped Him. Then they went on to find the disciples and tell them to leave for Galilee to meet Jesus there.

Mark 16:1–8

1 When the Sabbath was over, Mary Magdalene, and Mary the mother of James, and Salome, bought spices, so that they might come and anoint Him. 2 Very early on the first day of the week, they came to the tomb when the sun had risen. 3 They were saying to one another, "Who will roll away the stone for us from the entrance of the tomb?" 4 Looking up, they saw that the stone had been rolled away, although it was extremely large. 5 Entering the tomb, they saw a young man sitting at the right, wearing a white robe; and they were amazed. 6 And he said to them, "Do not be amazed; you are looking for Jesus the Nazarene, who has been crucified. He has risen; He is not here; behold, here is the place where they laid Him. 7 But go, tell His disciples and Peter, 'He is going ahead of you to Galilee; there you will see Him, just as He told you.'" 8 They went out and fled from the tomb, for trembling and astonishment had gripped them; and they said nothing to anyone, for they were afraid.

Like any eyewitnesses to a great event, different people emphasize the importance of different things. This is true of the Gospel accounts of Jesus' birth, life, death, and resurrection, but the main details are constant. As Mark heard it, Mary Magdalene, Mary the mother of James and Jesus, and Salome, the mother of James and John, all went to the tomb after the Sabbath. The women were planning on anointing Jesus' body, but Mark notes they were concerned how they were going to be able to roll the massive stone away to get into the tomb.

When they got there they were likely shocked to see that the stone had already been rolled away! They went on into the tomb, where they met an angel sitting there. The angel calmed them with the assurance that he knew why they were there—to care for the body of Jesus. They were amazed to hear that Jesus had risen from the dead. They were even shown the place where His body had been laid to rest. Then the angel instructed them to go inform the disciples, making it a special point to mention Peter's name.

Peter, we recall, had denied Jesus—not once, but three times. Peter was the one follower who had spoken his conviction (noted in Matthew 16) that Jesus was indeed the Messiah. Jesus wanted Peter to know that His forgiveness was complete.

When Matthew heard about what happened at the grave, he used the terms "fear and great joy" to describe what the women had felt. Mark expressed their feelings as "trembling and astonishment." In the grip of these emotions, these women said nothing to anyone. We might think that such amazing news couldn't be kept silent, but "trembling and astonishment" closed the mouths of the witnesses according to Mark.

Luke 24:1–12

1 *But on the first day of the week, at early dawn, they came*
to the tomb bringing the spices which they had prepared.
2 *And they found the stone rolled away from the tomb,*

> 3 *but when they entered, they did not find the body of the*
> *Lord Jesus.* 4 *While they were perplexed about this, behold,*
> *two men suddenly stood near them in dazzling clothing;*
> 5 *and as the women were terrified and bowed their faces to*
> *the ground, the men said to them, "Why do you seek the*
> *living One among the dead?* 6 *He is not here, but He has*
> *risen. Remember how He spoke to you while He was still*
> *in Galilee,* 7 *saying that the Son of Man must be delivered*
> *into the hands of sinful men, and be crucified, and the*
> *third day rise again."* 8 *And they remembered His words,*
> 9 *and returned from the tomb and reported all these things*
> *to the eleven and to all the rest.* 10 *Now they were Mary*
> *Magdalene and Joanna and Mary the mother of James;*
> *also the other women with them were telling these things*
> *to the apostles.* 11 *But these words appeared to them as*
> *nonsense, and they would not believe them.* 12 *But Peter*
> *got up and ran to the tomb; stooping and looking in, he*
> *saw the linen wrappings only; and he went away to his*
> *home, marveling at what had happened.*

The women entered the tomb expecting to find Jesus' body, but were instead met by *two* angels, not one as in the other accounts. Luke uses the word *terrified* to describe the reactions of the women when they met the angels. Jesus had predicted His death and resurrection on a number of occasions, but none of His followers completely understood what He was saying, which is why the women were shocked to find that Jesus had, in fact, been raised from the dead!

Among these women were Mary Magdalene, Joanna (the wife of a man on Herod's staff), Mary (the mother of James and Jesus), and other unnamed women. They rushed to share the news with the apostles, who thought it was all nonsense! When Peter heard it, he ran to investigate. When he entered the tomb and saw only the linen wrappings, he went home mystified.

John 20:1–10

[1] *Now on the first day of the week Mary Magdalene came*
early to the tomb, while it was still dark, and saw the stone
already taken away from the tomb. [2] *So she ran and came*
to Simon Peter and to the other disciple whom Jesus loved,
and said to them, "They have taken away the Lord out of
the tomb, and we do not know where they have laid Him."
[3] *So Peter and the other disciple went forth, and they were*
going to the tomb. [4] *The two were running together; and*
the other disciple ran ahead faster than Peter and came to
the tomb first; [5] *and stooping and looking in, he saw the*
linen wrappings lying there; but he did not go in. [6] *And*
so Simon Peter also came, following him, and entered the
tomb; and he saw the linen wrappings lying there, [7] *and*
the face-cloth which had been on His head, not lying with
the linen wrappings, but rolled up in a place by itself. [8] *So*
the other disciple who had first come to the tomb then also
entered, and he saw and believed. [9] *For as yet they did not*
understand the Scripture, that He must rise again from
the dead. [10] *So the disciples went away again to their own*
homes.

John mentions that only Mary Magdalene spoke with him. There were several women who went to the tomb, which we know from the other Gospel accounts, but Mary was the only one who immediately left when she saw the tomb empty to report back to the disciples. She didn't see the angel there, for she ran back to the disciples in a panic because she was sure Jesus' body had been stolen.

When Peter and John heard what Mary said about the empty tomb, they ran to investigate for themselves. John beat Peter to the grave, but he was so awestruck that he didn't go in first; Peter did. John did peek in, though, and he saw Jesus' grave clothes lying there. Peter, when he entered the tomb, saw that the face-cloth was in a separate place and had been taken off, folded, and placed there.

That folded face-cloth was important for the disciples to see because it showed that the grave had not been rudely robbed in a rush. Instead, whatever happened was slow, calm, and deliberate. When Peter and John saw the face-cloth they "believed," yet they still didn't fully understand that Jesus had conquered death and was alive.

Confused and bewildered, they went to their own homes.

Witnesses to the Resurrection

Matthew 28:11–17

*[11] Now while they were on their way, some of the guard
came into the city and reported to the chief priests all that
had happened. [12] And when they had assembled with the
elders and consulted together, they gave a large sum of
money to the soldiers, [13] and said, "You are to say, 'His
disciples came by night and stole Him away while we were
asleep.' [14] And if this should come to the governor's ears,
we will win him over and keep you out of trouble." [15] And
they took the money and did as they had been instructed;
and this story was widely spread among the Jews, and is
to this day.*

*[16] But the eleven disciples proceeded to Galilee, to the
mountain which Jesus had designated. [17] When they saw
Him, they worshiped Him; but some were doubtful.*

Matthew 28:11 picks up when the women were on their way to tell the disciples about the empty tomb and their meeting with Jesus. It seems the Holy Spirit inspired Matthew to include solid evidence about Christ's resurrection to counteract any attempts to confuse the record. Matthew reports that when the soldiers who were at Jesus' tomb reported what they had seen to the chief priests, an assembly was called among the Jewish leaders to decide what to do. They bribed the guards to spread the rumor that Jesus' disciples stole the body in the middle of the night while the guards were asleep.

Meanwhile, the eleven disciples (Judas had taken his life at this point) had gone to Galilee as instructed, and there they saw Jesus. Some worshiped, but some doubted.

Mark 16:9–13

9 *[Now after He had risen early on the first day of the*
week, He first appeared to Mary Magdalene, from whom
He had cast out seven demons. 10 *She went and reported to*
those who had been with Him, while they were mourning
and weeping. 11 *When they heard that He was alive and*
had been seen by her, they refused to believe it.

12 *After that, He appeared in a different form to two of*
them while they were walking along on their way to the
country. 13 *They went away and reported it to the others,*
but they did not believe them either.]

According to Mark, Jesus appeared first to Mary Magdalene. She was at the tomb early to care for His body. Upon the Lord's instructions, Mary hurried to where the eleven were gathered to make them aware that Jesus was alive. Sadly, His followers didn't believe her report.

Mark also mentions that Jesus appeared to two of His followers "in a different form" (v. 12) later on. Scholars don't know exactly what that means. It could be that they were so unprepared to see Jesus alive, that they didn't recognize Him. Even so, they must have recognized Jesus somehow because they went and told the others that they had seen Jesus.

Luke 24:13–35

13 *And behold, two of them were going that very day to*
a village named Emmaus, which was about seven miles

*from Jerusalem. 14 And they were talking with each other
about all these things which had taken place. 15 While they
were talking and discussing, Jesus Himself approached
and began traveling with them. 16 But their eyes were
prevented from recognizing Him. 17 And He said to them,
"What are these words that you are exchanging with one
another as you are walking?" And they stood still, looking
sad. 18 One of them, named Cleopas, answered and said
to Him, "Are You the only one visiting Jerusalem and
unaware of the things which have happened here in these
days?" 19 And He said to them, "What things?" And they
said to Him, "The things about Jesus the Nazarene, who
was a prophet mighty in deed and word in the sight of
God and all the people, 20 and how the chief priests and
our rulers delivered Him to the sentence of death, and
crucified Him. 21 But we were hoping that it was He who
was going to redeem Israel. Indeed, besides all this, it
is the third day since these things happened. 22 But also
some women among us amazed us. When they were at
the tomb early in the morning, 23 and did not find His
body, they came, saying that they had also seen a vision
of angels who said that He was alive. 24 Some of those who
were with us went to the tomb and found it just exactly
as the women also had said; but Him they did not see."
25 And He said to them, "O foolish men and slow of heart
to believe in all that the prophets have spoken! 26 Was it
not necessary for the Christ to suffer these things and to
enter into His glory?" 27 Then beginning with Moses and
with all the prophets, He explained to them the things
concerning Himself in all the Scriptures.*

*28 And they approached the village where they were going,
and He acted as though He were going farther. 29 But
they urged Him, saying, "Stay with us, for it is getting
toward evening, and the day is now nearly over." So He*

went in to stay with them. [30] When He had reclined at the table with them, He took the bread and blessed it, and breaking it, He began giving it to them. [31] Then their eyes were opened and they recognized Him; and He vanished from their sight. [32] They said to one another, "Were not our hearts burning within us while He was speaking to us on the road, while He was explaining the Scriptures to us?" [33] And they got up that very hour and returned to Jerusalem, and found gathered together the eleven and those who were with them, [34] saying, "The Lord has really risen and has appeared to Simon." [35] They began to relate their experiences on the road and how He was recognized by them in the breaking of the bread.

In Mark's report, he tells us that the two men whom Jesus appeared to didn't, for some unexplained reason, recognize Him. Here, Luke says that "their eyes were prevented from recognizing Him" (v. 16)—not because God made them spiritually blind, but likely because Jesus looked different from what they remembered. They also didn't expect to see Him.

The two men on the road to Emmaus had been in Jerusalem during the crucifixion and had heard the reports that Jesus' tomb was empty. Like the others, they were mystified. As they walked toward Emmaus and talked about all they had seen, they met Jesus (although they didn't know it was Him), and He started traveling with them. Jesus challenged them about their reluctance to accept what the Scriptures had to say about the suffering, death, and resurrection of Christ.

As they neared town, they persuaded Jesus to join them for supper. As He broke the bread and blessed it, they recognized Him! In their excitement, Luke says that Jesus suddenly vanished. Then they went to find Jesus' eleven disciples to share what had happened.

John 20:11–18

*11 But Mary was standing outside the tomb weeping; and
so, as she wept, she stooped and looked into the tomb;
12 and she saw two angels in white sitting, one at the head
and one at the feet, where the body of Jesus had been lying.
13 And they said to her, "Woman, why are you weeping?"
She said to them, "Because they have taken away my Lord,
and I do not know where they have laid Him." 14 When she
had said this, she turned around and saw Jesus standing
there, and did not know that it was Jesus. 15 Jesus said
to her, "Woman, why are you weeping? Whom are you
seeking?" Supposing Him to be the gardener, she said to
Him, "Sir, if you have carried Him away, tell me where
you have laid Him, and I will take Him away." 16 Jesus said
to her, "Mary!" She turned and said to Him in Hebrew,
"Rabboni!" (which means, Teacher). 17 Jesus said to her,
"Stop clinging to Me, for I have not yet ascended to the
Father; but go to My brethren and say to them, 'I ascend to
My Father and your Father, and My God and your God.'"
18 Mary Magdalene came, announcing to the disciples,
"I have seen the Lord," and that He had said these things
to her.*

Mary Magdalene stayed by Jesus' tomb weeping after Peter and John went home. When she bent down so she could see into the tomb, she was amazed to see two angels. These angels must not have been present when Peter and John were there, since they made no mention of seeing anything other than Jesus' grave clothes.

The angels asked Mary why she was weeping, and as she was explaining why, Jesus came behind her. Mary didn't recognize Him initially; in fact, she thought He was the gardener! But when Jesus said her name, she immediately knew it was Him.

Jesus told Mary to stop clinging to Him, and there's a lot of conjecture on why He said that. Perhaps He knew that if she hugged Him, she would want to stay with Him, keeping Him with her. But Jesus knew that He was soon to return to His Father, and He needed to be diligent with His time to complete what He had to do before that appointed time.

Jesus told Mary to go tell the others what He had said to her. Following Jesus' instructions, Mary found the disciples and delivered the message He had entrusted to her.

Jesus Appears to His Disciples

Mark 16:14

> [14] *Afterward He appeared to the eleven themselves as they were reclining at the table; and He reproached them for their unbelief and hardness of heart, because they had not believed those who had seen Him after He had risen.*

Mark does not give us an exact address of where the disciples were eating, but Jesus found them where they were and challenged them for not readily believing the reports brought to them by Mary and the other women. Mark doesn't mention how the disciples reacted when they saw Jesus.

Luke 24:36–43

> [36] *While they were telling these things, He Himself stood in their midst and said to them, "Peace be to you."* [37] *But they were startled and frightened and thought that they were seeing a spirit.* [38] *And He said to them, "Why are you troubled, and why do doubts arise in your hearts?* [39] *See My hands and My feet, that it is I Myself; touch Me and see, for a spirit does not have flesh and bones as you see that I have."* [40] *And when He had said this, He showed*

them His hands and His feet. [41] *While they still could not believe it because of their joy and amazement, He said to them, "Have you anything here to eat?"* [42] *They gave Him a piece of a broiled fish;* [43] *and He took it and ate it before them.*

The two men who had met Jesus on the road to Emmaus, and then recognized Him as they were eating dinner together, found the eleven disciples and told them what had happened. In the middle of their story, Jesus appeared to them.

The disciples were afraid because they thought they were seeing a ghost. In order to show them that He was real, that He had really come back from the dead, Jesus showed His disciples the scars on His hands and His feet and invited them to touch Him to see that He was actually human. Then, to further prove His humanity, He asked them for some fish and ate it in front of them. If He were a ghost, why would He need to eat?

John 20:19–31

[19] *So when it was evening on that day, the first day of the week, and when the doors were shut where the disciples were, for fear of the Jews, Jesus came and stood in their midst and said to them, "Peace be with you."* [20] *And when He had said this, He showed them both His hands and His side. The disciples then rejoiced when they saw the Lord.* [21] *So Jesus said to them again, "Peace be with you; as the Father has sent Me, I also send you."* [22] *And when He had said this, He breathed on them and said to them, "Receive the Holy Spirit.* [23] *If you forgive the sins of any, their sins have been forgiven them; if you retain the sins of any, they have been retained."*

[24] *But Thomas, one of the twelve, called Didymus, was not with them when Jesus came.* [25] *So the other disciples were*

saying to him, "We have seen the Lord!" But he said to them, "Unless I see in His hands the imprint of the nails, and put my finger into the place of the nails, and put my hand into His side, I will not believe."

[26] *After eight days His disciples were again inside, and Thomas with them. Jesus came, the doors having been shut, and stood in their midst and said, "Peace be with you."* [27] *Then He said to Thomas, "Reach here with your finger, and see My hands; and reach here your hand and put it into My side; and do not be unbelieving, but believing."* [28] *Thomas answered and said to Him, "My Lord and my God!"* [29] *Jesus said to him, "Because you have seen Me, have you believed? Blessed are they who did not see, and yet believed."*

[30] *Therefore many other signs Jesus also performed in the presence of the disciples, which are not written in this book;* [31] *but these have been written so that you may believe that Jesus is the Christ, the Son of God; and that believing you may have life in His name.*

John gives us more insight into Jesus' appearance to the disciples. He tells us that the disciples had locked themselves together in a house because they were afraid of the Jewish leaders who had executed Jesus. The Gospel writer makes it a point to say that the doors were locked (and most scholars believe they were barred from the inside, too). This detail becomes especially interesting when John notes that Jesus simply "appeared" in the house among the disciples—bolted doors and all! Jesus showed them His hands and His side where the spear had pierced, and "the disciples rejoiced when they saw the Lord" (v. 21).

What Jesus said about forgiving sins and retaining sins is very similar to what He said in Matthew 16:19: "I give you the keys of the kingdom of heaven; and whatever you bind on earth shall have been bound in heaven, and whatever you loose on earth shall have been loosed in heaven." Disciples of Jesus have an awesome responsibility to do things on earth that have an eternal impact. Disciples cannot forgive sin, but we can introduce sinners to the Forgiver.

For some reason not explained to us, Thomas was not with the other disciples when Jesus appeared to them. When the disciples told him what had happened, Thomas was adamant that unless he saw Jesus for himself, he absolutely wouldn't believe what they were telling him. Thomas had a problem with doubting. He was skeptical about going with Jesus to Mary and Martha's home when Lazarus died. And when Jesus told the disciples they "know the way" to the Father, Thomas said, "Lord, we do not know where You are going, how do we know the way?" (John 14:4–5). And now Thomas was doubting again. Eight days after Jesus had appeared to them, the disciples were behind closed doors again when Jesus just appeared among them. Turning to Thomas, He offered His hands and His side to satisfy Thomas' doubts. When Thomas saw Jesus for himself, he worshipped.

Jesus took the occasion to make a point about faith. In verse 29 Jesus said, "Blessed are those who did not see, and yet believed." We get to count ourselves among the vast crowd of those who believe in Jesus even though we have never seen Him. Peter, who was there, gives us a reassuring word in 1 Peter 1:8: "Though you have not seen Him, you love Him, and though you do not see Him now, but believe in Him, you greatly rejoice with joy inexpressible and full of glory."

According to his own testimony, John was not able to record everything Jesus did—both before and after His resurrection—in his Gospel. What he did include, though, following the inspiration of the Holy Spirit, was recorded in order to help us believe that Jesus is the Promised One. He is, by many irrefutable proofs, the Son of God. Everyone who believes this is granted the fullest life—eternal life.

Jesus Visits His Disciples at the Seashore

John 21:1–25

[1] *After these things Jesus manifested Himself again to*
the disciples at the Sea of Tiberias, and He manifested
Himself in this way. [2] *Simon Peter, and Thomas called*
Didymus, and Nathanael of Cana in Galilee, and the sons
of Zebedee, and two others of His disciples were together.
[3] *Simon Peter said to them, "I am going fishing." They said*
to him, "We will also come with you." They went out and
got into the boat; and that night they caught nothing.

[4] *But when the day was now breaking, Jesus stood on the*
beach; yet the disciples did not know that it was Jesus.
[5] *So Jesus said to them, "Children, you do not have any*
fish, do you?" They answered Him, "No." [6] *And He said to*
them, "Cast the net on the right-hand side of the boat and
you will find a catch." So they cast, and then they were
not able to haul it in because of the great number of fish.
[7] *Therefore that disciple whom Jesus loved said to Peter,*
"It is the Lord." So when Simon Peter heard that it was
the Lord, he put his outer garment on (for he was stripped
for work), and threw himself into the sea. [8] *But the other*
disciples came in the little boat, for they were not far from
the land, but about one hundred yards away, dragging the
net full of fish.

[9] *So when they got out on the land, they saw a charcoal*
fire already laid and fish placed on it, and bread. [10] *Jesus*
said to them, "Bring some of the fish which you have now
caught." [11] *Simon Peter went up and drew the net to land,*

full of large fish, a hundred and fifty-three; and although
there were so many, the net was not torn.

12 Jesus said to them, "Come and have breakfast." None of
the disciples ventured to question Him, "Who are You?"
knowing that it was the Lord. 13 Jesus came and took the
bread and gave it to them, and the fish likewise. 14 This
is now the third time that Jesus was manifested to the
disciples, after He was raised from the dead.

15 So when they had finished breakfast, Jesus said to
Simon Peter, "Simon, son of John, do you love Me more
than these?" He said to Him, "Yes, Lord; You know that
I love You." He said to him, "Tend My lambs." 16 He said
to him again a second time, "Simon, son of John, do you
love Me?" He said to Him, "Yes, Lord; You know that I love
You." He said to him, "Shepherd My sheep." 17 He said to
him the third time, "Simon, son of John, do you love Me?"
Peter was grieved because He said to him the third time,
"Do you love Me?" And he said to Him, "Lord, You know
all things; You know that I love You." Jesus said to him,
"Tend My sheep.

18 Truly, truly, I say to you, when you were younger, you
used to gird yourself and walk wherever you wished; but
when you grow old, you will stretch out your hands and
someone else will gird you, and bring you where you do
not wish to go." 19 Now this He said, signifying by what
kind of death he would glorify God. And when He had
spoken this, He said to him, "Follow Me!"

20 Peter, turning around, saw the disciple whom Jesus
loved following them; the one who also had leaned
back on His bosom at the supper and said, "Lord, who
is the one who betrays You?" 21 So Peter seeing him said
to Jesus, "Lord, and what about this man?" 22 Jesus said

to him, "If I want him to remain until I come, what is that to you? You follow Me!" [23] *Therefore this saying went out among the brethren that that disciple would not die; yet Jesus did not say to him that he would not die, but only, "If I want him to remain until I come, what is that to you?"*

[24] *This is the disciple who is testifying to these things and wrote these things, and we know that his testimony is true.*

[25] *And there are also many other things which Jesus did, which if they were written in detail, I suppose that even the world itself would not contain the books that would be written.*

Earlier, John told us that Jesus made an appearance to His disciples to answer any doubts Thomas had about the validity of the resurrection. Now we read of another appearance by Jesus to some of His disciples by the Sea of Tiberias. This encounter further substantiated that Jesus had indeed risen from the dead. It's also a time of warm fellowship between Jesus and His disciples.

John notes that Peter, Thomas (we hadn't known that he was a fisherman), Nathanael (from the city where Jesus did His first miracle), James and John, and two other disciples were there. It would be interesting to know if the two unnamed disciples were from the original twelve or were more recent converts.

Peter suggested they go fishing and everyone joined him. They fished all night but caught nothing. In the breaking dawn, they noticed a man on the beach. He called out to them to see if they had caught anything. John says that they did not recognize that it was Jesus. When the frustrated fishermen answered that they hadn't caught anything, Jesus told them to cast their net on the right side of the boat. They did what He said and caught so many fish they couldn't haul them all in.

At this point John recognized that the man on the beach was Jesus! When he said that it was the Lord, Peter dove into the sea and swam to land. He and the sons of Zebedee may have remembered the time they had fished all night and caught nothing until Jesus told them to "put out into the deep water and let down your nets for a catch" (Luke 5:4). After doing that, they caught so many fish that their boats could scarcely stay afloat! This time they had an equally spectacular catch, netting 153 fish and managing not to tear their net.

A fire greeted them on the shore with fish and bread cooking. Jesus had prepared breakfast for them. John doesn't tell us where the bread came from. It's possible Jesus produced it miraculously, as He had done before when feeding the 5,000 and the 4,000.

After they had finished breakfast (another proof that Jesus wasn't an apparition), Jesus turned to Peter and asked him the same basic question three times in slightly different ways: *Do you love me?* Each time, Peter answered that he did. Peter had denied Jesus three times and now he affirmed his love for Jesus three times. Jesus wanted to restore Peter, and He wanted Peter to know that he was restored.

Jesus told Peter that a time was coming when he would no longer be able to do what he wanted to do, but would be under the control of others. John tells us that Jesus said this to prepare Peter for the kind of God-glorifying death he would die. Peter became concerned about what would happen to John, and Jesus told him not to worry about that but to simply, "Follow Me" (v. 19).

John closes his Gospel with a word about the reliability of his testimony. He was there when all this happened, so we can trust that what he recorded is accurate. He closes his Gospel with the truth that Jesus did much more than what he recorded: "And there were also many other things which Jesus did, which if they were written in detail, I suppose that even the world itself would not contain the books that would be written" (v. 25). The story of Jesus continues to be written in and through the lives of His countless followers, who continue to spread the good news of the gospel in His name.

The Great Commission and the Ascension

Matthew 28:16–20

> [16] *"But the eleven disciples proceeded to Galilee, to the mountain which Jesus had designated.* [17] *When they saw Him, they worshiped Him; but some were doubtful.* [18] *And Jesus came up and spoke to them, saying, 'All authority has been given to Me in heaven and on earth.* [19] *Go therefore and make disciples of all the nations, baptizing them in the name of the Father and the Son and the Holy Spirit,* [20] *teaching them to observe all that I commanded you; and lo, I am with you always, even to the end of the age.'»*

When Jesus first met Mary at the tomb, He told her to inform the disciples that He would meet them in Galilee. Rumors were rampant in Jerusalem about what might have happened at the tomb. Despite those rumors—and fortified by the times they had met with the risen Jesus—the disciples journeyed up to Galilee.

The disciples—after meeting with Jesus on the beach at the Sea of Galilee—returned to Jerusalem, where they heard Jesus challenge them with what we have come to know as the "Great Commission." Jesus said to them, "All authority has been given Me in heaven and on earth" (v .18), assuring them that He had the authority to give them such a commission. On the basis of that unparalleled authority, these disciples were to go to every nation with the gospel. They would never lack for encouragement and support, for Jesus committed to "be with you always, even to the end of the age" (v. 20).

Mark 16:15–20

[15] *And He said to them, "Go into all the world and preach*
the gospel to all creation. [16] *He who has believed and has*
been baptized shall be saved; but he who has disbelieved
shall be condemned. [17] *These signs will accompany those*
who have believed: in My name they will cast out demons,
they will speak with new tongues; [18] *they will pick up*
serpents, and if they drink any deadly poison, it will not
hurt them; they will lay hands on the sick, and they will
recover."

[19] *So then, when the Lord Jesus had spoken to them, He was*
received up into heaven and sat down at the right hand
of God. [20] *And they went out and preached everywhere,*
while the Lord worked with them, and confirmed the
word by the signs that followed.

This ending to Mark's Gospel (vv. 9–20) is not included in some of the earlier manuscripts, so there is some debate as to whether it should be included. In any case, the person who gave Mark these details seems to have been impressed with the signs that would accompany the preaching of the gospel. We aren't sure if these signs would accompany any evangelist or just these initial eleven and the early apostles like Paul. We do know from Luke's account in Acts that another disciple was added to fill the void Judas left (Acts 1:26), and that Paul was used to bring about healing (Acts 19:11–12)—in fact, we know that Paul survived a viper bite! (Acts 28:3).

Just after He had delivered this mandate, Jesus was "received up into heaven and sat down at the right hand of God" (v. 19). Mark assures us that these disciples did go, just as their Lord had commissioned them to do.

Luke 24:44–53

[44] *Now He said to them, "These are My words which I spoke*
to you while I was still with you, that all things which are
written about Me in the Law of Moses and the Prophets
and the Psalms must be fulfilled." [45] *Then He opened*
their minds to understand the Scriptures, [46] *and He said*
to them, "Thus it is written, that the Christ would suffer
and rise again from the dead the third day, [47] *and that*
repentance for forgiveness of sins would be proclaimed in
His name to all the nations, beginning from Jerusalem.
[48] *You are witnesses of these things.* [49] *And behold, I am*
sending forth the promise of My Father upon you; but you
are to stay in the city until you are clothed with power
from on high."

[50] *And He led them out as far as Bethany, and He lifted*
up His hands and blessed them. [51] *While He was blessing*
them, He parted from them and was carried up into
heaven. [52] *And they, after worshiping Him, returned to*
Jerusalem with great joy, [53] *and were continually in the*
temple praising God.

Jesus told the disciples, as He had in the past, that the Old Testament prophecies about Him had to be fulfilled. They had not fully understood how the Scriptures pointed to Him. As He "opened their minds to understand the Scriptures" (v. 45), they must have been filled with amazement.

Since the disciples were witnesses to these prophetic events, their testimony would be the most undeniable and effective. They were instructed to wait in Jerusalem for the promised Holy Spirit, who would remind them of the things Jesus said and empower them for mission. They must have been both excited and a little mystified by Jesus' instruction to stay in the city "until you are clothed with power from on high" (v. 48).

After Jesus told the disciples about the coming Spirit, they walked together the few miles from Jerusalem to Bethany, where Jesus lifted His hands to bless them. As He was pronouncing His blessing, He was carried up into heaven. Luke adds to this account in the Book of Acts, chapter 1.

Acts 1:4–11

> 4 *Gathering them together, He commanded them not to leave Jerusalem, but to wait for what the Father had promised, "Which," He said, "you heard of from Me;* 5 *for John baptized with water, but you will be baptized with the Holy Spirit not many days from now."*
>
> 6 *So when they had come together, they were asking Him, saying, "Lord, is it at this time You are restoring the kingdom to Israel?"* 7 *He said to them, "It is not for you to know times or epochs which the Father has fixed by His own authority;* 8 *but you will receive power when the Holy Spirit has come upon you; and you shall be My witnesses both in Jerusalem, and in all Judea and Samaria, and even to the remotest part of the earth."*
>
> 9 *And after He had said these things, He was lifted up while they were looking on, and a cloud received Him out of their sight.* 10 *And as they were gazing intently into the sky while He was going, behold, two men in white clothing stood beside them.* 11 *They also said, "Men of Galilee, why do you stand looking into the sky? This Jesus, who has been taken up from you into heaven, will come in just the same way as you have watched Him go into heaven."*

While the disciples watched Jesus ascend into heaven, they were interrupted by two angels who told them Jesus would return the same way. We look forward to the day of Christ's return, living in the assurance that He is coming back again to set everything right, once and for all.

It was while "they were continually in the temple praising God" (Luke 24:53) that the disciples received what Jesus had promised—the outpouring of the Holy Spirit. The sending of the Spirit on the day of Pentecost (Acts 2) propelled these initial witnesses to do their work so effectively that the church exploded and continues to spread across the earth some thousands of years later.

A lawyer named Saul was one of those who was affected by the witness of these disciples. Saul's life was so transformed that he became the great apostle Paul and went on to plant churches and write a large portion of the New Testament. In Philippians 2:10–11, Paul wrote, "At the name of Jesus, every knee will bow, of those who are in heaven and on earth and under the earth, and that every tongue will confess that Jesus Christ is Lord, to the glory of God the Father." This is the same Jesus who the angels stated would "come in just the same way as you have watched Him go into heaven" (Acts 1:11).

It is just a matter of God's timing before this promise becomes reality.

Scriptural Index

OLD TESTAMENT

NEW TESTAMENT

www.ingramcontent.com/pod-product-compliance
Lightning Source LLC
Chambersburg PA
CBHW051414090426
42737CB00014B/2655

* 9 7 8 1 6 3 2 9 6 0 8 8 7 *